POETRY, THE MAGIC LANGUAGE

POETRY, THE MAGIC LANGUAGE
Children Learn to Read and Write It

MAUREEN W. ARMOUR

1994
TEACHER IDEAS PRESS
A Division of
Libraries Unlimited, Inc.
Englewood, Colorado

Copyright © 1994 Maureen W. Armour
All Rights Reserved
Printed in the United States of America

No part of this publication may be reproduced, stored in a retrieval system, or transmitted, in any form or by any means, electronic, mechanical, photocopying, recording, or otherwise, without the prior written permission of the publisher. An exception is made for individual library media specialists and teachers who may make copies of activity sheets for classroom use in a single school. Other portions of the book (up to 15 pages) may be copied for in-service programs or other educational programs in a single school.

TEACHER IDEAS PRESS
A Division of Libraries Unlimited, Inc.
P.O. Box 6633
Englewood, CO 80155-6633
1-800-237-6124

Project Editor: Kevin W. Perizzolo
Copy Editor: Diane Hess
Proofreader: Ann Marie Damian
Typesetting and Design: Kay Minnis
Indexing: Nancy Fulton

Library of Congress Cataloging-in-Publication Data

Armour, Maureen W.
   Poetry, the magic language : children learn to read and write it / Maureen W. Armour.
   xvii, 215 p. 17x25 cm.
   Includes bibliographical references and index.
   ISBN 1-56308-033-8
   1. Poetry--Study and teaching (Elementary) 2. Poetry--Authorship--Study and teaching (Elementary) I. Title.
LB1576.A712   1994
372.64--dc20
93-49104
CIP

For my daughter Kit
Who made it possible

CONTENTS

ACKNOWLEDGMENTS xiii

INTRODUCTION xv

1—THE POETRY WORKSHOP 1
  How Poetry Workshop Began 1
    Inspiration from Outdoors 3
    The Bat Poet 4
    Finding Rhyme 6
  Workshop Structure 8
    Reading Poems Provides Models for Writing 9
    Writing and Conferring 9
    Revision in the Workshop 10
    Writing About Writing 12
  Publication and Celebration 16
    Final Editing 16
    Adding Visual Interest 17
    Putting It All Together 19
    Celebration! 19
      Planning the Event 19
      The Guest List 20
      Poetry Reading Rehearsal 20
      Food! 21
      The Day Arrives 21
    Revising Teaching 22
    What to Write About 23
    The Reading/Writing Connection 25
      Where to Hold a Poem 26
      Planning for the Workshop 26
  Beyond the Workshop 27
  References 27

2—POETRY IS EVERYWHERE 29

- The Primary Years 29
  - Big Books 31
  - Poetry Sources 32
  - Poetry Writing in the Primary Grades 34
    - Poems by the Very Young 34
    - Helping Children Find Their Poems 35
    - Getting Poems on Paper 37
    - Models Help Writing 38
    - Second-Graders Show Growth 40
- Special Challenges 42
- Poetry and ESL Learners 43
  - Poetry Bridges Cultures 44
    - A Multilingual Kindergarten 44
    - Building Self-Esteem with Poems 45
  - Helping ESL Learners Write Their Own Poems 46
- Multicultural Poetry 49
  - Native American Writers 49
  - African American Writers 51
  - Poetry by Hispanic Writers 52
  - Multicultural, Multilingual Books 53
- The World of Poetry 54
- References 54

3—THE SHAPE OF A POEM: FORMS AND CONVENTIONS 58

- Lines and White Space 58
  - Revising Lines 59
    - Computers Make It Easy 60
    - Another Way to Revise Is Invented 60
  - Form Fits Content 60
  - Hearing the Lines 61
  - Stanzas 62
- Poetic Devices and Structures 64
  - Rhyme 64
  - Repetition 66
  - Unrhymed Poems 67
  - Personification 67
  - Punctuation 69
  - Teaching Poetic Terms 70
    - Similes 71
    - Metaphors 71
    - Onomatopoeia 74
    - Alliteration 75

Poetic Forms 76
   An Analogy for Poetic Forms 78
   Teaching Poetic Forms 78
      Rhyming Couplets 79
      Limericks 80
      Cinquains 80
      Haiku 81
      Narrative Poems 82
      Forms That Play with Words 83
   Handle with Care 85
References 85

4—ORAL POETRY: SINGING, PERFORMING, AND DISCUSSING POEMS 87

The Music of Words 88
Oral Experience Promotes Learning 89
   Discussion Furthers Comprehension 89
      Middle-Grade Poetry Discussions 90
      But Be Careful Not to Overdo It 92
   Add Interest with Poets' Lives 93
   Poets Reading Poems 93
   Lively Parts of Speech 94
Memorizing Poems 97
   Poems Just for You 97
   Making Memorization Student-Friendly 98
   Fitting Poems In 100
Choral Speaking 101
   You, the Conductor 101
   Beginning Choral Speaking with Your Class 102
   More Possibilities 103
   Beginning the Year with Chants 103
   Chants in a Child's World 104
   Benefits of Choral Speaking 105
   Taking Choral Speaking to Larger Audiences 106
Poetry Readings 107
   Children Read the Poems They Write 107
   Going Public with Poetry Readings 108
   More Ways to Perform Poetry 109
   Act It Out 110
   Center on a Theme 111
   Poetry in Harmony 111
   Visual Enchantment 112

4—ORAL POETRY: SINGING, PERFORMING, AND DISCUSSING POEMS (*continued*)

Writing the Sound of Poems 113
    Sounds for the Fun of It 114
    Playing with Words and Sounds 115
Conclusion 116
References 116

5—GOING PUBLIC: REVISING, EVALUATING, EDITING, PRINTING, AND CELEBRATING POEMS 119

Choosing the Best Poems to Publish 120
    Children Choose Their Own 121
    When a Student Chooses Less Than the Best 122
Revision in the Workshop 122
    Revision Conferences 124
    Peer Conferences 124
    Are They Really Getting It? 125
    Revision Through the Grades 126
        First Attempts 126
        Is It Right? Is It Right? 127
        Revision at the Point of Utterance 128
        Older Children Revise 129
        Models Help Revision 130
        Critiquing Through Conferences 131
Evaluation 132
    Self-Evaluation 132
    Questions Are Crucial 134
    Standards: High Yet Attainable 135
    Grades and Report Cards 136
    Evaluation Conferences 138
Editing 139
    Spelling 139
    Editing Conferences 141
Writing As Reflection 141
Illustrating Poems 143
Production 144
Different Ways to Publish 144
Record Keeping 145
Party Time! 146
Polish, Publish, And Cherish 147
References 148

6—POETRY ACROSS THE CURRICULUM 149
Poetry: Both Fun and Facts 150
Poems for Science 150
Poems for Social Studies 152
Geography and Maps 152
Cities 154
Native Americans 154
History 155
Poems for Math Class 155
Spelling and Other Lessons 158
Poetry and Themes 159
Food 159
Weather 161
Wind 161
Rain and Fog, Thunder and Lightning 162
Rainbows 165
Snow and Ice 166
Space and Time 168
Space 168
Clocks and Calendars 170
The Animal Kingdom 171
Pets 172
Birds 175
Insects (and Spiders and Worms, Too) 177
Dinosaurs 180
Mountains and Volcanoes 180
Ocean 180
Trees 182
Families 185
Ecology 190
Conclusion 193
References 193

AFTERWORD: POETRY BEYOND THE CURRICULUM 197

INDEX 201

ABOUT THE AUTHOR 215

ACKNOWLEDGMENTS

An unexpected and delightful outcome of writing this book has been renewed contact with many of my former students who, just a few short years ago, sparked my teaching days with their energy and imagination. It gives me tremendous pleasure to bring their words to a larger audience and to reaffirm their power as authors. Their poems are the heart of this book.

I also want to thank the teachers who unstintingly shared with me their ideas and practices and their students' work. Edie Ziegler, a treasured colleague, heads the list. Marilyn London and Barbara Cullere in New Jersey and Tom Pipher, Carol Graham, Pat Nix, Alyce Watkins, and Agnes Homan in Florida gave invaluable help. Dr. Jane Kern, Lynne Powell, and the staff of Seacrest Country Day School in Naples, Florida, especially Joanne Hammond and Lynn Shearer, welcomed me to their school with justifiable pride.

Unending gratitude goes to the teachers who have taught me. Nick Aversa's inspired leadership in his New Jersey Writing Project workshop opened the first door. Dr. Joan Feeley of William Paterson College unlocked many others.

The bright flame of Professor Lucy McCormick Calkins's wisdom and convictions continues to illuminate my world of teaching and writing. Sessions at Teachers College led by her, Shelley Harwayne, and Georgia Heard inspired and informed me and changed forever the way I saw the writing and reading processes.

A big thank you goes out to the children and students who authored the poems in Georgia Heard's *For the Good of the Earth and Sun*. Every effort has been made to contact the copyright holders and the students to reprint borrowed material. I regret any oversights that may have occurred and would be happy to rectify them with a printed correction.

Thanks go also to my editors Suzanne Barchers and Kevin W. Perizzolo for their patient guidance.

INTRODUCTION

Welcome to the poetry club! No meetings to go to, no officers to elect, no dues to pay; just the joy of reading and writing beautiful, powerful language—a magic language.

In high school and college I thought poetry was an exalted mystery, unrelated to my experience, unclear in its meaning, and beyond my capacity to write. As an English major and hopeful writer, this annoyed me and made me feel somehow left out. Later, as a teacher, I was determined that my students would learn to find pleasure rather than pain in poetry.

We rollicked through Edward Lear, A. A. Milne, Dr. Seuss, Shel Silverstein, and T.S. Eliot's *Book of Practical Cats*, and I learned to love poetry right along with the children. Without realizing it, they invited me into the poetry club, a community of readers and writers who have discovered the magic of that unique form of language.

Lee Galda's definition is clear and inclusive: "Poetry examines emotions and experiences carefully, with honesty and extraordinary clarity of vision, and presents these emotions and experiences through words that sing" (1992, 114). Children, too, grow to understand the special nature of poems. Howard, a fourth-grader, introduced his poem "Skiing" this way: "This poem describes what skiing is like. This poem will not tell you how to ski, but it will tell you how it feels."

James Britton sounds like a poet when he writes that real poetry is "words that are aflame with the fire of imagination" (1982, 10). We need to bring poems that sing and are aflame with imagination to the children in our classrooms. If you were fortunate enough to have had wonderful teachers of poetry when you were in school, you're probably already doing this. However, many of us, as children, learned to fear or dislike poetry; how peculiar that is, when the purpose of education is to enable us to use and enjoy art and information throughout our lives.

Perhaps that early aversion is the chief reason poetry is so often neglected in classrooms; other causes are the crowded curriculum and the demands of an increasingly technological culture that allows little time to savor the printed word. Pushing insistently against these pressures is the knowledge that poetry has been an integral component of human life perhaps since language began; indeed, poetry, with its ability to transform experience, is part of what makes us human. It's up to us to make sure the children in our classes aren't left out of the poetry club, even given all the pressures we face. They have the right to experience poetry, to learn to read and write it, and to find pleasure in it all their lives.

How can we as teachers help this happen? Our experience as students can be informative: Perhaps our teachers made us memorize poems that had no connection to our lives and sounded uncomfortably strange. Maybe we had to write in complete sentences what the message of a poem was, knowing that our chances of hitting the right one were slim. Or perhaps we had teachers who recited beloved poems with "the fire of imagination" in their eyes, who engaged us in the music and magic of poetry because they wanted to share the joy it gave them.

So first, we must find poems we love. It won't take long because poems are usually short. (For example, all unattributed poems in this book were written by me.) The children's poetry shelf in the library is a wonderful place to find all kinds of poems—funny, sad, exciting, soft, jangly, scary, poignant, nonsensical—and most of them are good poems, which is to say their words are vivid and vibrant and speak directly and honestly to the experiences of children. Good poems are not silly, sticky-sweet jingles that patronize kids or try to teach unwelcome lessons.

I don't believe there's such a thing as a children's poet. There are good and bad poets, however, and the good ones have written much that children can understand and enjoy. Good poets whose books are aimed at children have written poems we all can understand and enjoy because we all contain the child we once were. Part of the joy of sharing poetry with your students is the chance to get back in touch with that child.

My concepts of how best to help students learn to read and write poetry rest on the principles of child-centered, literature-based instruction with emphasis on what is called the reading and writing process. By child-centered I mean that the child has the responsibility to make choices and be actively engaged in learning, and that the child's intentions and purposes are essential in structuring that learning.

The writing process, as we read in the books of Donald Murray, Donald Graves, and Lucy McCormick Calkins, is simply the way writers have pursued their craft over the centuries. They think about what to write; they write; they think about what they've written; and they rewrite. We can call those actions rehearsal or prewriting, drafting, and revision. Editing is the final polishing a piece gets before going public. None of this takes place in orderly steps but is recursive, with the writer constantly moving around among the parts of the process.

It now seems strange that we used to try to teach kids to read and write by giving them workbook exercises *about* reading and writing. The evidence that children learn these processes best by doing them rather than filling in blanks on worksheets is virtually indisputable. When a teacher establishes the framework in which reading will take place, when children read well-written material that is meaningful to them and that they have some say in choosing and write their own responses and discuss what they've read with teachers and peers, then they're really learning to read.

When they write about topics of their own choosing, confer with teachers and peers about the clarity and beauty of their work, and strive to make it better because they have invested themselves in it and are inspired by the pride of ownership, then children really learn to write. Throughout these processes, the teacher is indispensable, but as a knowledgeable guide and mentor rather than an authoritarian commander.

For me, poetry fits seamlessly into this approach to teaching. Its diversity and singularity demand that each poem be looked at as a unique whole. The brilliant leaps that characterize wonderful poems vault over sequential logic and defy the rules of written prose. The subjective quality of poetry empowers every reader's and writer's thoughtful interpretation and vision. There is no place for the traditional teacher role of handing down rules and right answers, and there is every opportunity for children to be actively and responsibly involved in their own learning processes.

In an integrated curriculum or whole language classroom, it's hard to separate and identify the subjects being studied. Poetry, for instance, is often a recurring element in the day rather than a separate subject. Similarly, although the chapter headings list the contents of this book, I've found it difficult to chop up the ways of reading and writing poetry and to keep them in separate chunks. For example, revision is treated mainly in chapter 5 but is also discussed in chapters 1 and 3; in fact, chapter 1, "The Poetry Workshop," has a little bit of everything you'll find discussed in detail further on.

So, just as the writing process is recursive, you'll find similar ideas and practices recurring throughout the book. Using a child-centered approach and an integrated curriculum demands a holistic design, and that model has imprinted itself on the structure of this book.

Let me tell you a first-day-of-school story. A few years ago, I conducted the usual first-day guided tour of the classroom. One of the stops was the fish tank, a small aquarium inhabited by guppies. I explained that these fish gave birth to live young, and, indeed, one of the females looked as if she might deliver baby guppies that very day.

Later on, my fourth-graders chose from a variety of activities while I worked with individuals. One of the options was to observe the fish tank. In one of those rare moments when everyone happened to be silent at the same time, I heard Lenny's voice rise from the group of guppy watchers.

"*Push!*" he urged. "*Push!*"

I hope you won't feel I'm pushing you too hard to share poetry with your students! But I believe passionately that poetry is an essential part of every child's experience, and if there isn't yet a chapter of the poetry club where you teach, I hope you'll form one as soon as you can.

REFERENCES

Britton, James. "Reading and Writing Poetry." In Gordon M. Pradl (ed.), *Prospect and Retrospect*. Montclair, NJ: Boynton/Cook, 1982.

Eliot, T. S. *The Complete Poems and Plays*. New York: Harcourt, Brace, 1952.

Galda, Lee. "Giving the Gift of a Poet's Words." *Fanfare* 1 (1992): 105-16.

Chapter 1
THE POETRY WORKSHOP

Nine-year-old Tomoki walked to the front of the classroom without looking up at the audience of fifty-three fourth-graders and twenty-eight adults sitting before him. The paper in his hands trembled slightly. He took a deep breath and began to read. "Fireworks:

>In front of the black curtain
>A huge flower appears
>And disappears.
>There's a bang
>Then a beautiful flower.
>But before you can say something
>It hides behind the huge curtain.
>One by one
>In different colors
>In different sizes
>The huge flowers flash
>And lighten the night sky. ❖

by Tomoki Moriyama," he finished, as applause filled the room. With a quick glance at his beaming parents and a smile of happiness and relief, he sat down and prepared to listen to the next young writer of poems.

HOW POETRY WORKSHOP BEGAN

The poetry reading was the high point of our poetry publication party, attended by parents, teachers, our principal, and every other member of the school staff who was free. The excitement in the air was palpable. "If we could just bottle this, the energy crisis would be over," our principal said.

A mother known for her skepticism shook her head in wonderment. "Imagine," she said, "fourth-graders getting this excited about *poetry*!"

Some eight weeks earlier when I announced to both my fourth-grade writing classes that we'd be writing only poems for a while, the mood was far less joyful. The children tried to be polite, but I heard a collective murmur of protest salted with individual objections.

"I can't write a poem."

"Poems? I want to write a space story."

"Poetry's yucky."

"*Only* poems?"

"Yes, only poems," I answered as I dropped a few large safety pins on each table. Trying to ignore their humorous speculations about what the pins were for, I asked them to look closely at the familiar objects. What did they notice about the safety pins? Already aware of the importance of details from the minilessons, conferences, and sharing that had made up our writing workshop since the beginning of the year, they began to scrutinize their pins.

"This one's shiny. I guess it's new."

"Look, it's all one piece of wire. It starts here and goes around and around at the bottom and comes up to the point."

"Ouch!" Kristen had tested her pin's sharpness on her neighbor.

"Listen to what a poet named Valerie Worth thought when she looked at a safety pin," I said, and read this poem to them:

Safety Pin

Closed, it sleeps
On its side
Quietly,
The silver
Image
Of some
Small fish;

Opened, it snaps
Its tail out
Like a thin
Shrimp, and looks
At the sharp
Point with a
Surprised eye. ❖

While they thought this over, looking again at their safety pins and commenting to their neighbors, I wrote the poem on the chalkboard. "Listen to it again," I said and reread it slowly while we all looked at the words as we heard them.

"Safety Pin" from *More Small Poems* by Valerie Worth. Copyright © 1976 by Valerie Worth. Reprinted by permission of Farrar, Straus & Giroux, Inc.

"It looks weird, the way it goes up and down," Mark commented.

"What do you mean, Mark?"

"Well, I thought it would go like a sentence, you know, from one side to the other, but it goes from top to bottom."

"Yes, that's the way a poem is," I said. "You write it in lines instead of sentences."

"And you have to start every line with a capital letter?" Jenny asked.

"You don't have to, but lots of poets do. Let's read it together now." I moved my hand under the words as we read the poem in unison. Then I showed them Valerie Worth's book *All the Small Poems* and read some of the titles: "Slug," "Seashell," "Garbage," "Pebbles," "Acorn," and "Toad." I promised in response to requests (especially for "Garbage") that we'd read more of them later.

Inspiration from Outdoors

"Poems can be about small, everyday things, you see," I went on. "In a minute, we're going to go outside"—I was interrupted by a cheer—"to look for something we can bring inside to write a poem about. It can be anything that catches your eye, that looks interesting to you: a little stone, a twig, a leaf, anything. We'll have about ten minutes to look." After a brief discussion warning them away from appropriating anything belonging to the cars in the parking lot or the properties that bordered the school grounds, we put on our coats and set out on our search.

A surprising variety of found objects came back to the classroom with us: a scrap of aluminum foil with an interesting patina, a rusty nail, a red button, several bits of rock (one, an astonishing shade of blue), a twig in the shape of the letter *T* (found by Timmy), and leaves of many shapes and colors. The children examined their objects carefully, turning them over and around, holding them up to the light, talking to each other about their attributes.

"Write down what you see that's interesting or unusual. See if you can make it into a poem," I said. By the end of workshop time, all the children were well into writing their own small poems. Laura, who had found the blue rock, worked on hers for several days. Six weeks and many revisions later, she chose it as the one she wanted to publish in our poetry book.

Blue Rock

A rock that looks like it was from a fish tank once,
With fish swimming over it all day
All night.
Or maybe it was a tooth
Of a monster
Long ago,
And has turned blue from decay.
Or maybe it fell off a woman's ring
Because the glue had worn away.
Or maybe it was chipped off an ancient fossil
From Egypt or India or Greenland.
Or maybe it's a valuable rock
And was stolen from a famous museum.
Or maybe it was the stone
In that story "Stone Soup."
Well, one thing is true,
It's mine—
Forever. ❖

Laura Woodson
Grade 4

The Bat Poet

On the second day of poetry workshop, I began reading aloud Randall Jarrell's *The Bat Poet*. This is a wonderful book to read to your class at any time, but especially when you're working with poetry. Tucked into the story are several poems by Jarrell that, in addition to being fine works in their own right, give the reader hints about how a poem comes to be.

The Bat Poet is a short book; wanting to make it last, I read a small part at a time. When we got to the little bat's poem about the chipmunk, I gave everyone a copy so they could see as well as hear it and reread it at will.

The Chipmunk's Day

In and out the bushes, up the ivy,
Into the hole
By the old oak stump, the chipmunk flashes.
Up the pole
To the feeder full of seeds he dashes,
Stuffs his cheeks,
The chickadee and titmouse scold him;
Down he streaks.
Red as the leaves the wind blows off the maple,

Red as a fox,
Striped like a skunk, the chipmunk whistles
Past the love seat, past the mailbox,
Down the path,
Home to his warm hole stuffed with sweet
Things to eat.
Neat and slight and shining, his front feet
Curled at his breast, he sits there while the sun
Stripes the red west
With its last light: the chipmunk
Dives to his rest. ❖

A few days later, Paolo wrote this poem:

My Squirrel

My squirrel looks like a fur coat
As he runs on top of our balcony
And jumps on a tree.
He sits on a branch as his fluffy tail
Hangs down and he nibbles on a nut.
Like lightning he jumps on our greenhouse
And disappears
Running, he jumps into his hole
And doesn't come out till the next day. ❖

Paolo Mangonès
Grade 4

Gradually, the images and rhythms of poetry were working their way into young eyes, ears, and minds.

I hoped the children would enjoy the story of the little brown bat who followed his own poetic vision in the face of being ignored by his fellow bats and criticized by the mockingbird, the self-appointed arbiter and authority on poetry. I also hoped they would internalize the message that strict forms inhibit the beginning poet and are unnecessary for the writing of perfectly good poems.

With that in mind when we finished the book, I asked them to write what they thought the bat learned. Maybe the message I wanted to get across had registered somewhere, but it wasn't uppermost in the children's minds. Most of the responses reflected their empathy with the little bat as a beginning poet, reminding me of what was more important than forms or the absence of them: the essential, humanizing effect of good literature, whether prose or poetry.

"The Chipmunk's Day" by Randall Jarrell from *The Bat Poet* © 1963. Permission granted by Mary von S. Jarrell.

6   *The Poetry Workshop*

Carl was succinct: "The bat poet learned that writing poems was fun and it's hard to find a good audience." David's observation rings true for many of us: "I think he learned that poems are not always what they seem . . . and it's hard to get ideas all the time." Michael was realistic: "If you are a poet it doesn't mean you can always write a poem." Shain wrote, "He learned that it's hard to make a poem about something when you know nothing about it."

Although the first part of Eric's statement was probably intended literally, it's also interesting metaphorically: "I think the bat was inspired because he opened his eyes and saw all the colors. When he wrote a poem, he learned that you can make poems with any subject."

Adam's response was prophetic for all of us who participated in the poetry workshop. He wrote, "I think the bat learned more than he expected."

Finding Rhyme

The rhyme question cropped up on the first day. The most capable writers, remembering their success with rhymed poems in earlier grades, wanted to continue the practice. My memory was of too many efforts like this one: "I was there when a fool / Had a duel in a pool. / I was there when the king / Got his swing," and so on.

Anticipating the problem, I had chosen Valerie Worth's poems as our first models precisely because they didn't rhyme. Then I explained that, although listening to rhyming poems is delightful, writing good ones is very difficult. We talked this over and some of the children recalled the frustration of not being able to come up with rhyming words that made sense and fit into their poems. I told them that sometimes rhymes just happen, which is wonderful, and can come anywhere in the line, not just at the end.

Andrew's poem "The Sky" provided me with material for a minilesson about occasional rhyme and then led us on to consider alliteration.

It throws down
Snow as white as a wedding gown,
Sleet as solid as sugar cubes. . . .❖

Andrew Friedman
Grade 4

After we enjoyed "down" and "gown" because they were exactly the right words for his poem and also happened to rhyme, I pointed out the two *W*'s in line 2 and the *S*'s in line 3. I said that sometimes poets like to put together words that begin with the same letter sound. Jody suggested that it was a little like rhyming, only at the beginning of the word instead of the end. I told them that the ten-dollar word for that was *alliteration*, drawing out the syllables with zest. My aim was to present a term simply as a big, interesting word; perhaps it would lodge in a few schemas so that when they met up with *alliteration* in a more formal, future setting, a useful connection could be made.

Then we noted, to Andrew's surprise, that the repeated *s* sounds in the next line made us think of the sound that sleet actually makes when it falls. "I didn't know I did that!" the author said, beaming. I was glad to see, in the days that followed, children reading their poems to each other with greater attention to the sounds of words.

In a later group sharing time, Shain read:

When leaves fall
Off the trees
They swingle around
Down to the ground. ❖

> *Shain Marke*
> *Grade 4*

"Swingle" seemed to be the perfect word for the erratic path a leaf takes to the ground, and all the *ow* sounds were pure pleasure as they rolled out of his mouth.

As time went on, more children experimented with occasional rhyme. I especially enjoyed Charlie's poem, partly because he had not always experienced success in traditional language arts instruction.

Birds

Birds are sweet
With a really sweet sound
They fly
With the sky so high
If I didn't know
Any better
I would think it
Was a rainbow.

A bird could be mistaken for a
Plane so high with its wings
Spread out and when he sings
His engine is turned on. ❖

> *Charlie Griffin*
> *Grade 4*

When we listened to Charlie read his poem at sharing time, we noticed that he had fit three rhyming words into just two lines, a remarkable feat, but we were even more impressed with "wings" and "sings," which sounded perfect for where they were and what they meant.

Timmy discovered in his poem, which poignantly evokes the childhood fear of being lost, that words can look like they rhyme even if they don't sound exactly alike, as with "come" and "home."

Compass

When you have a compass
You always know where you are
You never get lost
Except when you drop it in the ice cold frost.
Your mother calls you
But you don't come
Because you can't find your compass
And you can't find your home.❖

Timmy Celfo
Grade 4

The next poem made Chris an instant celebrity.

Girls

Some girls are cool
Some are fools
Some girls are plump
Some are as thin
As a pin
Some girls are brawny
Some act like weenies
But the ones I like best
Are the ones in
Bikinis!❖

Chris Harvey
Grade 4

WORKSHOP STRUCTURE

Poetry workshop followed the same structure as our writing workshop had from the beginning of the year: minilesson, writing time (which included conferences), and sharing time. Minilessons often consisted of the next installment of *The Bat Poet* or the reading of a published poem or two. *Miracles* and *Those First Affections*, both collections of poetry written by children, provided models that were particularly accessible to fourth-graders. Hearing poems that were printed in a book yet written by children their age or younger added a dimension of possibility and importance to their own work.

Reading Poems Provides Models for Writing

Much good poetry can be read on more than one level, including, sometimes, fourth-grade level. William Carlos Williams's poems appealed to some of the children; others felt that they weren't really poems. The works of Carl Sandburg, e. e. cummings, Robert Frost, and Langston Hughes were heard in minilessons as well as those of poets who write chiefly for children. We read many of Valerie Worth's small poems and, while enjoying their sight, sound, and meaning, found much that was useful in them.

Several children brought poetry books from home or the library and read favorite poems from them. When a poem had special appeal, it was copied and kept in the child's folder for later rereading. In *Those First Affections* we found "Snow Falling," written by Gillian Hughes when she was only six. Its image of the snowy sky as a piece of paper with lines drawn on it by telephone wires made it a December favorite.

From these models, we learned everything we needed to know about writing poems: possible topics, metaphor, simile, punctuation, writing poems in lines, and more. They showed us that poems could be about images, experiences, feelings, people, or places. They could be serious or happy (or both at once), sad or funny. Often a child's discovery or problem would provide the next day's minilesson.

Sometimes we listened to audiotapes of poets reading their work or talking about how they wrote their poems. After hearing Kenneth Koch say that you can write even crazy things in a poem, Steven wrote about the moon as a witch. He said he really believed there was a witch in the moon when he was little but thought it was so crazy that he'd been embarrassed to write a poem about it.

Minilessons were as short as I could make them so that we could quickly get to the good part, which was writing. Before poetry workshop began, we had emptied out all our writing folders and transferred their contents to the all-year files. Now, because poems were usually short and written one to the page, the folders rapidly filled up again, and the children loved to watch them grow. Like most writers, they prided themselves on the physical evidence of their efforts.

Writing and Conferring

One day a couple of weeks into the workshop, I stole a minute to observe the class. Every writing behavior was visible, from frantic activity to writer's block. Five children were working at computers, using the Bank Street Writer; Ali was reading her poem to an attentive friend; Brian was reading to himself and laughing; Ronda was staring out the window; Eric was writing with great concentration, his nose almost touching the paper.

Usually I was too busy with conferences for the luxury of class-gazing. Compared with our personal narrative-writing workshops, poetry conferences went quickly. There was less content to deal with and closure was easier to reach. Just as poetry freed the children from the logical and structural constraints of prose writing, it allowed me to respond more spontaneously to their writing.

When a child called me over to hear a poem, my reaction was often nonverbal: smiles, sighs, or laughter. Verbal responses were usually questions or exclamations: "What a great image!" or "That gave me chills!" As well as being genuine requests for information, my questions were a way to suggest revisions or, as Donald Graves says, to nudge the writer. Here are some that recurred.

Can you think of some unusual words to use here?

What can you say that nobody else knows about this?

Can you compare this with something else?

Where's a good place to break this long line?

Are there some words you can take out?

What makes a poem good?

Can you write a longer/shorter poem this time?

How did you get that great idea?

Revision in the Workshop

Just as poetry had picked up the pace of conferences, the children seemed more willing than before to proceed quickly to revision or to a new topic, perhaps one suggested in a conference or sharing session. Peer conferences were also more successful than in earlier workshops. It was easier for both writer and responder to stay with the writing and not get sidetracked into discussions that didn't move the writing forward. Images were manageable units that could be talked about, reworked, and savored.

Jody's poem "Winter," contained these lines:

And little birds' footprints look
Like skis for the snowflakes.❖

She read it to Tally, who thought a minute and said, "But ski tracks are long and straight. Birds have toes." After some discussion, the lines became

And little birds' footprints
Look like
Little snowshoes
For the snowflakes.❖

Group sharing sessions benefited most from the brevity of poems. Five children could be heard in the time it would have taken just one to read a story. The listeners had less to hold in their minds until they could respond and had little chance to become bored or fidgety. As in conferences, the impact and sincerity of their spontaneous responses were deeply satisfying to the writer.

When it was time to publish, the children used the feedback they had received from conferences and sharing sessions to choose the poem to be printed in our book, and we moved on to the final revision and editing. Suzanne couldn't decide whether she liked *Stars* or *Moon* better. In an earlier conference, she had described how Venus looked so big it was almost like a bright, little moon. As we talked, she realized she could combine the two poems, using a few lines about Venus as the connection.

Jamie's early draft of "Summer and Winter" contained these lines:

In summer I go swimming
In winter I go sled riding.
When it's summertime I have water fights with my brother
When it's winter I have snowball fights with my sister. ❖

After reading her poem aloud in several conferences, she wrote her final draft:

In summer I jump in a pool
In winter I jump on a sled.
When it's summer I love to throw water bags on my brother
When it's winter my brother throws snowballs on me. ❖

When I asked Jamie for the details of how she went about revising her poem, her answer was simply, "It just sounds better this way." Thinking it was a valid standard for judging a poem, I almost let it go at that. I wanted to stay far away from acting like the mockingbird in *The Bat Poet*, whose belaboring of the uses of feet, meter, and rhyme exasperated the little bat. But I went on to tell Jamie that, for me, her use of "jump" sparked the first two lines, and the way she wove the activities in the last two lines made the images and the rhythm flow smoothly. She probably thought something like, "That's what I said—it just sounds better," but she nodded and smiled.

Some of the children wrote about their revision processes. Robert wrote this about his poem "Wild Classroom": "My poem went through a lot of revisions and editions. Sometimes it was wrong punctuation or it didn't make sense, or just something that I could change that would make it sound better. My friends helped me with this part, like advising certain changes."

Timmy, whose poem "Compass" appears earlier in this chapter, learned that sometimes writers have to quit and start again from scratch. "At first I wrote something about a compass is a place finder. Then I started all over again and wrote a much better poem!!!!"

Andrew's comment showed he took the revision process seriously: "When I was revising and adding on, I had to make very big decisions." Here is his final draft:

My Two Parakeets

My two parakeets have wings that go up and down
Like windshield wipers
When they eat
They swallow their food like a vacuum cleaner
My two parakeets' colors are aqua and white and
When they sit next to
Each other their colors blend into a whirlpool
When they tweet their voices echo
When they fly it seems like a cloud
Flying at the speed of light, and
When they play with each other their wings feel fresh. ❖

Andrew Karalian
Grade 4

Editing and publishing became almost painless with the Bank Street Writer word processor and our Apple //e computers. Words could be changed or moved with ease, and line breaks could be rearranged by pressing a key or two, thus eliminating finger-numbing copying and recopying. We no longer had to petition secretaries and aides to turn stacks of handwritten pages into typewritten copy. Instead, the kids printed out final drafts that were ready for the copying machine.

Writing About Writing

When I asked in conferences, "How did you get that idea?" the answers were like spotlights shining on the poems, making them glow with color and sharpened images. These discoveries were so exciting that I asked both classes to write about the origins of their poems. When they read these accounts in peer conferences or at sharing time, chain reactions were set off. The listeners, reminded of similar experiences or bemused by the unexpectedness of what they heard, found new possibilities for their own writing.

Often, they wrote of experiences that stuck in their memories: walking on the beach, going outside at night to watch fireflies, the first day of kindergarten, or a family trip. The memory that led to Laura's poem "Balloons" was unearthed because she was known to her classmates as a good speller. She wrote, "I got the idea for my poem when I was sitting down thinking about what to write and someone came over and asked me if you spell balloons with one or two *l*'s in it. Then I remembered. When I was in kindergarten the whole school let go of helium balloons. I remembered looking up and seeing them all floating together. It was a bright, sunny day."

Some found inspiration by imagining impossible things, others by looking around them at the real world with new eyes. Robert wrote this poem:

Wild Classroom

The brown and black pencil sharpener
I see,
Looks like a chipmunk scurrying up a
Tree.
The green carpet I stride on all day
Is like moss, where the animals play.
The tables are tree stumps
That you can move around,
Unlike the real ones
That are stuck in the ground.
My classroom is a fun place where I
Work and play,
But I wouldn't want to be stuck
In a forest all day!❖

Robert Ratish
Grade 4

He explained his writing process this way: "I got the idea of writing my poem by noticing that some of the smallest things that I see every day can be much different when I really think about them. I also got little ideas from poems that other people wrote."

Matthew also wrote about common objects; he began matter-of-factly and then let his imagination fly:

Paper Clips

Paper clips could do lots of things.
For example: they could hold things together,
You could bend them into different shapes like an S,
A snake, or even a seahorse. . . .❖

Matthew Cudrin
Grade 4

His explanation of how he went about writing his poem shows he understood how ephemeral thoughts can be: "One day I was thinking of a poem. I saw a paper clip on the shelf. Then I said to myself, 'Wouldn't that be a good topic for my poem?' I got a piece of paper fast because if I waited a long time I might forget all my idea."

I knew Christina had recently gotten a new puppy, so I wasn't surprised by the topic of her poem:

Puppies

Puppies flash across the room!
The blur can be any color,
But the blur depends on the color of the puppies!
Puppies can be crazy
And play with yarn like kittens do
They can fall down from a bed
Or jump from a couch.
Some things never change about puppies,
And some things do. ❖

Christina Oltmann
Grade 4

Her account of how she got her idea reminded me that children's attention is not necessarily where we think it is: "When Mrs. Armour was talking to the class, I was thinking, what was my puppy doing! Then I got the idea of writing a poem about him." It also reminded me that poetry writing lets us spin the gold of daydreams into the stuff of learning.

Delia recalled a special time at the beach:

A Night at the Beach

Picture a glittering sea,
The sea is as calm as a cloud
There are no BIG waves,
Just ripples,
Seagulls sing.
The cool wind blows by
With a snapping,
Snoring and shaking song.
The wind tickles your nose.
The sand is also glittery,
Like stars in the night sky.
If you go to the beach
On a late night
I'll bet you will find
Something special inside
Yourself. ❖

Delia Hayden
Grade 4

She used her past writing as a source of inspiration and as a memory-jogger: "I was looking through a story that I wrote a while ago. The title was 'Long Beach Island.' When I was reading it I didn't know what to write about, so I wrote about the best part of the trip. That's how I found my poem."

Hope worked for a long time on her poem "Trees," which appears in chapter 3. She struggled to frame her entire poem around a metaphor and, when she was finally done, explained it simply: "I got my poem by thinking very hard." Tomoki, whose poem opens this chapter, showed he had experienced the writer's constant dilemma of what to leave in and what to leave out: "I tried to remember small details, and wrote it. I also wrote what it seemed like. There were a lot of small details, so I wrote only what I think is good."

The ocean was a favorite topic, and that's what I thought Lee had in mind when he wrote this poem.

Fish

Fish are like scuba divers
Who have an endless air supply,
Swimming in all kinds of caves and cracks,
And almost never getting lost.
Little fish digging for food in the sand
At the bottom of the sea
And the big fish eating the little fish.❖

Lee Land
Grade 4

If Lee hadn't written about his composing process, I might never have learned that he had begun with the guppies in our small classroom aquarium and used them as a springboard to a larger and more dramatic setting. He wrote, "The way I thought of my poem was one day during writing class I looked at our fish. I thought if I wrote about them I could make an interesting poem. So I started to write about them. Then I looked at them again and they were digging in the rocks at the bottom of the fishtank. So in my poem I wrote, 'digging for food in the sand at the bottom of the sea.' Then I wrote the rest of my poem and I finished it." Notice the way that last line resonates with the writer's satisfaction at closure!

Akiko's explanation of how she wrote her poem gives us another example of the value of daydreaming. "I got my poem by thinking back about last summer when rabbits used to come to our back yard and nibble at the berries that grow in my yard, and how the butterflies fluttered with the dragonflies in the air. I can remember my brother running to catch the butterflies and the fun things we used to do. I can't wait until summer."

But the resultant poem is more than just another paean to the joys of summer. Filtered through Akiko's memory and shaped by her daydream, its images capture a warm summer day and draw us into it.

Animals

The rabbits lay motionless
Flattened against the ground
And the blackberry brambles.
The mice took care not to
Leave their holes in the ground.
Honey and the bumble bees hummed
The butterflies fluttered
Through the thin air
The dragonflies hovered
Like wonderful airplanes. ❖

Akiko Murasaki
Grade 4

PUBLICATION AND CELEBRATION

A natural outcome of any writing workshop, publication offers a satisfying closure that you can call on when it's needed. When I began our poetry workshop, I planned for it to last about six weeks; this stretched into two months, and even then some children didn't want to stop. But it's possible that other groups might not find the same gratification that this one did, and quitting time might have to be moved up. In any case, the activity of publishing a book creates enthusiasm as it brings the workshop to a close.

Final Editing

The last step in getting ready to publish our book of poems was the final editing conference. We did this at the computer with the author of the poem at the keyboard and me sitting alongside. I made suggestions about form and mechanics, and the student typed in the changes—if my suggestions were accepted.

In the beginning of the workshop, I told my classes that one of the appeals of writing poetry was that punctuation could be more flexible than in prose. By now, the children had so much ownership invested in their poems that punctuation (or the lack of it) was there because they wanted it there for their own reasons, and my opinion was of secondary importance. My consolation for being overruled by a fourth-grader was the recognition of having reached a major goal: The children were exercising full ownership of and responsibility for their own writing.

These editing conferences were, of necessity, lightning fast. Our self-imposed deadline raced toward us at a frightening speed, and the usual unexpected crises (power outages, a jammed printer, a fire drill) were reliably present. I spent a couple of lunch hours in the classroom, eyes fixed on the computer screen, while the children cycled themselves in and out of the room for their conferences.

An aide who was in tune with the process would have been a treasure beyond price; I urge you to recruit and train volunteers early in the year and wish I had done so. Of course, it's possible to be more relaxed than I was about where a classroom book lands on the road to perfection. I wanted all the children's poems to appear in the best possible form and remembered with a pang the distress of a child whose poem had been published the year before with its last line missing. I also remembered adding all those last lines by hand. I was determined that when our manuscript went to the "printer" (i.e., the office copying machine), it was going to be as error-free as we could make it.

Adding Visual Interest

The previous year's class had published a collection of poems, and although the content was wonderful, the pages lacked visual interest. We decided to illustrate our poems and immediately discovered that we faced a new set of decisions. I believed the kids' descriptions of how they had written their poems were essential, so there were three elements to be arranged. Could the poem, picture, and explanation fit on one page? Short poems posed no problem, but several were so long that they took up most of the page.

When we decided to allot two pages to each poem, we faced still more questions. How big should the illustration be? Which page would it look better on? What was the best drawing style for this sort of presentation? It would have been easier, or at least faster, if I had made these decisions myself, but the children would have missed the experience of considering aesthetic choices and being involved in a significant part of the publishing process.

We concluded that the poem should have one whole page to itself and that the illustration could share the other page with the explanation. We knew that it would be difficult to draw the pictures right the first time, so we cut pieces of unlined paper in half to practice on. I encouraged the kids to sketch their ideas first and treat them like poems: to try out a few drafts, then revise the one they liked best to make a good picture. I reminded them that the copying machine needed very dark lines and unfortunately was color-blind, so they could use shading in their pictures but the colorful markers could stay on the shelf.

The illustrations were eye-openers! Tomoki's fireworks burst beside the many-windowed twin towers of the Trade Center in lower Manhattan. Christina's puppy jogged on two legs across a kitchen floor. Donald's picture for "Baseball" showed batter, catcher, umpire, and the stadium walls, complete with beer signs. Chris illustrated his poem "Girls" with examples of the topic. Charlie's picture for "Birds" made me think of an Escher drawing with its arc of six shapes that changed, little by little, from bird to airplane.

When all three parts were completed, I took the collection home for assembling. It was fun to place the illustration on a page with the explanation in a way that seemed to fit best (the puppy went at the bottom of a page; on another, sun and clouds went at the top) and provide a little visual variety. Clear tape held the parts together. Because the poem was the focus, it went on the right-hand side. We wanted our book to be printed on both sides, the way regular books are, so I clipped page fronts and backs together and numbered them carefully at the bottom.

About halfway through the arranging and taping, I noticed something that sent my heart on a free-fall: The kids' names didn't appear with their poems! When they were working at the computer, they all had their own diskettes, so there was no need to sign each poem. Names had been hurriedly written on the backs of pages to identify them, but we had completely overlooked the need to give the author's name in the most important place: on the page with the printed poem.

Facing the unpleasant prospect of everyone going back to the computers to type in their names and then reprinting the pages, I took the manuscript to school in the morning and told the kids what we had forgotten to do. I wish I could remember which inspired child said, "Why don't we just sign our names under the poems?" Brilliant! Not only did that wipe out the need to go through the computer and printer again, but the handwritten signatures added a distinctively personal touch. For once, a mistake had turned into an improvement!

When the children had made books of their own writing earlier in the year, they had enjoyed creating colorful, exciting covers. Now we faced a critical selection: Who would create the cover for our poetry book? The best solution we could think of was to hold a contest. Everyone who wanted to would make a cover and we would vote to choose the one to go on our book.

The thing I don't like about contests is that there's usually only one winner and all the rest are losers, but there didn't seem to be an alternative. We set a deadline and when it arrived, I collected the potential covers and taped them in an impressive row across the chalkboard.

The conversations I listened in on as I did this told me we had to have a brief discussion about choosing the best cover instead of the cover made by your best friend. I didn't expect aesthetic considerations to overcome loyalty completely, but at least campaigning was kept to a minimum. We voted by secret ballot, which also encouraged independence of judgment.

The winning design captured us with its enthusiasm. In the top right corner was drawn a large medal on which was printed, "*GREAT! 1st Prize Poems.*" Beside it the title proclaimed, "The Fourth Grade's Poems Are Great," and below this were drawn three pages. Each had two eyes, a mouth, and squiggly lines to represent print. The eyes of one page dripped tears, and a balloon coming from its mouth said, "Sad poem!" Another had a pleasant expression and a balloon that said, "Good, I like it!" The page in the middle winked at us and said, "GREAT!" The exclamation mark looked like a heart.

The runner-up, a computer graphics design that showed a scroll, a pen, and an inkwell, was more conservative, proclaiming in Gothic type, "Our Fourth Grade Poems." It looked polished and elegant. We decided it was too good to leave out and made it the back cover.

Putting It All Together

We were learning that there's more to publishing a book than just writing it. An office aide was able to run our manuscript through the copying machine, but the machine did not collate pages. Nor was collating part of our aide's job description, so she brought us 2,800 pages, printed on both sides, in several stacks. Turning them into books was up to us. The book held the work of two fourth-grade classes, and the class that met first in the day was the one who had the job—and the excitement—of putting it together.

This is the only time I can remember finding the assembly line method useful and acceptable in the classroom. We pushed our tables and desks into a large oval and set out piles of pages on them. The first stack was front covers; the next stack had page 1 on the front. This was the introduction, which would be on the right when the book was opened. On the back was page 2, the first poem's explanation, which would be on the left. The next stack was of pages 3 (the first poem, also on the right-hand side) and 4 (the second poem's explanation), and so on.

Thirty-five stacks of our book's pages and covers ringed the room. Twenty-seven fourth-graders lined up behind the back cover and proceeded counterclockwise around the oval, picking up a page and putting it on top of the last one, until they reached the front cover. Just beyond it I sat with a stapler, waiting to bind each book with staples at top, middle, and bottom.

Unfortunately, it was a hand stapler. The line of kids kept circling around until the stacks of pages had been collated into books. By the time the eightieth copy reached me, I was trying to remember what I had read about carpal tunnel syndrome. But when we finally finished and sat back to look at all those great fourth-grade poetry books, fatigue and boredom were overcome by pride, and we settled down to read and admire our newly published anthologies.

Celebration!

All elementary school teachers know that *party* is one of the few magic words that never fail to get everyone's attention immediately. When I had suggested a poetry publication celebration a couple of weeks earlier, everyone thought it was an excellent idea. Now, as we looked back on nearly two months of work, we knew we truly deserved a party.

Planning the Event

After we agreed that food was the primary consideration, we talked about whom to invite and what else we could do to celebrate our work. I told about a poetry reading I had gone to where poets stood up before the audience and read their poems, and everyone applauded them. Afterward they signed their books of poems for people who had bought copies.

This sounded appealing to most of the children, and we began to consider having our own poetry reading. Two of our class members who had read their poems the year before at the regional poetry festival told us it was fun, but it took a lot of practice to be ready to stand up in front of an audience and read your poem. Riding on a wave of confidence born of seeing our book in final form, we decided a poetry reading would be the centerpiece of our celebration.

The Guest List

When we listed the names of people to invite, we began to wonder if we might have to print more copies of our book, because we planned to give one to each guest. Our guest list included parents, our principal, the superintendent of schools, all the teachers (we knew most of them would be busy with their classes, but some might be free for at least part of our program and all would certainly receive a copy of our book), our custodian, the librarian, the nurse, lunch ladies, the secretaries, classroom and office aides, student teachers, and the crossing guards. At this point I should have realized that it was time to book the auditorium and make it an all-school assembly, but I was still locked in the mind-set of a small, classroom reading.

Composing the invitations was a collaborative, whole-group project for each class. I wrote the children's suggestions on the board, and when we were sure we had included all the necessary information about place, time, and the nature of the event, the children carefully copied invitations for their families. The ones who wrote their first invitations neatly, accurately, and quickly (not an easy combination to achieve) got to write and deliver another one to a school guest of their choice.

Poetry Reading Rehearsal

The next day we began to rehearse for the poetry reading. The children read their poems to each other in pairs or groups of three, working to develop expression and smoothness, before reading for the whole class. Shyness and self-consciousness kept voices low and speed of delivery high at first, but that wore off with repetition.

Someone raised the question of whether we should memorize the poems or read them. "I already know mine," Carina said. Several other authors of short poems said they knew theirs, too.

"I think I know mine, but I'm afraid I'll forget a word," Eric said. Tomoki nodded agreement, looking worried.

"Either way is fine," I said. "Take a copy of your poem with you if you want." My mind produced a brief flashback of the distant past, when less flexible ways of presenting a public performance held sway, and stage fright could lead to trauma. Thank goodness that time is past, I thought.

Later I gave up some flexibility and took on the authority of a coach, firmly insisting that words had to be said slowly and distinctly enough to be understood from the back of the room. The kids who had read their poems at the poetry festival said they'd used a microphone, but it was a little scary and weird to hear your voice that way. We decided to stay unamplified.

Getting the kids to keep their voices up for the entire line and not swallow the last word was an ongoing problem. I repeated the line with an exaggerated lift of tone and volume on the last word and especially at the end of the poem and had them imitate this. We taped and played back some of the poems so the kids could hear their voices as the audience would but soon realized we didn't have time to do that for everyone. The party date was almost upon us. I made a mental note to ask the speech teacher how I could be a more effective coach in the future.

Food!

The day before the celebration, we discussed the order in which we'd do things. Jody, always nervous about speaking before a group, said, "Let's do the poetry reading first and get it over with," and a chorus of voices agreed.

"Then we can give our guests their books," I said. "You can each give one to your parents if they're here, and then to whoever else you took an invitation to."

"Then we eat!" said Chris, and the chorus of agreement was louder than before. Good grief, I thought. I'd forgotten about the food! Always a firm believer in planning and organization, here I was on the day before the celebration with no lists of who would bring what, no refreshment committees, and no cleanup cadres!

Suppressing a touch of panic and hoping the loaves and fishes principle would come through for us, I said, "Bring whatever you want to. I'll take care of the fruit punch."

The Day Arrives

Before school the next day, I stood in my empty classroom, reflected on the poetry-saturated weeks that had gone before, and wondered. Would others think the poems in our book were as good as we thought they were? Should I have taught more poetic forms? Did we spend too much time on oral activities and too little on quiet writing? Should I have emphasized memorization? And, above all, would the children continue to enjoy poetry, either as readers or writers, in years to come?

The arrival of the children rescued me from that bottomless pit of questions without answers. Now there was no time for worry or wondering. We pushed back the movable divider between our two fourth-grade classrooms, moved desks and tables to the sides, and arranged chairs in rows facing the chalkboard. At the front of our mini-auditorium was a desk topped with a portable lectern. We had used it in our final rehearsal as a refuge for the most nervous: a place to stand behind or to rest a paper held by shaking fingers. Braver kids stood beside or in front of it.

Without benefit or constraints of committees and assignments, everyone hustled around and got everything done. The right amount of pretzels, chips, cookies, and popcorn appeared on the tables, to my relief. Some children had dressed up for the occasion, some wore their usual clothes, and one or two were downright scruffy. No matter; all were happy and excited, though a little nervous. Our books sat in splendor on a front table, waiting for their wider audience.

A few minutes before our guests were to arrive, Laura pulled on my arm and whispered, "Look at Tomoki." I followed her gaze to a far corner of the room where he stood with his back to all our hubbub, in a cocoon of quiet, rehearsing his poem one last time.

Before long, the room filled up and our program began. One after another, children of both fourth-grade classes rose, stood before an audience of about eighty adults and peers, and read the poems they had selected as their best works. Applause filled the air again and again as the exhilaration of high achievement built in our hearts. Poetry gave wings to our spirits as well as our words.

Revising Teaching

This model of a poetry workshop is only one of an uncounted number. It stood at a point on the unending continuum of revision that represented my teaching process. I hope you'll begin your own version of a poetry workshop soon if you haven't done one before; if you're an old hand at this kind of teaching and learning, I hope you've found some ideas that contribute to your ongoing revision.

The basic workshop structure is hard to improve on: minilesson, reading/ writing/conferring, group sharing time. Even that simple structure is flexible; you won't always need a minilesson, and sometimes you'll run out of time before the sharing session. Within that basic structure, however, flexibility is rampant.

Minilessons ideally are short, as their name tells us—perhaps five minutes or less—but they can stretch occasionally so long as we're careful not to make a habit of extending them into reading/writing/conferring time. You can use them for direct instruction, such as defining and giving examples of similes or showing how to handle line breaks. They can be as simple as the reading of a poem you love that matches the needs of your kids at that time. On another day, a minilesson could be a five- or ten-minute discussion of a poem heard earlier. A student's brief explanation of how he or she changed a line from ordinary to unique can be a wonderful minilesson.

The minilesson launches students into the heart of the workshop: reading, writing, and talking about poetry. Grouping arrangements are limited only by the number of kids in your class and range from a child working alone to the whole class composing a collaborative poem. Pairs, permanent or ad hoc, can work together; larger groups can be fluid, forming and reforming according to the work at hand. You might choose to organize your whole class into response groups, give each a copy of a poem, let them read and discuss it, and then meet as a whole class to share what they found.

Conferences, integral to this part of the workshop, are also infinitely elastic. They can be as short as a smile and a pat on the shoulder in recognition of a student's having solved a problem you worked on the day before. Rarely, you might find yourself spending most of the scheduled time with one writer whose need requires continuity of attention from you. The student can have a conference with you, a peer, or, when everyone in the room is busy, a passerby corralled by a student who needs to discuss a poem at that very minute.

Obviously, this won't be a silent environment. Teachers often speak of the "workshop hum" created by the voices and movement of children who are engaged in productive activity. Marilyn London, who teaches fifth grade, says she likes her classroom to sound like a college library—not too quiet, not too noisy. Some teachers insist that a silent writing time be part of the workshop. All teachers must find the noise level they and their students can work best with; it will vary from teacher to teacher and class to class.

But don't mistake all this flexibility for excessive permissiveness and lack of discipline. A well-run writing workshop is purposeful and productive with a structure that is understood and accepted by teacher and students. The ground rules are simple but firm: Everyone writes and everyone's writing is respected. Within this framework, children and adults work together and share responsibility for learning. Because children write for their own, authentic reasons, they have an investment in the success of the workshop.

What to Write About

Teachers, fearful that children won't know what to write about, sometimes assign topics or maneuver their classes through exercises designed to produce a certain kind of poem. They run the risk of teaching children to go through the motions of writing with little personal involvement and deny them the valuable experience of searching their own minds and memories to find the unique poems that only they can write.

A standard component of most writing workshops is a minilesson of questions that help children find topics they want to write about. One of the most effective for poetry topics is, "What sticks in your memory—can't be forgotten—keeps popping up in your mind?" As children talk about their persistent memories, connections click in the minds of listeners, who quickly jot a reminder for writing time. These lists, or topic banks, are added to periodically and provide a continuing resource.

For me, ideas for topics come best from my own experience, something real that I perceive or have done, so I encouraged my classes to search for topics in their personal lives. Other teachers use arranged experiences in the classroom with success. Gregory Denman calls his approach "wordsmithing" and describes a series of encounters with words that helped primary-grade children write poems individually and collaboratively. He and the children read poems together and made collections of the words they relished the most, which then were available for use in their writing.

Donald Graves suggests a number of strategies to get teacher and child started on writing, such as list poems, starters ("I am the person who . . ."), and finding poetry in prose. Florence Grossman, in *Getting from Here to There: Writing and Reading Poetry*, names each chapter according to the topic of the poems discussed. Chapter 1, "Lists," provides a wonderful variety of ways to approach writing list poems. The next chapter,"Then," is about recalling childhood memories; "Things" shows us poems that hide in ordinary objects. "Look long enough at a pencil and the poem will begin," she writes (1982, 30). Here is a poem by a child about a pencil.

Word Wake

A tall piece of wood
with a rock at the end,
a pointed rock,
a rock that sails
on paper,
making dark trails
behind it.
A tree
with no branches,
just a tip,
pointing to God. ❖

Kyle Cummings
Grade 3

Kenneth Koch (1980) tells how inner-city kids in his classes used his topic groups of wishes, lies, and dreams to write strong, startling poems. In *Rose, Where Did You Get That Red?* he describes his use of poems by Blake, Shakespeare, and Whitman, among others, as models for children's poems. These models were springboards, however, not recipes, and led to original works rather than imitations.

Joanne Hammond, who teaches at Seacrest Country Day School in Naples, Florida, used Koch's modeling strategy with her students. Although the debt the next two poems owe to William Blake and William Carlos Williams is clear, they stand firmly as poems in their own right.

Poem

Snake, snake who made you?
Who gave you your beady eyes?
Snake, Snake why do you live?
Why do you have deadly fangs?
Snake, Snake who taught you to strike?
Who taught you how to hide?
Snake, snake tell me, who made you? ❖

Katherine Scarborough
Grade 4

Rain

The
rain
ruined your
baseball game

I
knew
it meant a
lot to you

But
when
the sun
came out

The
rainbow
was worth it ❖

> Katie Dubrule
> Grade 4

The Reading/Writing Connection

The single most effective way to help children find topics to write poems about is to immerse them in poetry. The more poems they hear and read, the more ideas they'll find for their own poems. Start the day by reading a poem, post poems around the room, hang up those the kids have written, and use poems to fill empty moments spent standing in line or waiting for the next event.

Poetry circles, groups of children who meet to read, talk about, and enjoy poems they've chosen, develop a sophisticated understanding and appreciation of poetry. They can develop from your having conducted similar sessions with the whole class; even if just one group wants to continue on its own, the activity will be worthwhile. It's possible for circles to focus only on reading poetry, but it's more likely that one or more members will move into writing it as well.

When we discuss a poem we've read with a group, it's important to remember that there's no single correct meaning of a poem. Indeed, to think of a poem primarily as "meaning" can detour us into the dead end of paraphrasing it in prose. Research tells us that reading is a transaction between reader and text in which the reader reconstructs the text in terms of her or his own experience.

Consider Tomoki's poem, which opens this chapter. It arose from his experience of watching fireworks on a summer night in the city. In Tomoki's mind, the images are specific, clearly remembered, but their details are unknown to us. In my mind, the curtain is black velvet and hangs in a huge theater, and the flowers become magenta waterfalls as they disappear. In your mind, the images will be different. None of us can see exactly what Tomoki sees, and that is at once the magic and the paradox of poetry.

To insist on just one interpretation of a poem would kill it as effectively as dissection does. The richest discussions of poems are among readers who all have different impressions to share and are encouraged to express them, secure in the knowledge that all opinions will be respected.

We know that reading poems as models is a powerful way to foster the writing of poetry. There's another more subtle way that reading and writing connect. I find that after reading a lot of poetry, my speech and writing begin to sound more poetic than usual. It's as if the words from the page enter my mind, look for friends, and persuade them to join their poetry club. Immersing your kids in poetry can help to organize their thinking into poetic modes and increase their fluency when they write.

Where to Hold a Poem

Manila folders have long been the container of choice for children's pieces of writing, but sometimes poems and the collected objects that inspire them refuse to fit into folders. Primary-grade children are especially likely to need a place for the assorted small objects that matter to them and are therefore the stuff of poetry. I've seen teachers use everything from cereal boxes to plastic dishpans for this. Portfolios (the kind with accordion-pleated sides and a flap that keeps the contents from falling out) hold a lot, are portable, and appeal especially to older children.

Lucy Calkins describes using notebooks as holders of bits and pieces of our lives that will later be woven into writing. Anything the child sees, hears, or thinks of that seems worth saving can be written in a notebook. Entries don't have to be drafts or even sentences but rather become a vein of ore to be mined later. A poetry notebook can hold phrases, sketches, labels, photos—anything that whispers to the writer's imagination.

Calkins tells how children carry their notebooks with them everywhere, ready to add nuggets of possibility. They reread their notebooks often and reflect on their contents, mining them for images and ideas to be refined into the shining metal of a piece of writing. Notes and early drafts can escape from a folder and be lost; a notebook holds all efforts and shows the history of each piece of writing through all its forms.

Planning for the Workshop

Just as the form of the poetry workshop is flexible, so must the planning of it be. I began with a broad outline of a six-week project, listing introductory activities, titles of books and poems I wanted to use, concepts I wanted to develop in minilessons, and the final outcome (our published anthology).

It was impossible for me to write detailed plans for a week in the future because each day's work grew from the events of the day before. Minilesson topics answered specific needs as we discovered them; occasionally no needs presented themselves, and I chose from my list of concepts or strategies one that seemed to fit in best.

Planning in advance for conferences was impossible, too, in that they usually arose spontaneously. Follow-up conferences developed from the notes I made during the initial discussion, so the planning for them was tied closely to record keeping. (Record keeping is discussed in chapter 5.) Sharing sessions led to more record keeping, which led to further planning. A writing workshop is a river that refuses to break up into separate streams; all its parts flow together.

BEYOND THE WORKSHOP

A workshop is an excellent way to begin reading and writing poetry for the first time. We can see it as a contained, manageable unit with a beginning and an end, and a purpose and theme understood by all. It gives teacher and students a shared, intensive experience in the genre.

Actually, it's just the beginning, which I learned from one of my fourth-graders. When our poetry workshop was over, I told the kids they could now write anything they liked. Kevin came up to me a little later and said hesitantly, "Can I write poems? I started one after we finished our book and I want to write another draft." I was so pleased I just stood there and beamed at him.

Once you've freed poetry from its undeserved reputation as a difficult, unpopular subject, it becomes a treasured accompaniment to the classroom day. I think of my Siamese cat: When she's sleeping and I'm working at the computer or in the kitchen, I forget about her. But when I need the beauty of her blue-eyed gaze or the warm softness of her fur in my arms, I stop and pick her up for a moment. When we play, the grace and hilarity of her movements fill me with delight. And sometimes she comes to me and simply demands that I pay attention to her.

Poems are like that in the classroom. They bestow moments of beauty on us; they comfort us with words that crystallize our emotions and tell us we are not alone; they make us laugh, filling our hearts and minds with lightness. Whether we read or write them, they demand and deserve our attention.

REFERENCES

All unreferenced quotes are from conversations with the author or observations of the author.

Calkins, Lucy McCormick, with Shelley Harwayne. *Living Between the Lines.* Portsmouth, NH: Heinemann Educational Books, 1991.

Denman, Gregory A. *When You've Made It Your Own: Teaching Poetry to Young People.* Portsmouth, NH: Heinemann Educational Books, 1988.

Graves, Donald. *Explore Poetry*. Portsmouth, NH: Heinemann Educational Books, 1992.

Grossman, Florence. *Getting from Here to There: Writing and Reading Poetry*. Montclair, NJ: Boynton/Cook, 1982.

Jarrell, Randall. *The Bat Poet*. New York: Macmillan, 1963.

Koch, Kenneth. *Rose, Where Did You Get That Red?* New York: Vintage Books, 1973.

———. *Wishes, Lies and Dreams: Teaching Children to Write Poetry*. New York: HarperCollins, 1980.

Lewis, Richard. *Miracles: Poems by Children of the English-Speaking World*. New York: Simon & Schuster, 1966.

Rogers, Timothy, ed. *Those First Affections*. London: Routledge & Kegan Paul, 1979.

Worth, Valerie. *More Small Poems*. New York: Farrar, Straus & Giroux, 1976.

———. *All the Small Poems*. New York: Farrar, Straus & Giroux, 1987.

Chapter 2
POETRY IS EVERYWHERE

Most teachers would agree that children in the middle grades—from age eight or nine to about eleven—are naturals at writing and reading poetry. They've mastered most of the basics, so they can focus on meaning and handle concepts such as metaphor or personification, and their attention hasn't yet fallen hostage to the demands of adolescence.

But poetry can and should be a source of pleasure and learning for all schoolchildren. It should have a place in the lives of kindergartners and first-graders, inner-city children, children who are learning English as a second language, and children with emotional or developmental difficulties. They all have the right and the capacity to be enriched and delighted by hearing or reading other people's poems and writing their own.

THE PRIMARY YEARS

Nancy Larrick (1993) writes about a sixteen-month-old child whose family made music an integral part of the day, from good-morning songs to lullabies. Not yet a year and a half old, little Sara showed how much she already knew and loved about music by waving her arms in time to the rhythm like a conductor, even pausing appropriately at the ends of stanzas.

Babies and small children meet poetry and song as one. Mother Goose and counting rhymes, "Twinkle, Twinkle, Little Star" and "This little piggie went to market"—these and more are beloved by preschool children who are captivated by their rhyme, rhythm, and repetition. Early childhood teachers know this and foster their children's enjoyment of poetry by reading these old favorites and many new poems to them. Anthologies of this kind of material are everywhere; a particularly good one is Lee Bennett Hopkins's *Side by Side: Poems to Read Together*, with a tremendous variety of poems new and old, long and short, about animals and holidays and weather and more.

Young children, unfettered by self-consciousness, respond spontaneously to poetry. They move their hands, heads, and bodies to the rhythm and chant the repeated refrains. This is the time to make poetry an integral part of their lives so that it never becomes the stranger or, worse, enemy that too many high-schoolers see when they open their anthologies.

Perhaps you, like many primary teachers, read poems to your class as a daily part of your language program. Christine Duthie and Ellie Kubie Zimet, first-grade teachers in Trumansburg, New York, sit in a circle with their children every day and read a poem chosen to fit their classes' interests and needs. The teachers make multiple copies of the poem, one for each child's personal poetry book at home and one to put in a loose-leaf notebook, which becomes the classroom anthology.

Christine and Ellie also encourage their students to read poems of their own choice to the class. In their experience, poetry is often neglected in classrooms. But they found that teachers who love poetry and share it with their classes teach their children to love it, too. These children read and write poems with joy and confidence.

Regie Routman, in *Transitions*, describes how she and other primary-grade teachers in her school use poetry as a regular part of the writing and reading program. From the beginning of the year, they read poems to their classes. These are poems the teachers themselves love, and this love is contagious. Each week they choose four or five new poems to introduce, so that by the end of the year, the children have read more than 150 poems.

Children illustrate their own copies of the poems, read the words to and with each other (many can do this by early November), and take them home to share with their families. Parents are delighted to see their children reading and reciting poems, sometimes on the phone to distant relatives. It's visible, audible proof that their children are indeed learning to deal with the written word, often an anxiety-causing concern for parents of young children.

The use of poetry to foster early reading is far from new, especially of the rhyming, rhythmic variety. The compilers of basal readers have always included it, beginning with McGuffey. James Moffett wrote, "Rhyme in particular is helpful for reinforcing phonics instruction"; he suggests that teachers write a poem on a transparency, read it first to and then with the children, and finally, "When rhythms and repetitions are still pounding in their ears, and images swirling through their heads, send the children to paper to write their own nursery rhyme or ballad or limerick" (1973, 122-23).

The difference today is in the way we select and use poems. We look for poems that will engage young children's imaginations and resonate with their experience. Understanding that learning takes place more effectively when children are actively involved and have a sense of self-determination, we use materials and strategies to further this process.

Big Books

Teachers who practice whole language strategies often read to their classes from big books; many narrative poems are available in this format, from "I Know an Old Lady" and "The Three Little Pigs" to Sendak's *Chicken Soup with Rice: A Book of Months*. Regie Routman tells of using this book to introduce the months of the year, beginning the first week of school. As children memorize the poems through repeated readings, they see themselves as readers and tackle the learning process with confidence.

Big books have the advantage of enabling children to see words at the same time they are hearing and sometimes saying them. Bill Martin Jr.'s *Brown Bear, Brown Bear, What Do You See?* and Joy Cowley's *Mrs. Wishy Washy* are among a large group of big books, beloved for their simple but satisfying texts and wonderful illustrations, that help first-graders learn to read through rhyme, rhythm, and repetition.

When their teacher announces it's big book time, children hurry to get a good spot on the floor in front of the reading chair. There's no nonchalance of the blasé fifth-grader here! Little kids welcome a well-loved poem like a good friend, happier to see it the tenth time than the first. As their teacher reads and moves a hand below the line of text, they chant the repeated refrain, forming connections between the sight and sound of words. If their teacher pauses before the last word of a rhyming couplet, they supply it gleefully, using context and their knowledge of initial consonants as clues.

An observer watching a group of kindergartners or first-graders having such a wonderful time would scarcely connect their activity with the arduous task of learning to read, yet that is just what's happening. Rhyme and repetition make these poems predictable and therefore foster letter-sound connections and word recognition. The rhythm of the words accompanied by repeated body movements such as hand clapping or foot tapping help build neuronal patterns and connections that underlie the reading process. Recurrent pleasurable experiences that connect hearing, seeing, and saying the written word build solid reading skills.

The active involvement we know is necessary in order for learning to take place is obvious in this process. Often children in whole language classrooms choose to make small copies of a cherished big book or collaboratively compose their own version of a narrative poem that is made into an original big book. By emulating these models, they develop their burgeoning reading and writing abilities.

It's important to provide poetry-reading time when children can choose from these materials and printed poems, take them to a comfortable place, and, alone or with a friend or two, reread their favorites. And it's all right if their reading is sometimes more a matter of paraphrasing; we can think of this as a kind of invented reading, a precursor to the accurate representation of words rather than errors that must be corrected.

Poetry Sources

Fortunately, there's a proliferation of beautiful books for young children that include rhyme, rhythm, and repetition. An inclusive bibliography of such books for beginning readers is given in Regie Routman's *Transitions*.

A useful anthology is Jack Prelutsky's *Read-Aloud Rhymes for the Very Young*, a wide-ranging collection of more than 200 poems that are perfect for kindergarten through second grade. *Me!*, compiled by Hopkins, is a collection of poems about bumps, itches, friends, pets, and lost teeth, all topics of immediate interest to young children. It includes "Everybody Says" by Dorothy Aldis, which is about the child's resemblance to several family members and ends with the line, "But *I* want to look like ME!"

Poems like these appeal to little kids' love of surprise and the ridiculous and speak to their experience of being only five or six years old in a world of big people. I remember a book I read when I was little in which an independent-minded schoolchild was asked to read a poem that contained this line: "Birds in their little nests agree."

"Oh, but they don't!" she objected. "They fight like anything!" Her outraged teacher punished her severely for daring to contradict authority. Such a poem is unlikely to be found in today's classrooms where children's knowledge of their world meets with respect rather than punishment.

Shel Silverstein's outrageous poems in *Where the Sidewalk Ends* are great crowd-pleasers in primary classrooms (and with older kids as well). "Ourchestra" says it doesn't matter if we don't have instruments, we can just play our bodies—beat bellies for drums, play noses for horns, and clap hands for cymbals. "Thumbs" extols the delights of sucking your thumb and "One Inch Tall" begins, "If you were only one inch tall, you'd ride a worm to school."

Silverstein's work arouses strong responses in readers of all ages. It's hard to find a child who doesn't love the poems but easy to find adults who disapprove of them. Parents and teachers are sometimes put off by his subject matter, which includes, for example, sticking your finger in your nose, spitting down from a tall building, and the conflict between God's gifts and Ma's commands. Not every teacher has the grace and flexibility, as does a colleague of mine, to greet with equanimity a first-grader who came to school wearing a toilet plunger on his head, inspired by Silverstein's poem "Hat."

Of course, part of his powerful appeal for children springs from just this irreverence. Literature that tweaks propriety and the establishment comes to us from the ancient Greeks, Chaucer, and Shakespeare; contemporary writers who write in this mode know it's going to bring them trouble in some form. If the child within you delights in a little iconoclasm, you'll share your classes' enjoyment of Silverstein's poems. If they offend you, you have the prerogative of not including them in the poems you bring to your classes.

Teachers sometimes object to these poems on the grounds that they don't provide suitable models for children to use when writing their own poems, not because of the subject matter but because the rhyme, rhythm, and wordplay are too sophisticated to be accessible. This is true of much of the poetry young children love, from Mother Goose on, and if we excluded all such poems, it would impoverish us. Few of us are painters, poets, or composers, yet we love and are enriched by works of art for their own sake, not because we hope to be able to emulate them.

Part of helping kids of all ages to write poetry is convincing them that it doesn't *have* to rhyme. As we saw in chapter 1, there are a number of excellent unrhymed poems to present as models when your children begin to write poetry. I've talked to several first-grade teachers who use Valerie Worth's books for this purpose. But for listening, chanting, and illustrating, such Silverstein poems as "Upstairs," about a family of wrens living in the speaker's hair, or "Recipe for a Hippopotamus Sandwich" are hard to beat.

Another author whose genius for rhythm and rhyme appeals to all ages from prereaders on up is Theodor Geisel, the beloved Dr. Seuss. Parents who read to their children from babyhood can recite chunks of *Green Eggs and Ham* from memory. When, in 1992, an actor on a television sitcom said, "I do not like them, Sam-I-am," the audience chuckled with recognition at words that first appeared in print more than thirty years earlier.

Green Eggs and Ham gives us an interesting illustration of the importance of quality in poetry for children. Dr. Seuss produced this classic after Bennett Cerf, his editor at Random House, bet him he couldn't write a book using only fifty words (Moje and Woan-Ru Shyu 1992). We're all familiar with the mind-numbing dullness of some controlled-vocabulary texts; yet Dr. Seuss created one that has delighted generations.

In *The Cat in the Hat*, written three years earlier, he used less than 250 words to tell a story that he expected to be a snap, something he could toss off in two or three weeks. But it wasn't until more than a year later, after a great deal of writing and rewriting, that the book was finished. Probably a less-talented writer *could* have done the job in a few weeks, but I doubt the result would have found an audience.

Dr. Seuss's books have everything for the beginning reader: rhyme, rhythm, zany characters, intriguing stories, and wildly imaginative illustrations. The limited vocabulary and predictability of repetition help young children develop reading skills more effectively than any number of worksheets can do. As with the work of Silverstein, teachers read these verse narratives to their classes for the joy of hearing and chanting their words rather than as models for writing.

Today we are fortunate to have available a tremendous variety and amount of poems that are in harmony with children's lives, needs, and interests. There's no reason to inflict on them poetry that is obscure, at odds with their experience, or poorly written. If, by chance, your early encounters with poetry were not happy ones, now as a teacher you have a wonderful opportunity to reverse a negative event as you choose poems for your kids that you wish your teacher had chosen for you.

Poetry Writing in the Primary Grades

I've asked a number of first-grade teachers about how they use poetry in their classrooms and not one has said that it isn't used at all. A few, however, have said something like, "They can't write it, of course, but I read poetry to them all the time." I've wished for a magic carpet that could whisk those teachers to Barbara Cullere's classroom in Closter, New Jersey, to see first-graders write poems like this, by one of Barbara's students.

Rain

> A big storm
> sounds like bombs
> crashing against the ground.
> And a little shower
> is like salt
> pouring out of a jar. ❖
>
> *Mike Gallagher*
> *Grade 1*

Writers have said that writing can't be taught and poets have said that poetry writing definitely can't be taught. Certainly the didactic method of direct instruction that imposes external and sometimes arbitrary rules for the learner to follow seldom teaches students to write authentic poems. Perhaps the teachers who didn't believe their children could write poetry had experienced that sort of instruction as school children and quite rightly recognized that it couldn't possibly work with first-graders.

There's considerable evidence that it didn't work well with older children either in that so few adults who were taught in that way think themselves capable of writing poems. In *Those First Affections*, a remarkable collection of poems composed by children from the ages of two to eight, the accompanying notes written some years later tell again and again of children giving up the writing of poetry when they were taught it in school.

Poems by the Very Young

Teacher education courses that show how to help children write poems are scarce. As it was in the early days of teaching writing as a process, teachers have to search out for themselves books, articles, workshops, or like-minded colleagues in order to find effective strategies. Perhaps the first and biggest step is recognizing that poems are simply words arranged in striking, original ways that touch our emotions and make us see the world in ways we never dreamed of. For young children, words and their views of the world are still fresh and new, and poetic language comes naturally.

If you're a parent, you've probably been delighted by your small child's sayings and perhaps you've written some of them down—or wished that you had, before they were lost to memory. The poems in *Those First Affections* by children younger than six or so were first spoken or sung by their composers and then written down, fortunately, by mothers. Patrick Buxton was just three and a half, sitting in the back seat of his parents' car as they drove home across Bodmin Moor one night, when his mother heard him chanting a poem to himself. She later wrote down his words as a three-line poem "On Bodmin Moor," an eerie evocation of the spirit of night in that desolate place.

Making poetry must be experience-linked, especially for young children. When Lynn Shearer led her fourth-graders to Karen Masell's kindergarten, they could smell the popcorn before they opened the door. Munching happily, they settled into prearranged pairs of one older and one younger child to talk about popcorn. The fourth-graders were prepared to elicit words through the kindergartners' senses with questions: "What does it smell like?" one asked. "Does it smell bad, like onions, or. . .?"

Another older member of a pair asked, "How does it feel? What do you hear? We put it up to our ears and we hear a little—cracking?" (Obedient answer: "Yeah, cracking.") The nine-year-olds took their responsibility seriously, squelching off-task behavior and quickly writing down the words their younger partners provided.

"It feels fluffy—it smells like fluffy!"
"It sticks like Spiderman."
"It sounds soft—it's a bumpy little cloud."

Whether or not finished poems emerged from this activity, the foundation for poetic thinking was being laid.

Helping Children Find Their Poems

Edie Ziegler conducts an innovative, interage program in Closter, New Jersey. After immersing her primary classes in poetry of all kinds, she watches for signs that her kids are ready to begin writing their own poems. Then she focuses on feelings as a starting point. She reads *Feelings* by Aliki to the children and encourages them to talk about feelings they've experienced.

Young children, unfettered by years of hearing similar word patterns repeated, unwittingly speak in poetic modes. When a child offers a striking phrase, Edie exclaims, "That sounds like poetry!" and writes it down. As more phrases are celebrated and recorded, enthusiasm builds. The sight of their own words in print (first publication, even if just on the chalkboard!) and the sound of their teacher and peers repeating those words combine to send a powerful message: I can write a poem.

Edie suggests to her kids that feelings can also create images in their minds and asks, "What do you see when you think about your feeling? Close your eyes and tell me." Soon, the children move away from the group to make their own poems, either by writing them down or by telling them to a partner. On another day, Edie brings in poems about feelings on transparencies and shares them with her class so they can see and talk about how a poem looks on a page, as well as note the special ways the poet chose to capture feelings in words.

Donald Graves tells us we can help children discover poetry in their prose writing (1992, 37). When very young children use invented, or temporary, spelling to write in their journals, you have an opportunity to find poems they didn't know were there. "And if we refrain," James Britton writes, "from drawing too clear a distinction between what is poetry and what is prose in their reading, encourage them to exploit the binding power of repetition and avoid that of rhyme (which is a device beyond their control in the early stages), and allow freedom as to what they write and when they write, we shall find a good deal of poetry is being written in school" (1982, 13).

Sometimes a bit of writing might hold only a hint of a poem. Barbara Cullere, when she finds a promising entry in a child's notebook, sometimes asks, "What would be an interesting or unusual way of saying that?" Repeated, brief experiences like these will develop an awareness of poetry and prepare your kids for a more intensive workshop or unit in the spring.

By then most first-graders will be knowledgeable enough to produce temporary spelling that you'll be able to read without their help. Barbara schedules her poetry workshop at the end of the school year partly because she wants to be sure of their exact words—paraphrasing won't do—but also because, "I know how hard it is for them. Poetry's different from the way we always speak." A first-grader in Trumansburg, New York, confirms this: "Poets work hard; they don't just stick words together" (Duthie and Zimet 1992, 15).

As do most primary-grade teachers, Barbara brings poems into the classroom throughout the year, beginning with Mother Goose. Reading and writing workshops are also ongoing parts of the day, and for two weeks before poetry writing begins in earnest, reading time focuses on poetry. Children often choose to read in pairs for the pleasure of sharing and to get help with figuring out words.

In conferences and minilessons, Barbara points out parts of poems that are said in particularly beautiful and surprising ways. Her room fills up with poetry. Poems on chart paper can be seen and read from anywhere in the room. The children's illustrations of poems they love glow on bulletin boards. Books of poetry are everywhere and individual copies of familiar poems wait in the Poetry Box for someone to reach in and pick one out to read. Letters go home asking parents to send in family favorites.

Barbara invites her kids to write poems during these two weeks and celebrates the ones that appear. By the time the poetry workshop begins, everyone has a clear concept of what a poem is and of their own potential as writers of poems. Now the line between reading and writing time blurs as the class studies what poets do when they write poems and the children proceed to write their own.

A strategy Barbara uses to help kids focus on what works in poetry was suggested to her by Lisa Lenz, a teacher and researcher. She chooses three poems linked by theme or structure, depending on the attribute she wants to concentrate on. For example, they could all be "sandwich poems," with first and last lines the same, or the content could deal with feelings, or they might be filled with alliteration. She makes copies for everyone in the class.

After the poems are read aloud, children work in pairs to find parts that stand out for them and are special in some way. They underline words and phrases they like a lot. Then Barbara puts each poem on an overhead projector and marks it up as she and the class pool their observations, often exclaiming, "Oh, look what the poet did here!"

When all three poems have been examined, the children individually choose one to glue in their writing notebooks. They read it again and decide how to respond to it, whether by writing what they noted about its words, sounds, form, or what it reminded them of in their lives, or by illustrating it. Sometimes a child writes a poem in response. The choice is left to the child and provides for all levels of ability.

Getting Poems on Paper

Even prewriters can compose poems if someone can be found to write their words down. You might want to set aside a time for your kids to compose poems orally and then dictate them to you, parent volunteers, classroom aides, or older children with whose teacher you have a collaborative arrangement. If children in higher grades use word processors, typing younger kids' poems not only gives them keyboard practice but, more important, provides both partners with the benefits of cooperative learning between students of different ages.

But for dictation to succeed as a way of getting early learners' poems on paper, you need to have enough writers available to prevent classroom gridlock, when children spend more time waiting in line than composing. You'll also want to make sure that your kids move on to doing their own writing using temporary (invented) spelling as soon as possible so that they don't become dependent on scribes.

You might also try to develop some way for children to save their poems as they are born. A tape recorder is one possibility if you have one that's easy for young kids to operate themselves. Learning to recognize a poem when it pops into their heads and mastering the procedures of recording it can give your children valuable experience in becoming independent, responsible learners.

In schools where whole language is understood and supported, all staff members are accustomed to serving as impromptu audiences. If your school is like that, you can encourage your children to take pencil, paper, and their newborn poems to the nearest available adult for transcribing. As with everything you teach, some of your kids will be able to carry out these procedures effectively and some won't, at least at first. All of these strategies are temporary measures to allow very young children to save poems as they are born. They become unnecessary as children learn enough of the written alphabet to record their ideas on paper themselves.

More and more studies are showing that first-graders can compose on a word processor. If you have even one computer in your room, consider using it as a poetry center for part of the day. Let children work in pairs to compose poems cooperatively. In addition to abetting each other's imaginations, they'll benefit from collaborating on the intricate choices they have to make in syntax, spelling, punctuation, capitalization, and keyboarding.

Models Help Writing

If you teach writing as a process, you know how important models are in helping children learn to write. They're especially necessary for primary children who have less experience with the written word than older kids. Georgia Heard, when she comes to kindergarten classes to help teachers as well as children find out about writing poems, uses poems written by other kindergarten children as models, and new poems grow from old poems in a flowing circle.

Untitled

Tigers lay in flower beds,
Dead until the sun rises. ❖

Ellen Catch

Butterflies

three butterflies
flap their wings
long
skinny
tongues
licking sugar water ❖

Tanya

Heard encourages the use of rhyme and repetition in the early grades much more than with older children, using familiar nursery rhymes as models. She finds that kindergartners' idea of rhyme is still so fresh and new that they don't produce the forced clichés that older kids sometimes resort to. The important thing "is to get the children immersed in the pleasure and power of poetry" (1989, 103), and to give them many options as they explore the reading and writing of it.

Among the options Heard suggests is showing them poems written by other children in their own handwriting to encourage the belief that they too can write. She suggests we let them know about the great variety of topics available to them: "Feelings, something they can see, things they're curious about, pictures in their minds" (1989, 105). She gives them variety in materials, too, with paper in many sizes and shapes.

Christine Duthie and Ellie Zimet also use published poems as the center of minilessons. The topics of their minilessons might surprise anyone who has no experience of what first-graders can do when their teachers know how to help them write poems. Some of them are

Focusing on a single image

Repetition

Sound words

Lining

Invented words

Stanzas

Couplets

Titles

Which to teach and when to teach it depend on the needs and interests of their students.

First-graders who hear and see lots of poems learn to use poetic figures of speech that don't appear in the curriculum until several grades later. Barbara Cullere found that Valerie Worth's poems helped her kids invent similes and metaphors.

My Brother

I love my brother.
He is delicate as glass.
He is as cuddly as a puppy dog.
I love my brother. ❖

Danny Richards
Grade 1

Wind

Wind is an invisible man
    pushing me the way he wants to. ❖

Kate Clark
Grade 1

Barbara's minilessons, especially early in the workshop, include much talk about feelings. These and other discussions generate word banks that are posted on the walls for kids to refer to when they're composing. As she moves around the room conferring, she watches for writing in which the child has used ideas from the minilesson. Any examples of this are cause for enthusiastic acclaim, which encourages not only the writer but those nearby as well.

If, in a conference, a child stares at a poem in dissatisfaction, unable to find or bend words to fit the mental image, she might ask, "Well, could you say it this way?" and give a possible word or phrase. Often the child says, "No, that's not it," and she goes on to, "Maybe you could say it this way . . . Or maybe this way. . . ." Usually the writer of the poem at some point says, "Yeah! That's it!" and jubilantly starts to write. Barbara is careful to maintain the child's sense of ownership of the poem, emphasizing to her students that she's there to help them find the words they need, not tell them which ones to use.

Second-Graders Show Growth

By the time these children are in second grade, they can astound us with their vision and skill.

Night

A shadow covers
over the sky.
Yellow diamonds
stand in place.

The moon is like a
flashlight,
guides my way.
The night crawls out.
Morning walks in. ❖

Jessica Fazekas
Grade 2

Pinwheel

As the person
jerks the pinwheel
      upward
with multi-starbright
      colors
      swoosh!
The person watches closely.
The wind whispers
      in his
        ear. ❖

Jeffrey Latzer
Grade 2

The energy of the next poem can never be found in a worksheet on verbs:

Salmon

As the shiny salmon
approaches the twitching lure,
he'll strike
and dance out of the water
and back in.
He'll swim round and round,
struggling to get loose.
He'll slap the water
with his fearsome tail
and pounce
into the net. ❖

Mike Accordino
Grade 2

The content of second-graders' poems is more likely to involve feelings and reflective thought, as do these from Edie Ziegler's classes.

It Isn't Fair

Just because
my sister
is shy and
she talked
in school,
she gets
a toy
from my
mommy and
daddy, that's
why it isn't
fair. ❖

Janet Lee
Grade 2

The next poem contains similes, internal rhyme, and unstated but powerfully implied emotion. Think of the challenge of being seven years old, when you're struggling to master difficult physical skills and at the same time find your place as a person in an ever-widening world. Kenneth shows us the vulnerability of that age and the fragility of pride.

Skating

I skate around the rink
like a bird soaring
through the air
some little kids
fall or slip
But I
stand straight
and tall
but sometimes
fall. Like a bird
being shot
down. ❖

Kenneth Stroger
Grade 2

Primary-grade teachers whose children write wonderful poems share certain practices. Many of them use the workshop structure, having found that, like Santa Claus's bag, it can hold whatever is required over the year. They search for and find lots of poems they can't wait to read to their kids and they share these poems every day. They risk the ultimate challenge for teachers—doing what they ask their students to do—and write poems themselves.

They understand that reading and writing are processes, not subjects, and that the more their students use these processes, the more proficient they will become. They teach with enthusiasm and good humor and are constantly on the lookout for original, exciting language in their classes. When they discover these bits of poetry, they celebrate them and all evidences of progress, knowing that the teacher's validation of the child as a learner is a powerful motivator.

SPECIAL CHALLENGES

Jane Beaty uses good literature to help her third-, fourth-, and fifth-graders become more successful readers. At the beginning of the school year, she reads from an anthology poems she knows they'll like. She makes student copies of the ones that become favorites and uses them in minilessons. Soon, she's reading story poems by Prelutsky and others to an enthusiastic audience. Sounds familiar, doesn't it? What is remarkable here is that Jane's students are classified by the state as "either learning disabled, seriously emotionally disturbed, or educable mentally retarded" (Feeley et al. 1991, 181).

The same qualities of poetry that succeed with so-called regular classes are effective with special education students. The poems Jane chooses for reading minilessons are short and easily mastered, giving her kids the experience of prompt success as readers. Story poems, with their predictable refrains and engaging humor, become familiar through frequent rereadings by the teacher and are soon in demand as independent reading material. *Bringing the Rain to Kapiti Plain* is a special favorite both with Jane, who likes the way it fits into her class's study of weather and climate, and her students, who "beg to take their copies home to share" (Feeley et al. 1991, 184).

In Perry, Florida, Alyce Watkins uses poetry throughout the year with her primary Chapter I class, focusing on poems with strong rhyme and rhythm. She found that working with isolated phonic skills was difficult, but when her children heard and repeated entire poems, they caught on rapidly to such concepts as rhyming sounds and letter-sound correspondence. Alyce uses big books a great deal and emphasizes that the kids need to hear *lots* of rhyming poems, repeated often.

Good, carefully chosen poems convey a sense of joy and freedom that appeals strongly to children who experience more failure than success in school. Poems can contain information, of course, but they're more likely to be rooted in emotion, and educationally challenged children especially need this. Poetry not only builds important reading skills but can unlock the mystery of writing as children find that even their small, quiet thoughts can become poems.

The poet Jim Daniels expresses what writing poetry meant to him as a child whose inability to produce certain speech sounds correctly set him apart from his classmates. "I often think that I started writing poetry at such an early age because of my speech defect, but I probably would have come to it eventually, speech defect or no, because I became addicted to the freedom of the page, to saying whatever I wanted without having to think about what other people thought. Eventually, I did have to be concerned with that, but early on, it was just me and the paper, the paper that didn't make fun of what I said or how I said it" (Janeczko 1990, 46).

POETRY AND ESL LEARNERS

To travel through Europe was always a dream of mine, and when at last I did it, in the midst of the pleasure and excitement came an unexpected sense of fear and isolation. It took me a while to realize that the disorientation I was feeling stemmed, naturally enough, from having to cope with cultures and languages different from my own. How much more frightening it must be for children of elementary school age to be dropped into an environment where most of the rules are strange and the words are incomprehensible.

The struggle is on both sides. Those of us who have had ESL (English as a second language) learners in our classrooms, and this is the majority of teachers today, share the children's frustration. We search constantly for strategies and materials that will help them learn enough English to benefit from instruction in other subject areas and at the same time become assimilated into the social structure of the classroom.

From *The Place My Words Are Looking For*, Paul Janeczko, Editor, Bradbury Press, 1990.

Evidence is accumulating that ESL students learn effectively in classrooms where teachers use whole language strategies (Lim and Watson 1993). Second-language learners acquire speaking, reading, and writing skills readily when they participate in content-rich activities that stem from authentic purposes and when they have teachers who encourage social interaction as a means to understanding. Student-centered, meaning-focused instruction fosters second-language learning, enabling ESL students to function in their classrooms in an integrated way. Although the process is usually rapid, those first few weeks are full of questions that occupy much of our time and attention.

Poetry Bridges Cultures

Poetry, a form of language uniquely accessible to ESL students, can give us many answers. Poetry is by nature out of the ordinary, even mysterious. It sets the stage for children's acceptance of other mysterious things such as another culture and language. ESL students are supported in their task of learning to speak and read English by the same elements of poetry that help beginning readers. Rhyme, rhythm, and repetition make it easier to identify letter and word patterns. The oral practice necessary for successful choral reading strengthens their skills.

Several factors that enhance language learning (McCauley and McCauley 1992) fit easily into choral reading in the classroom. When children read or recite poems in unison, especially short, funny ones, they escape many of the hazards facing ESL students. First, they are sheltered by the other voices. Errors that would be embarrassing if the child were speaking alone are blurred and hardly noticeable. Choral reading or speaking integrates them safely into a group. All these conditions lower children's anxiety and permit them to engage more effectively in the learning process than when they're the only ones answering the teacher's questions.

Dramatic presentation of poems also helps the ESL child. Theory of ESL instruction states that language learning takes place within a zone of proximal development, that area where the child knows enough to function within a group but is attacking the unknown. Acting out poems as they're being read in unison adds contextual clues to meaning, giving the ESL child additional input to support learning in that zone.

A Multilingual Kindergarten

Of the twenty-three children in Tom Pipher's kindergarten class in Immokalee, Florida, only seven learned English as their first language. Most of the residents of this agricultural community work in the surrounding fields of vegetables and fruit trees, and many of them migrate with the growing seasons. Tom's kids come to school with little experience of books or the language they contain, and his aim is to provide that experience by "inundating them with literature."

Midway through the school year, they know and love dozens of books, big and small, many of them containing poems. When Tom asks which one they want to read, several voices begin to chant, "Chicka chicka boom boom! Chicka chicka boom boom!" They sit facing the reader's chair in concentric semicircles on the floor, cross-legged, and begin to clap hands and slap thighs in unison as Tom reads the first line of Martin and Archambault's alphabet book, in which the letters follow each other to the top of a coconut tree. The children repeat each line, copying their teacher's inflections exactly, especially relishing the refrain, "Chicka chicka boom boom! Will there be enough room?" and the ensuing tumble of all the letters out of the tree.

When Tom holds up JoAnne Nelson's *Follow Me* and says, "Do you remember how it goes?" several kids sing out, "I went for a walk and what did I see?" After they sing the entire book, Raul stands beside his teacher to read his adaptation of the story, which he has made into a foldover book with flaps that open to show the birds and animals he decided to see on his walk. Another version begins, "I went for a swim and what did I see? A mean big shark was following me!"

Big charts, suspended from wire coat hangers, hold other modified versions of books they've read. After repeated readings have made the children thoroughly familiar with a book, Tom leads a brainstorming session in which they make up their own adaptation, following the pattern of the original. In October, "Teddy bear, teddy bear, turn around" became "Scarecrow, scarecrow, turn around." After the children reread each line, they act out the motions with enthusiasm.

Another chart begins with "Seven little snowmen riding on a sled," inspired by Eileen Christelow's *Five Little Monkeys Jumping on the Bed*. Each line is written on a strip of tagboard that slips into a clear plastic pocket so that it can be taken out and held up separately. Tom begins by asking, "Do you remember how many snowmen are in the poem?" and goes on to, "What letter does seven start with? What letter does snowmen start with?" and "Is snow*men* one or more than one?" before leading the unison reading of the poem.

Four languages are represented in Tom's class: Spanish, Haitian Creole, a native Guatemalan dialect, and English. Only a few children have progressed to sound-letter correspondence for initial consonants. Yet they "read" book after book with enthusiasm and vigor, using all their senses and every learning mode. Rhyme, rhythm, and repetition are helping to build the background every beginning reader needs.

Building Self-Esteem with Poems

In *The Art of Teaching Writing*, Lucy Calkins tells of Morat, a boy whose native language was Russian; at the beginning of the year, he was embarrassed by this and resisted anything to do with Russian. But in the poetry workshop in the spring, Morat shyly read a poem he had brought with him from Russia, and its reception by the class was altogether positive.

The children found beauty in the sounds of the unfamiliar language that transcended their inability to understand its meaning and happily listened to Morat read the poem again and again. Later, he translated the poem into English (think of the language learning involved in that!) and later still, other children brought in poems from their native cultures. Recognition of the value of these works enhanced the worlds of all children in the class.

Throughout the grades, using language successfully as a member of a group builds the trust and confidence that will enable ESL children to stand alone in the spotlight occasionally. Ask them to bring to class copies of poems in their own languages (with accompanying translations if possible), particularly children's poems. Most cultures have their equivalent of Mother Goose verses. Encourage the child to teach one of these to the class, or to help you do it if the solo task seems too daunting at first.

This practice accomplishes lots of wonderful things. The ESL child gets positive recognition as the introducer of something interesting and different from the everyday stuff of learning. She or he gains the respect of classmates through being able to read with great ease words that are incomprehensible to everyone else. Rather than being on the bottom of the totem pole, he or she is now an authority.

The rest of the class experiences the difficulty of dealing with a different language, and this develops empathy for the ESL learner. At the same time their horizons are stretching to include another culture. The ESL child can copy the poems and their translations during writing time, thereby being able to engage in the same activity as the rest of the class and to gain practice in writing and reading meaningful English.

Helping ESL Learners Write Their Own Poems

When your ESL students understand enough to know what you mean when you ask them to write poems, they can write them in their own language, inserting any known English words that happen to fit. The poems can be taken home for translation by family members or friends, which is a good way to get the family involved in the school. If there are children or staff members in your school who speak the language, they can be enlisted as translators. Bilingual parents who have volunteered as aides are a natural choice for this job.

When the child is comfortable enough, he or she can read the poems in both languages during group sharing time, again reaping the social benefits already mentioned. This also provides the opportunity for you and the children, including the ESL child, to recognize the progress being made as more English words appear over time. Encourage the use of temporary, or invented, spelling while giving assurance that the child will learn correct spelling as time goes on.

Another way to strengthen home-school ties is to encourage the ESL learner to write poems in her or his first language for family members to mark special occasions or just to serve as affectionate messages, then take them home and read them to the family member. Next day, invite the child to tell the class what happened. This serves to further integrate the ESL child and to extend the class's understanding of the similarities of family life among cultures.

Even after children have been in the United States for a year or more and have mastered the basics of English, their use of it will be flavored by their first language. Like all children, ESL kids want to belong, to be an accepted member of their social group. They need the help of their schools and their families to retain their first language and culture at the same time that they are making their way in new ones. Poetry is an excellent vehicle for achieving this.

Kenneth Koch in *Rose, Where Did You Get That Red?* tells how he included in the poems he taught to his kids at PS 61 in New York City some by Federico García Lorca. He chose them for "their dreamy use of colors and their sense of magic places" (1973, 163) but also to give his Spanish-speaking students beautiful poems in their own language while letting the rest of the class experience poetry in an unknown tongue. He first read the English translations, then gradually added words and phrases in Spanish. The children enthusiastically savored the sounds, deciding, for example, which word expressed a color more intensely: blue or azul, green or verde.

Some of the poems they went on to write were completely in Spanish; some contained just a few Spanish words among the English and others had many, depending on the writer's facility.

Because originality is valued over the strict observation of rules and regulations in the writing of poetry, ESL kids can capitalize on their fresh views of their new language. Like kindergartners, they choose and combine words in ways that surprise and delight us. Their similes are never trite. Kun Byul Kim, a fourth-grader, wrote, "The moon has craters as big as / Ninety whales! / And the craters of the moon are like / enormous garbage cans."

Their topics, though, fit right in with those of their classmates, in this case fourth-graders, and help to strengthen their sense of belonging.

My Most Comfortable Place

> My room is messy,
> sometimes clean.
>
> Many books
> my favorite toys
> my stuffed animals
> my bed
>   and
> many other things
> are in my room.
>
> The most comfortable place
> my room is. ❖
>
> *Naoya Iguchi*

Chairs

Chairs, chairs
they are nothing special
but when I sit on one
I feel like it got happy. ❖

Akiko Tsuda

Perhaps the experience of listening carefully to an unknown language sharpens the child's awareness of sound as distinct from and yet supportive of meaning.

Boots

Boots are splash
Colors of darkness
Clunk-a-da-pic
Go your boots.
Stepping in mud
Like a hawk
Boots look like black snow
Then melt away to mud
They protect your feet
From the water.
When you take them off
Away fly your boots!
Footprints like black junk
Or black paint,
Dirty boots,
You put them on your feet
You see your feet are brown like mud
Clunk-a-da-pic Clunk-a-da-pic
Clunk-a-da-pic
With your boots! ❖

Helen Cho

Perhaps, too, having the literature of two cultures to draw upon broadens the child's capacity for creating striking images, as in this poem.

Icicles

Icicles shine through the night
Like silver swords,
They hang on the rooftop of the snow
Like beautiful crystals on a rock.

In the morning
They glitter and sparkle,
Like a golden ring fallen from heaven. ❖

Kenzo Tatsuno

Experimentation, looking for new and different ways of saying something, is at the heart of writing poetry. Your encouragement and guidance help all your students become strong enough to take the risk of experimenting when they write poems. ESL students are faced with risks throughout the school day, always having to deal with new and different ways of speaking and living. In the poetry workshop, risk-taking is supported as a valued behavior, helping ESL learners feel less isolated.

This is not to say that children who are learning English as their second language don't need instruction in the mechanics of spelling, sentence construction, and punctuation. Of course they do; but a steady diet of skill-based tasks leaves children hungry for the spice and color they can find in poetry.

Poetry nurtures the whole ESL child socially, emotionally, intellectually, and spiritually. It helps students feel more at home in their native cultures and languages as well as the new ones; it enables them to extend their use of English and express their own unique feelings and experiences. Few areas of school learning speak to the mind and heart of the ESL child as vividly as poetry does.

MULTICULTURAL POETRY

In our multicultural world and age, teachers are searching for literature by writers from other countries and cultures. The drought of poems from such writers now shows signs of lessening but is far from over. Probably your best source of such works is the children in your classroom. As suggested earlier, asking them to bring poems from home has many positive effects and, over time, will enable you to make your own collection of poetry from other cultures. Below is a small sampling of books you can find in libraries.

Native American Writers

The Whispering Wind: Poetry by Young American Indians, edited by Terry Allen, contains poems that can serve as models in a writing workshop or as expressions of parts of the Native American experience. "I Am Crying from Thirst" by Alonzo Lopez of Arizona speaks of the sky beginning to weep at the sight of the poet singing and dancing for rain on the dry earth.

This poem by Calvin O'John, Ute-Navajo from Colorado, contains a richness of ideas and images that kids can discuss on several levels.

Afternoon and His Unfinished Poem

> Afternoon sits down on an old rocking chair
> and starts writing his poem.
> The sun drops by and adds a
> few bright words.
> All is going well.
> Then, unexpectedly,
> out of the gray sky
> comes wind, his huge cheeks puffed up.
> He lets out a burst that carries
> Afternoon's unfinished poem
> across the corn fields.
> Afternoon is angry.
> He gets up from the old rocking chair
> and chokes wind's throat so he can't
> blow any more.
> The wind dies down.
> Afternoon goes and searches
> for his unfinished poem. ❖

First, as a whole, it addresses the frustration writers of all ages feel when a poem starts out well and then falls flat, when the initial idea doesn't carry through to a satisfactory ending. Older children especially will appreciate O'John's metaphor of afternoon as a poet and a summer storm as the expression of a poet's frustration. Someone—perhaps you—will probably remark that he used the experience of not being able to write as the basis of a successful poem.

Children from the early elementary grades on will enjoy the images of nature. I can imagine talking to my class about afternoon in an old rocking chair and asking what images those words create in their minds, what season of the year they think it is, what mood they feel when they close their eyes and see afternoon sitting there, and what afternoon looks like.

We'd also appreciate the sun's bright words and the wind's huge, puffed-up cheeks. I hope the violence of afternoon's solution to his problem doesn't disturb you, because here it fits the poet's need beautifully and is, after all, purely allegorical. I know kids will relish the direct action of afternoon becoming justifiably angry, throttling the wind, and going to search for his poem. After they have enjoyed the excitement of the literal narrative, you might need to prompt their recognition that the poem is rooted in the reality of a summer storm.

"Afternoon and His Unfinished Poem" by Calvin O'John. From *The Whispering Wind*, edited by Terry Allen. Copyright © 1972 by the Institute of American Indian Arts. Used by permission of Doubleday, a division of Bantam Doubleday Dell Publishing Group, Inc.

"Fishing" by Agnes T. Pratt, Suquamish from Washington, tells of an experience that is shared by many children and does it with an intense sensitivity to the emotions of a child.

Brother Eagle, Sister Sky is an adaptation of the words Chief Seattle spoke when he was presented with a document enacting the purchase of his people's lands by the U.S. government. It begins, "How can you buy the sky? / How can you own the rain and the wind?" Beautifully illustrated by Susan Jeffers, who also wrote this adaptation, the book evokes not only the spirit of the Native Americans' respect for the earth but the beliefs of those who, today, want to protect the natural environment. It also provides an interesting example of writing that blurs the line between prose and poetry.

In the Trail of the Wind: American Indian Poems and Ritual Orations is a rich anthology of poems from more than forty tribal languages of the original inhabitants of North and South America, best to use with older children. The poetry in Virginia Driving Hawk Sneve's *Dancing Tepees* combines present-day experiences with traditional attitudes of Native Americans from this continent.

African American Writers

Eloise Greenfield's books of poems give voice to African American children's lives and are a unique treasure for every classroom. In *Nathaniel Talking*, "Nathaniel's Rap" begins with the lines "It's Nathaniel talking / And Nathaniel's me."

"Mama" and "Missing Mama" are about a child's coming to terms with a mother's death, a subject that is seldom treated in children's poetry. The latter poem ends, "sometimes I cry / but mostly / I think about / the good things / now." On the next page is "Making Friends," a joyful view of a kindergarten child welcoming a "new girl," followed by "When I Misbehave," which describes with undeniable authenticity a child's feelings about having to stay after school.

Music joins with poetry in "Grandma's Bones," about the rhythm Nathaniel's grandma can produce when she holds two sticks in one hand and makes them go "clack clack clackety / clackety clack." "My Daddy" and "Watching the World Go By" are written in the twelve-bar blues form, and Greenfield shows how the rhythm works in a diagram so that readers can see how they might construct such a poem themselves.

Night on Neighborhood Street, also by Greenfield, is a collection of poems, some rhyming and some not, showing positive aspects of an African American child's life in a neighborhood where families are intact and adults hold community meetings and go to church. At the same time, the topics are realistic. In "The Seller," children go inside when the drug dealer is on their street. As in *Nathaniel Talking*, the illustrations by Jan Spivey Gilchrist are large and colorful, making these books excellent choices for reading aloud to a group of children gathered around you.

Some of the Days of Everett Anderson by Lucille Clifton is a short series of poems, one or more for each day of the week, that illuminate events in the life of a six-year-old African American boy with energy and sensitivity. Although it's not a big book, the striking illustrations are large enough to be appreciated by your class as you read the poems aloud.

The emotions from which the poetry springs, universal among children, will be especially evocative for kids in the primary grades who live in the city. Conversation can easily lead to writing poems with similar topics. The pattern of using a child's full name (which all of these poems do) can be an appealing starting point.

Nightfeathers by Sundaira Morninghouse is a collection of poems written about the experiences of African American and Hispanic children living in the city. "Jambo" tells the reader rhythmically that *jambo* means "hello"; "Besito" combines Spanish and English in a lullaby-like chant. "Dogs on the Corner" speaks to the fear any small child might feel when confronted by two strange dogs.

Older kids will appreciate the works of Langston Hughes, one of America's most notable poets. "Mother to Son," with its memorable line "Life for me ain't been no crystal stair" appears often in anthologies but is only one of his hundreds of poems. When your class is learning about the civil rights struggles of the 1950s and 1960s, read "Ku Klux" to them for the immediacy of its narrative and "Daybreak in Alabama" for its lyrical expression of longing for a better time and place. "My People," just six lines long, has the mystical quality of a chant and ends with "Beautiful, also, are the souls of my people."

Hughes's poems paint authentic pictures of Harlem and the excitement and beauty of living there as well as the sadness and hardship. Many of them sing with the rhythm and sounds of jazz and bebop. "Vagabonds," though written in the first half of this century, speaks eloquently for today's homeless people.

Also best for older children are Maya Angelou's poems. "Woman Work" is a lyrical cry for comfort by a hard-working country woman. The narrator of "On Aging" speaks with strong dignity, rejecting pity and sympathy and affirming personal identity in spite of old age. Children in the middle grades and beyond might find an unspoken message in "Life Doesn't Frighten Me"; younger kids will enjoy it at the surface level.

Poetry by Hispanic Writers

Gary Soto's *Neighborhood Odes* is a collection of poems that celebrate life in a Mexican-American neighborhood as experienced by a child. "Ode to Los Raspados" is about the delight of snow cones in summer, ending with "And the juice runs / To their elbows, / Sticky summer rain / That sweetens the street." Other poems create vivid, eloquent evocations of objects, events, and places that are important in all children's lives: cherished pets ("Ode to Mi Gato," "Ode to Mi Perrito"), favorite foods, tennis shoes, the library, and the water sprinkler. Soto's poems will probably be best appreciated by middle-graders.

For younger readers, look for *Arroz Con Leche*, a collection of nursery rhymes and songs in Spanish and English. *The Tamarindo Puppy, and Other Poems*, also a blend of Spanish and English, is a picture book that celebrates everyday events in verse. Arnold Adoff's *Flamboyan* and *Today We Are Brother and Sister* are set in Puerto Rico and evoke the experiences of children living on that island. *Tortillitas Para Mama: And Other Nursery Rhymes, Spanish & English* is a bilingual collection that includes lullabies and radiates a comforting warmth sure to appeal to the youngest readers.

Multicultural, Multilingual Books

We teachers are increasingly aware of our responsibility to help children develop global awareness and understanding, and poetry from a variety of cultures in a variety of languages is a useful resource. A book remarkably rich in such diversity is *If I Had a Paka: Poems in Eleven Languages*; some of the eleven are Swahili, Samoan, Japanese, and Yiddish. Each poem is translated into English as well.

For me, a major ingredient of helping my classes learn about other cultures has always been amazement. We were amazed by the strangeness of exotic and heretofore unimagined lives of children in other parts of the world and in the next instant we were amazed by the similarities between their lives and ours. Most of the similarities involved family life, and in *Grandparents' Houses; Poems About Grandparents*, children can find poetry about families from Hispanic, Zuni, Yiddish-speaking, and Chinese backgrounds that illustrates those similarities and differences.

The same-different aspect of multicultural poetry is evident in Jane Yolen's *Street Rhymes Around the World*, a collection of children's street rhymes from everywhere that are given in both the original language and translation. *Coconut Kind of Day* by Lynn Joseph takes the reader into the life of a young girl who lives in Trinidad with poems about family, friends, school, and the special qualities of that Caribbean island.

More of us live in urban environments than in suburbs or the country today, and city living is a culture all its own. Nancy Larrick's anthology *On City Streets* contains poems by a wide range of authors: T. S. Eliot, Eve Merriam, Langston Hughes, Walt Whitman, and many more. A special appeal of this collection is that the poems were chosen on the basis of their attractiveness to more than 100 schoolchildren in small-city as well as inner-city schools.

I Heard a Scream in the Street, another anthology selected by Larrick, is a collection of poems by city kids between the ages of ten and eighteen who write with the authority of experience. Their settings reach from subways to park playgrounds to city streets, and they write of the gritty realities of city life. X. J. Kennedy's *The Forgetful Wishing Well*, in a section called "In the City," provides additional contemporary poems about children's views of the urban experience.

THE WORLD OF POETRY

Just as music is a universal language, so is poetry a language that speaks to all children, no matter their age, educational status, or cultural background. Poetry's arms open wide and welcome us all in. It's important that we teachers remember this inclusiveness and not subvert it by expecting that only certain children are capable of reading and writing poetry with pleasure and success.

Whole language classrooms provide environments that foster inclusiveness. Teachers see the child as the center of the instructional model and mold the curriculum accordingly. Literature is everywhere. Learning experiences are authentic, not artificially contrived, and take place in an integrated way. When learning is seen as potential rather than as a fixed, predetermined sequence, every child can find a place of value. Poetry brings a special excitement to that place.

REFERENCES

All unreferenced quotes are from conversations with the author or observations of the author.

Aardema, V. *Bringing the Rain to Kapiti Plain.* New York: Dial Press, 1983.

Adoff, Arnold. *Today We Are Brother and Sister.* New York: Lothrop, Lee & Shepard, 1981.

———. *Flamboyan.* New York: Harcourt Brace Jovanovich, 1988.

Aliki. *Feelings.* New York: William Morrow, 1986.

Allen, Terry, ed. *The Whispering Wind: Poetry by Young American Indians.* New York: Doubleday, 1972.

Angelou, Maya. *And Still I Rise.* New York: Random House, 1978.

Bierhorst, John, ed. *In the Trail of the Wind: American Indian Poems and Ritual Orations.* New York: Farrar, Straus & Giroux, 1987.

Britton, James. "Reading and Writing Poetry." In Gordon M. Pradl (ed.), *Prospect and Retrospect.* Montclair, NJ: Boynton/Cook, 1982.

Calkins, Lucy. *The Art of Teaching Writing.* Portsmouth, NH: Heinemann Educational Books, 1986.

Christelow, Eileen. *Five Little Monkeys Jumping on the Bed.* New York: The Trumpet Club, 1989.

Clifton, Lucille. *Some of the Days of Everett Anderson*. New York: Henry Holt, 1970.

Cooney et al. *Tortillitas Para Mama: And Other Nursery Rhymes, Spanish & English*. Illus. by Barbara Cooney. New York: Henry Holt, 1981.

Cowley, Joy. *Mrs. Wishy Washy*. San Diego: The Wright Group, 1987.

Delacre, Lulu. *Arroz Con Leche*. New York: Blue Ribbon Books, Scholastic Inc., 1992.

Duthie, Christine, and Ellie Kubie Zimet. "Poetry Is Like Directions for Your Imagination!" *Reading Teacher* 46 (1992): 14-24.

Feeley, Joan, et al., eds. *Process Reading and Writing: A Literature-Based Approach*. New York: Teachers College Press, 1991.

Geisel, Theodor Seuss. *The Cat in the Hat*. New York: Beginner Books, Random House, 1957.

———. *Green Eggs and Ham*. New York: Random House, 1960.

Graves, Donald. *Explore Poetry*. Portsmouth, NH: Heinemann Educational Books, 1992.

Greenfield, Eloise. *Nathaniel Talking*. New York: Writers and Readers, 1988.

———. *Night on Neighborhood Street*. New York: Dial Books for Young Readers, 1991.

Heard, Georgia. *For the Good of the Earth and Sun*. Portsmouth, NH: Heinemann Educational Books, 1989.

Hopkins, Lee Bennett, ed. *Me!* New York: Seabury Press, 1970.

———. *Side by Side: Poems to Read Together*. New York: Simon & Schuster, 1988.

Hughes, Langston. *Selected Poems of Langston Hughes*. New York: Vintage Books, 1990.

Janeczko, Paul, ed. *The Place My Words Are Looking For*. New York: Bradbury Press, 1990.

Joseph, Lynn. *Coconut Kind of Day*. New York: Lothrop, Lee & Shepard, 1990.

Kennedy, X. J. *The Forgetful Wishing Well*. New York: Atheneum, 1985.

Koch, Kenneth. *Rose, Where Did You Get That Red?* New York: Random House, 1973.

Larrick, Nancy. *On City Streets.* New York: M. Evans, 1968.

———, ed. *I Heard a Scream in the Street.* New York: M. Evans, 1970.

———. "Poetry and Song for Young Children." *Fanfare: The Christopher Gordon Children's Literature Annual* 1 (1993): 97-104.

Lim, Hwa-Ja Lee, and Dorothy J. Watson. "Whole Language Content Classes for Second-Language Learners." *Reading Teacher* 46 (1993): 384-93.

Martin, Bill, Jr., and John Archambault. *Brown Bear, Brown Bear, What Do You See?* Toronto: Holt, Rinehart & Winston, 1982.

———. *Chicka Chicka Boom Boom.* New York: Scholastic, 1991.

McCauley, Joyce K., and Daniel S. McCauley. "Using Choral Reading to Promote Language Learning for ESL Students." *Reading Teacher* 45 (1992): 526-33.

Merriam, Eve. *It Doesn't Always Have to Rhyme.* New York: Atheneum, 1964.

———. *Fresh Paint.* New York: Macmillan Children's Book Group, 1986.

Moffett, James. *A Student-Centered Language Arts Curriculum, Grades K-13: A Handbook for Teachers.* Boston: Houghton Mifflin, 1973.

Moje, Elizabeth B., and Woan-Ru Shyu. "Oh, the Places You've Taken Us: *RT*'s Tribute to Dr. Seuss." *Reading Teacher* 45 (1992): 670-76.

Morninghouse, Sundaira. *Nightfeathers.* Seattle: Open Hand, 1989.

Nelson, JoAnne. *Follow Me.* Cleveland, OH: Modern Curriculum Press, 1989.

Pomerantz, Charlotte. *The Tamarindo Puppy, and Other Poems.* Illus. by Byron Barton. New York: Greenwillow Books, 1980.

———. *If I Had a Paka: Poems in Eleven Languages.* New York: Greenwillow Books, 1982.

Prelutsky, Jack, ed. *Read-Aloud Rhymes for the Very Young.* New York: Alfred A. Knopf, 1986.

Rogers, Timothy, ed. *Those First Affections.* London: Routledge & Kegan Paul, 1979.

Routman, Regie. *Transitions*. Portsmouth, NH: Heinemann Educational Books, 1988.

Seattle, Chief. *Brother Eagle, Sister Sky*. New York: Dial Books for Young Readers, 1991.

Sendak, Maurice. *Chicken Soup with Rice: A Book of Months*. New York: HarperCollins Children's Books, 1962.

Silverstein, Shel. *Where the Sidewalk Ends*. New York: Harper & Row, 1974.

Sneve, Virginia Driving Hawk. *Dancing Tepees*. New York: Holiday House, 1989.

Soto, Gary. *Neighborhood Odes*. New York: Harcourt Brace Jovanovich, 1992.

Streich, Corinne, ed. *Grandparents' Houses; Poems About Grandparents*. New York: Greenwillow Books, 1984.

Yolen, Jane, ed. *Street Rhymes Around the World*. Honesdale, PA: Wordsong/Boyds Mills Press, 1992.

Chapter 3

THE SHAPE OF A POEM

FORMS AND CONVENTIONS

On the second day of our poetry workshop, my fourth-graders and I looked again at Valerie Worth's "Safety Pin," still on the board from the day before (see chapter 1). We had already heard the poem, read it, and talked about it. Now it was time to see its shape.

LINES AND WHITE SPACE

"Mark, yesterday you said you thought this poem looked weird. Who remembers why?" I asked.

"Because it goes up and down in little, short lines," Julie answered.

"That's right," I said. "Valerie Worth wrote it in short lines instead of sentences. What else do you see?"

"All the lines begin with capital letters."

"But there's only one period—at the very end."

"It isn't indented, like a paragraph is."

"Maybe it's *all* indented!"

"Great!" I said, breaking into the stream of responses. "You noticed a lot about how a poem looks. It's written in lines, they can begin with uppercase letters, and you don't have to put punctuation at the end of each one. These are some things that make the shape of a poem special. And there's something else."

I held up my copy of *The Lion, the Witch and the Wardrobe*, open to two densely printed pages. "If it isn't poetry, we call it prose. What do you notice about the way prose looks compared with poetry?"

"There's a lot of it!" Brad said.

"But the poem, there's just one on the whole page," Michiko said.

"Yes, look at all this white space," I said, referring back to the screen. "The poem is almost like a picture that's hanging on a white wall with nothing else around it. I think that helps to make it special; it helps us see it in a special way. When you write your poems, you'll write them in lines, too, and you can leave lots of space around them."

That ended our first minilesson on the shape of a poem. As the children wrote that day, they played with the possibilities of ending lines in different places and enjoyed the freedom of deciding that for themselves. As always, though, the price of changing their minds was much erasing and rewriting or enough rings and arrows to make a poem look like a briar patch. It showed me the way to the next day's minilesson.

Revising Lines

"What did you pay special attention to yesterday when you were writing your poem?" I began.

The responses were varied, of course, but most were about lining. "How many changed your mind and wanted to end a line in a different place after you wrote it?" About half the class raised their hands. "How did you do that?" I asked.

After several children described their revision methods, I said, "Here's an easier way that a lot of poets use. Last night I started to write this poem." I wrote these lines on the chalkboard.

> Blue cat eyes gaze at me
> And blink twice.
> I blink back.
> Is this a secret cat code
> That I don't know?
> And if it is—what did I say? ❖

"When I read it again, I thought maybe it would be more interesting if I ended the first line after 'gaze,' so I put a slash mark after it, like this:

> Blue cat eyes gaze / at me

"And I thought I'd like to end the next line after 'blink,' so I put another slash mark there, like this:"

> And blink / twice.

"That way I didn't have to erase or draw rings and arrows to show where I wanted my line breaks to be. And if I change my mind again later, I'll just have little slash marks to erase. Try that today on your poems and let me know how it works for you."

Computers Make It Easy

The lucky group whose turn it was to use word processors that day could change line breaks with just a keystroke or two. In fact, the advantages of using a computer for writing were most notable when we worked on poetry. The clarity of print, whether on screen or on paper, emphasized the visual quality of the poems. The children weren't distracted by the mechanics of handwriting, margins, spacing, and so on. Of course we still had to deal with the mechanics of using a word processor, but they proved easier to regulate than pencils in ten-year-olds' hands.

Because poems are usually short and are written one to a page, our printer chattered constantly, and the satisfaction of achievement put a smile on many young faces. A turn at the computer consisted of writing one poem, so several children got a chance to use a word processor each day, often as many as half the class.

Another Way to Revise Is Invented

On a day when Sharon did not get a turn at a computer and was writing the old-fashioned way with pencil and paper, she devised an ingenious method of literally reconstructing her poem. I first noticed it when I was passing her table and picked up a narrow slip of paper from the floor. "Oh, thanks!" she said. "I wondered where that went."

"What is it?" I asked.

"It's the third—well, maybe the fourth line of my poem. I put in the slashes like you showed us but it was hard to imagine how the line would look. So I cut the lines apart and then I cut where the slash lines are, and now I can put it together just the way I want, see?" I watched as she arranged the paper strips into a poem.

"That's a good idea," I said and turned to a small group of kids sitting nearby. "Did you see the way Sharon changes her lines? Sharon, show them how you do that," and a new revision strategy began to spread.

Form Fits Content

Donald found a way of forming his baseball poem into a structure that seemed particularly appropriate to the content.

Baseball

When someone
hits a baseball

        It goes soaring
        across the field

And lands on
the soft grass

        And rolls for ten
        or more seconds,

And someone goes
running after it

picks it up
       and throws it
       to first base
But he's too late
the runner's already home. ❖

Donald Welch
Grade 4

  The staggered pairs of lines, moving back and forth on the page, suggest visually the movement of the ball and runners on the field. Notice how the line "picks it up," stops our eyes by breaking the pattern on the page in the same way that the ball and runner stop and change their direction. Now, I'm not about to say that Donald thought of all this or would find a lot of sense in my analysis of his lining of the poem, but neither can weekend golfers analyze verbally all the technical components of every swing. They do, however, have a feel for what's right, and children, given experience, also know what's right in their poems. Donald, for whom traditional language arts learning activities were a chore, described his process this way: "When I wrote my poem I thought what baseball was really like, then wrote it in a line and then another line."
  At sharing time on the day of the slash-mark minilesson, the children sitting nearest the reader hovered so close that the reader nearly disappeared behind them. When I asked them why they were so anxious to see the poem as well as hear it, they said, "We want to see the line breaks!" I was delighted not only by their enthusiasm and keen awareness of lining but also because they pointed me to the next minilesson.

Hearing the Lines

  The following morning I began, "Remember yesterday at sharing time when you wanted to be able to see where the line breaks were in the poem you were hearing? Well, when poets read their work to an audience, lots of times you can *hear* the line breaks—but just barely. You know how when you read prose out loud, you pause at a comma? A line break is like that, but much less. When you come to it, you pause just the tiniest bit. It's kind of hard to do at first. I practiced reading 'Safety Pin' about five times so I could show you what I mean." I projected Valerie Worth's poem on the screen again and read it aloud. When I came to the end of each unpunctuated line, I kept the pitch of my voice up and paused almost imperceptibly.
  The children's responses were varied, of course. Some nodded sagely, some looked blank, some giggled. "It sounds funny that way!" was one comment. No doubt they had thought so the first time I read the poem, too, but either politeness or the newness of the experience had inhibited the giggles then.

"Yes, it does at first," I agreed. "It's another way that poems are special. You say them in a special way. You'll get used to it after a while." My choice to teach this form of oral poetry reading was a matter of personal preference. Many, but not all, poets read their work this way. In contrast, college professors often teach students to read through line breaks without pausing (Heard 1989, 55). Yet my kids wanted to know where those line breaks were; the visual and oral qualities of the poem belonged together for them. I think they're right. A poem is meant to be seen *and* heard, and what is important in one mode needs to be included in the other. But you decide for yourself. Try reading poems you like both ways, with and without tiny pauses at line breaks. Listen to recordings of poets reading their work. Think about what sounds most effective to you and try it out in your classroom. Ask your students what they think. They're our best teachers!

Stanzas

I mentioned stanzas to my class when we talked about reading poems aloud, explaining that I paused a little longer for the extra space than for the ends of lines. When it came to writing, I didn't teach stanzas as such, probably because of my built-in reluctance to formalize the poetry-writing process; but a simple minilesson could focus attention on this organization of content and use of white space. Valerie Worth's "Pebbles" would have been a good starting point for my classes. Its subject is appealing (I would have especially enjoyed sharing it with Laura, author of "Blue Rock" in chapter 1) and it clearly shows the organization of a poem into stanzas.

pebbles

Pebbles belong to no one
Until you pick them up—
Then they are yours.

But which, of all the world's
Mountains of little broken stones,
Will you choose to keep?

The smooth black, the white,
The rough gray with sparks
Shining in its cracks?

Somewhere the best pebble must
Lie hidden, meant for you
If you can find it. ❖

"pebbles" from *Small Poems* by Valerie Worth. © 1972 by Valerie Worth. Reprinted by permission of Farrar, Straus & Giroux, Inc.

The same kinds of questions that I asked when we first began to look at the shape of a poem would work here. I'm sure the children would notice that "pebbles" is in four "pieces," each with three lines and separated from the next by a space. Further discussion would bring out the unity of thought that each stanza expresses. On subsequent days, pointing out stanza divisions in other poems, including ones by the children, or asking them what they notice about a poem written in stanzas would reinforce the concept.

I was interested to find that the kids often chose on their own to arrange their poems in stanzas. Lindsay explained how she decided to use that structure. "I started to think of what poem to write about. And then suddenly I got the idea of seasons. I started to think of how I would write my poem. Then I decided I would write about each season in its own stanza."

Obviously, the children were receiving powerful instruction just from reading lots of poetry; I often thought we were getting closer and closer to the teacherless classroom. Left to his own devices, Brian organized the words of his poem into an unusual and effective pattern.

Spring to Summer

When I see the animals I also
Can see a beautiful spring
Ahead.

When I look up at the sun it
Blinds me but it still looks
Yellowish.

When I see the greenful leaves
On the trees I know that spring
Is here.

I look at the flowers and I feel
Like the heat is entering my
Body.

Now that summer is here the
Green grass is as bright as the
Sun.

When the brightful sun comes out
In the morning it lights up the
Whole world. ❖

Brian Siegrist
Grade 4

Brian, normally quiet and unassuming, was a bold writer of poems. In addition to using unorthodox spacing, he wasn't afraid to express himself in intensely personal terms or to make up words in order to convey his own vision of his subject. I believe his description of the process, beautifully simple, could apply to the experience of a great many poets, young or old: "One day in writing class I looked outside and it was beautiful out. When I looked outside something happened. I just felt like writing a poem about summer. Then I started to write."

POETIC DEVICES AND STRUCTURES

Rhyme

Rhyme is an important element in the form of a poem. The echoing of a sound at line's end satisfies what must be an ancient need, it is so deep and enduring a quality of poetry. Surely rhymes were spoken before they could be written, eons ago, and surely those long-ago people wanted to remember them. Imagine a prehistoric poet home from a successful hunt, flushed with the pride and passion of finding, killing, and bringing back enough meat for a week. When he last accomplished that, several days earlier, he was inspired to express his feelings in words. "That was a great poem I made up last week. Now, how did it go?" he muses, but the wonderful words are lost, vanished from his memory. "Guess I'll have to make up another one," he sighs, "but *this* one I'm gonna remember! Maybe if I used words that sound alike it would help. Hmmm—meat, feet, heat...."

Well, perhaps it didn't happen exactly that way, but we do know that rhyme has helped us remember poems for a very long time. In addition to its utility, rhyme is simply fun: It pleases our ears and minds. Consider Ogden Nash's " ... if called by a panther / don't anther" or Shel Silverstein's "Ickle Me, Pickle Me, Tickle Me too / Went for a ride in a flying shoe." When you read good rhyming poems to your classes, delight is equally shared between reader and listeners.

Here we come to a point where reading and writing poetry go somewhat separate ways for most young children. Reading and hearing good rhyming poetry are joys that none of us should be deprived of, least of all the kids in your classes. But writing good rhyming poetry is very difficult, as published poets will tell you. When my students and I talked about this early in our poetry workshop, examples of good and bad rhyming poems and recollections of their earlier attempts to write poetry helped them understand the concept.

Now, this doesn't mean that I outlawed the use of rhymes; that would have negated the whole idea of ownership and autonomy in writing, which is central to the teaching of the writing process. The only thing that was outlawed in writing workshop was denigrating anyone's writing, even the writer's own.

Yogi Berra is said to have said, "When you come to a fork in the road, take it." This is what we did where writing rhyming poems was concerned. When children found rhymes that fit and enhanced the meaning of their poems, we celebrated. But all of us were liberated from the constraint of believing that line ends *must* rhyme. We were free to follow the wonderful ideas and images that popped into our heads and free to work them into words that were just right, rhyming or no. Most of the children exercised that freedom and wrote wonderful unrhymed poems, but some seemed to have a natural affinity for rhyme.

Laura's "Blue Rock" in chapter 1 was inspired by her finding a small, bright blue stone. Andrew also picked up a stone when we went outside to find an object to write our first poems about, but his was an ordinary stonish color, mottled beige and white with an interesting texture. Although they didn't work together on their poems, Andrew was impressed and influenced by Laura, our chief writing expert. The similarities in the content of their poems are clear, but Andrew turned out to be our best role model for using rhyme without being limited by it. Read his poem aloud and listen to its internal rhymes, not all of which were consciously chosen.

Stone

> Stone could be a lone
>   stone out at sea
> Or a stone might be a bone
>   from someone's own body
> Or a little fish in a dish
>   of water
> Or maybe a delicious sundae
>   all bumpy with nuts
> Or maybe it was King
>   Tut's stone ❖
>
>   *Andrew Leach*

When Andrew read his poem at sharing time, finding the rhymes became an intriguing game. The children on the other side of the circle complained that they couldn't see the rhymes. "Wait a minute," I said, unaware that I was about to ask a dumb teacher question, "You *hear* rhymes. How do you mean you want to *see* them?"

They said they didn't exactly know, they just wanted to see what he wrote, and Andrew (who was from England) said, "I'll make a copy then, shall I?"

The next day when he projected his poem on the screen, it produced five minutes of delighted discovery as the kids murmured the lines to themselves, listening and looking for rhymes. "Oh, look, own goes with bone, stone, and lone!"

"Fish, dish, and de*lish*!"
"How about sea and bod*ee*?"
"Sund*ae* too!"
"Nuts and King Tut's!"

"I don't know—sundae and bumpy? They're not real rhymes but they're kind of alike." I fought back the urge to impose the word *assonance* on them and noted once again that learning sometimes happened best when I just got out of the way.

Repetition

Rhyme is repeated sounds, but repetition of words can also be a part of poetry. The refrain, a part of a poem or song that's repeated regularly, was probably invented by our prehistoric poet and it's been used ever since. A contemporary example is Maurice Sendak's *Chicken Soup with Rice: A Book of Months*, which is a series of poems, one for each month, that end in variations of the refrain "Going once, / going twice, / going chicken soup with rice."

Very young children are especially fond of refrains and love to chime in with repeated words in poems. Who could resist Ilo Orleans's

> There once
> Was a green
>   Little frog, frog, frog—
> Who played
> In the wood
>   On a log, log, log! ❖

Or this, by Anonymous:

> There's music in a hammer,
> There's music in a nail,
> There's music in a pussy cat,
> When you step upon her tail. ❖

(You can find both of these in Jack Prelutsky's *Read-Aloud Rhymes for the Very Young*.)

Kenneth Koch has used repetition to help children write inventive poems; one of his best known forms is the "I used to / But now" poem: "I used to be so big like an elephant / But now I am as lean as bacteria germs" and "I used to stay with angels / But now I am a star," for example. Another is the wish poem, in which every line begins with "I wish . . . ," a key that opens up the world of fantasy.

Poem by Ilo Orleans reprinted with permission of Karen S. Solomon.

Carolyn, a fourth-grader, wrote a twenty-four-line poem, part of which is below, using repeated words at the beginning of each line:

When you walk outside in the rain,
> you see puddles of cold chocolate
> floating down your sidewalk.

When you walk outside in the rain,
> you feel a cold breeze of whipped cream
> cloud coming toward you. . . . ❖

Carolyn Aibel
Grade 4

Repetition keeps the poem going, like the helpful push on a child's swing at the beginning of each forward arc.

Unrhymed Poems

Because of the inherent charm of rhyming poetry, that's the kind we usually find when we look for poems to read to our classes. Telling my kids their poems didn't have to rhyme wasn't enough. We needed models of unrhymed poems and found them in the work of such poets as William Carlos Williams, Langston Hughes, and Carl Sandburg. Sandburg's "Just Before April Came," for example, is an unrhymed poem full of images that resonate for children.

Valerie Worth's work is a treasure chestful of poems that don't rhyme. I showed her poem "Barefoot" to my classes in our poetry workshop and brought it out again when the weather got warm in the spring. It speaks of feeling the grass under bare feet, an experience dear to children who search out new grass to walk on in the early days of spring.

Published poems often provided springboards for the children by helping them think of topics to write about or providing fresh ways of looking at familiar sights or events. I don't know whether Michael was inspired by Worth's grass metaphor when he wrote, "It's like walking on paper needles / so soft and green," but I was impressed by the similarity in their contrasting the sharpness of teeth and needles with the soft and gentle texture of grass.

Personification

The following poem by Sandburg, as well as being unrhymed, can lead to minilessons on other procedures.

Bubbles

Two bubbles found they had rainbows on their curves.
They flickered out saying:
"It was worth being a bubble just to have held that
rainbow thirty seconds." ❖

You could teach a minilesson about the way Sandburg personified the bubbles by giving them sight and emotion and invite your class to find and share other examples of that poetic strategy. Valerie Worth often uses personification in her poems, and children like to point it out. Early in poetry workshop, James complained, "A safety pin can't look at itself!"

"*Duhh*!" (Brian often needed my reminder not to put anyone down.) "That's just pretending. Poems pretend a lot of stuff." Personification is a kind of poetic pretending that appeals to many children. Kelly used it effectively in her poem about shoes.

Who Am I?

I live in your closet and just
    sit
        sit
            sit
Like a lump on a log till you come and put me on,

Then you go outside and
            splash
                splash me in mud
Who am I? I am a shoe and all I do is sit
    sit
        sit
In your closet like a lump on a log! ❖

Kelly-Anne Laube
Grade 4

When asked how she got the idea for the poem, Kelly wrote, "I think I got my idea because I want a pair of shoes but I don't think the pair of shoes would like sitting in my closet like a lump on a log. I know I would not either." Personification speaks to the sensitivity and capacity for empathy we often find in children, particularly those between the ages of eight and ten, and gives these feelings a natural outlet. I fought down the teacherly impulse to tell everyone to

---

"Bubbles" from *Wind Song*, copyright © 1960 by Carl Sandburg and renewed 1988 by Margaret Sandburg, Janet Sandburg, and Helen Sandburg Crile, reprinted by permission of Harcourt Brace & Company.

try it, though, trusting that the models of Kelly's poem and other published works combined with the positive recognition she received would produce more genuine work than my exhortation.

Kelly could not express as clearly her reasons for the way she lined her poem. "I just like the way it looks," she said, when asked why she left white space in certain places and put each "sit" on a new line, indented by one space. An earlier draft of this poem was not arranged this way; the strikingly effective spacing was a result of her revision process. Reading and writing didn't come easily to Kelly, but in poetry workshop, surrounded by fine models and with the freedom to choose her own forms and topics, she showed remarkable sophistication in the use of poetry devices. She also benefited from discussing her work with her friends. "I had Christina, Farnaz, Akiko, Nicole, and Jody help me one or two times. I had Tally help me so many times I don't remember," she wrote.

Punctuation

The Sandburg poem "Bubbles" can also be useful on the level of mechanics as an example of the use of quotation marks and the colon. However, poets don't always follow the rules of punctuation. When the kids first discovered that, it was almost as good as waking up to hear that school was closed because of snow.

I began one minilesson with Eve Merriam's "Places to Hide a Secret Message" from *Fresh Paint*. It's just three lines long and devoid of punctuation and uppercase. Everyone loved the central image of tiny, appealingly impossible places to hide a secret, but soon a star pupil raised a hand and said, trying to be polite while correcting the teacher, "You copied it wrong, Mrs. Armour. You left out the capital letters and the periods."

"Actually, Eve Merriam left them out," I answered. "That's the way she wants it."

"Can you do that?" asked a less-than-star pupil in a voice that mixed doubt and hope equally.

"In poetry you can. Most poets do use punctuation and capitals, though, to help you understand the poem better. Sometimes they use them in ways you don't expect. Here's one that'll surprise you. This is the title of a poem," I said, drawing an exclamation mark on the board. Amid sounds of disbelief, I made a quick note to bring in e. e. cummings's *Hist Whist and Other Poems for Children* and show them "!" with its unorthodox use of typography and odd placement of uppercase letters that evoke the great roundness of the full moon in a completely original way.

Predictably, an epidemic of unpunctuated and uncapitalized poems broke out. The novelty soon wore off, however, and I showed them lots of poems that used those mechanics effectively. Their desire to communicate with their audience also helped return us to a reasonable state. Conferences with me or with peers provided motivation to use all available means to make their poems successful. I believe the outcome was a heightened awareness of the real purpose of mechanics and greater skill in their use. At the same time, children who were unsure of their ability in this area felt less restricted in their attempts to get the poem on the page.

Teaching Poetic Terms

We teachers are driven by the desire to "do the right thing." I worried constantly about whether I was teaching my kids everything they were supposed to know, either for life or for the standardized tests. Sometimes it was hard to work up enthusiasm for teaching something that seemed to apply only to the tests.

For example, simile and metaphor were terms that I was required to teach my fourth-graders when I was using a basal reading text. The experience illustrated the difference between teaching and learning. I did the teaching part the way the teacher's manual dictated but, according to the results of the accompanying tests, the learning part just hadn't happened.

Perhaps it seems to you, as it did to me then, that the concepts were too difficult for nine-year-olds. Certainly something was too difficult, but I think it was the context the terms were presented in. As often happens with textbooks, the explanation was largely unrelated to these children's experience. When I began poetry workshop, I argued with myself about whether to teach poetry terms at all. The very idea made me think of worksheets and short-answer tests and everything else that the writing process had delivered me from.

At the same time, those of us who have been teaching for some years find it almost impossible to escape entirely the pull to sink back into old didactic ways, particularly when we're dealing with straightforward information like poetry terms. Occasionally I slid into the role of authority and dispenser of knowledge. "A simile is a figure of speech in which we compare one thing to something else, often using *like* or *as*. Can anyone find a simile on this page?" My students' body language told me I was on the wrong track. They sank a bit in their chairs, faces grew blank, eyes began to glaze.

Yet terms do need to be taught, partly because of the curriculum and standardized tests, but mostly because they are part of the special language of poetry and we shortchange our students if we don't make them aware of this. Similes and metaphors, rhyme and alliteration refuse to be ignored when we read and write poetry.

I reminded myself not to throw out the baby (poetic terms) with the bathwater (fill-in-the-blank exercises) and thought instead about how to help children learn useful terms in meaningful ways. The method that evolved began with simply identifying the term when its example appeared in a poem. A day or two later we discussed the meaning of the term and eventually agreed on a definition that was then recorded on a page glued to the inside of everyone's poetry folder. The page was called Special Poetry Words and included, among others, poetry, prose, rhyme, and of course simile and metaphor.

Similes

Published poems are chock-full of similes, and their use comes naturally to children, if not immediately, then soon after they've spent some time with poetry. Akiko wrote, "The dragonflies hovered / Like wonderful airplanes." Steven began his poem, "The Wind and the Leaves," with "The wind blows across the earth / Like a giant fan" and Eric wrote this about comets: "They streak across the sky / Like beams from a flashlight." Here is Stephen's poem "Spring" in its entirety:

> Spring so peaceful as the summer's morning
> But so quiet as the feathers falling. ❖
>
> *Stephen Bluestein*
> *Grade 4*

With all these wonderful examples, the minilesson on similes almost taught itself; we identified and defined them on the same day. After we enjoyed the aptness of the comparisons and the images they created in our minds, I said, "Here's a five-dollar word for this kind of poetic writing." Earlier in my teaching career I might have said, "Do you want to know a five-dollar word for this?" but experience has taught me not to ask yes-no questions unless I'm willing to accept no for an answer.

I wrote *simile* on the board and pronounced it several times. Then I had the class say it several times to counteract their initial reaction, which was that I had put an extra letter in *smile*. After some discussion, we settled on the following definition: Simile: words that compare a thing with something else, usually with *like* or *as* in between. Although I couldn't defend this to a lexicographer, it made sense to the kids and was stated in their own words.

Metaphors

Metaphors were less abundant in the children's writing, so one day I began the minilesson with this poem by Langston Hughes.

Dreams

> Hold fast to dreams
> For if dreams die
> Life is a broken-winged bird
> That cannot fly.
> Hold fast to dreams
> For when dreams go
> Life is a barren field
> Frozen with snow. ❖

From *The Dream Keeper and Other Poems* by Langston Hughes. Copyright 1932 by Alfred A. Knopf, Inc. and renewed 1960 by Langston Hughes. Reprinted by permission of the publisher.

After we listened to it and looked at it, I asked, "What does this poem mean to you?"

Literal-minded Amy said, "After I wake up, I can't remember what I dreamed sometimes. But I can tell it was a good dream and I try and try to remember it. It's like I want to hold fast to it after I wake up."

"Mm-hmm," I murmured encouragingly, reminding myself that my interest in metaphor didn't mean that other interpretations of the poem weren't valid. "What else does this poem make you think of?"

"Maybe Langston Hughes means the kind of dreams you—well, it's like when you want something really bad, then it's your dream to have it," offered Efrem.

"And then what happens if you don't hold fast to your dream, if you let it die or go?"

This stumped the kids for a bit until Kirsten, one of our star pupils, said, "He says then life would be a broken-winged bird that couldn't fly. That's really sad."

"Yes, it is, isn't it! So your life would be sad if you let your dreams die. What else?"

Now it was easier. "And your life would be a barren—what does that mean again?" I had told them in the beginning, but Richie had forgotten.

"Nothing grows there," Matt reminded him.

"Yeah. So your life would be like a bare field, frozen, with just snow on it."

"Yes, and that's sad, too," I said. "You used the word *like*, Richie. That's what life would be *like*. Sometimes poets use the word *like* when they're comparing things ('Simile!' several voices volunteered) and sometimes they don't. Isn't it interesting the way Hughes says that life *is* a broken-winged bird or a barren field when you let your dreams die! That gives me a really powerful image and makes me feel how important dreams are. Read your poems over and let me know if you've said that one thing *is* something else, the way Hughes did in his poem. Or if you find a poem like that by someone else, show that to me, too."

Later that day, Hope brought me a poem. "I wrote this last week and I had lots of *likes* in it. So today I revised it and I took out the *likes* so it was more like the Langston Hughes poem. I mean the way he said something *was* something else." And she read this poem.

Trees

Trees are big men and women.
    The hair is the big green leaves.
    The arms are the branches.
    The woman's hands are flowers blooming.
    The man's hands are branches split up.
    The mouth is the hole in the bark.
    And the eyes are the dark brown holes carved into the tree. ❖

Hope Sperling
Grade 4

"Hope, I love it!" I exclaimed. "Especially the way the woman's hands are flowers and the man's hands are branches. Would you read this at the beginning of class tomorrow? I'd like to use it as an example of what we talked about today."

"Sure," Hope said with a grin, happy to be a minilesson assistant.

After Hope read "Trees" at the beginning of the next day's class and several children had pointed out her use of our new strategy, I said, "Here's another five-dollar word. Poets have a name for what Hope and Langston Hughes did. When you say that one thing *is* another thing, you call it a metaphor." I wrote the word on the board and we hashed out the following definition: Metaphor: words that compare one thing to another thing by saying it *is* that thing. Not very elegant, but sufficient for our purposes and meaningful to the young poets, it joined the definition of *simile* on everyone's Special Poetry Words page.

The concept and use of metaphor was not as accessible to the children as simile was (we missed those neat little flags, *like* and *as*), and poems with effective examples of that kind of comparison were harder to find, compounding our difficulty. I was delighted to discover several in Hilda Conkling's poems, which held special appeal for the kids because she was a child when she wrote them. Her lines "My thoughts are sea-foam and sand; / They are apple-petals fluttering" caused an electric silence in class as the children absorbed the unique images. "Dandelion," with its metaphor of the flower as a soldier wearing a gold helmet, also pleased them.

Langston Hughes's "Mother to Son" is excellent to use when you're illustrating metaphor. It begins, "Well, son, I'll tell you: / Life for me ain't been no crystal stair" and ends with "Don't you fall now— / For I'se still goin', honey, / I'se still climbin', / And life for me ain't been no crystal stair." This goes beyond imagery to make us think about the realities of human experience in a new way.

Eve Merriam, in *It Doesn't Always Have to Rhyme*, includes several poems that, if we were being very serious, we could label metapoetic because Merriam tells about a poetic form while using that form. For example, "Metaphor" presents morning as "a new sheet of paper" to be written on.

Given lots of models, the children wrote their own metaphors, which in turn became our models. Taka chose a topic that's central to writing poetry and gave it an unexpected slant with his closing metaphor.

Imagination

Imagination can do anything,
Make time machines
Or people with one hundred legs and one thousand hands.
Imagination is always in your brain,
So if you hear a ghost story
Your imagination will pop out
And erase your ghost story.
Imagination is an eraser of scary stories. ❖

Takafumi Ogasawara
Grade 4

Onomatopoeia

As a college freshman I was blessed with a demanding composition professor. My first paper came back peppered with her abbreviated comments, one of which was "awk." I was surprised; after rereading the sentence I could understand that it might cause a sensitive reader to squawk, but Dr. Smither didn't seem given to the sort of levity that would produce such a comment. My ear for onomatopoeia had overridden my word sense and it wasn't until next class that I recognized the abbreviation for *awkward*.

Children, closer to nature than we grown-ups are, listen to it with sharper ears and often choose words that fit its sounds. Stacy's poem evoked much positive feedback when she read it at sharing time; her audience liked the noises they heard in the words. (The italics are mine and mark the words we identified as sounding like what they meant.)

Rain and Thunder

When it rains you can hear the *tip tap* on your ceiling
And the thunder *roars* in the clouds like a spark is falling on the earth.
It looks like there are swords *clashing* in the sky hours on end.
The *smack* of its hands *shatters* the colorful earth piece by piece.
The might of its feet *rumbles* on the clouds . . .
The *plip plop* of the rain falls in the many puddles. ❖

Stacy Martinucci
Grade 4

When I wrote *onomatopoeia* on the board and told them it was the name for words like this, Mark said, "That's a *fifty*-dollar word!" Now, you can be sure I didn't write a test question on this term or even expect them to remember having met it, but its length and strangeness fascinated them so much that I'm sure many of them will, when presented with it in a later grade, remember their first encounter when they painstakingly entered it on the Special Poetry Words page. They certainly enjoyed pointing out their use of it and rolling its pronunciation around in their mouths. Howard began his poem about skiing with "Swoosh down the slope," and Shain wrote of a "gushing breeze" blowing away leaves that *rustle* and *crunch*.

The first stanza of Lilian Moore's "Telling Time," an excellent example of onomatopoeia, uses words such as *chime*, *ping*, *tock*, and *bong* to represent the sounds time makes. "I Speak, I Say, I Talk" by Arnold Shapiro is a comprehensive collection of words for animal sounds that begins, "Cats purr. / Lions roar. / Owls hoot. / Bears snore." Tony Johnston's "Jellyfish Walk" with its "phlup, phlup, phlup" demonstrates to kids that you can make up onomatopoeic words.

Alliteration

Another poetic practice I planned to present to the class was alliteration, which is the use of two or more words that begin with the same sound. Julie, though unaware of this, obligingly wrote these lines in her poem "Spring": "Grass grows green and shiny / Baby birds hatch / The fox has a family."

By now the children were used to my asking, "What do you notice about this poem?" and quickly pointed out Julie's repetition of consonants. The definition we entered on the Special Poetry Words page was: Alliteration: starting words with the same letter. I worried for a moment that it was too short and simple until I realized that those were virtues in a definition and would suit our uses well.

Nicole's poem "Sparkling Sea" began with this stanza.

> The sparkling sea shines
> Everywhere even in Africa.
> In the sparkling sea,
> There are some shells
> And animals.
> The sparkling sea is like
> A rock tumbler, it tosses the
> Rocks around
> And the sand is the grit. ❖
>
> *Nicole Vonthron*
> *Grade 4*

When we listened to the poem, sitting in the sharing circle, Julie was the first to call attention to the many *s* and *sh* sounds. Danny asked to hear it again and, having listened carefully to the second line, asked, "Do vowels count?" We decided they did and moved on to explore the extension of alliteration to include matching the sounds to what they represented. I asked, "What sound do the waves make when you're at the beach?" Several voices whispered "swish" and "splash," and it was easy to make the onomatopoeic connection between sound and substance. We went on to "bouncy, bumpy bus rides" and "marvelous marshmallow munchies."

Laura wrote a two-line poem called "The Sparkling Fields" that added to our understanding of sound matching subject:

> The sun shines upon the fields of white,
> Making them sparkle as if they were sprayed with stars. ❖
>
> *Laura Woodson*
> *Grade 4*

This time we talked about the sibilance (no, I did not impose that word on them) of frozen snow, which is the kind that sparkles most, and of the action of spraying, but not until we had marveled at the image her poem created in our minds.

You might want to use this poem by Carl Sandburg as an example of alliteration. It also gave me a chance to remind the kids about the effectiveness of repeating phrases at the beginnings of lines.

Grassroots

> Grass clutches at the dark dirt with finger holds.
> Let it be blue grass, barley, rye or wheat,
> Let it be button weed or butter-and-eggs,
> Let it be Johnny-jump-ups springing clean blue streaks.
> Grassroots down under put fingers into dark dirt. ❖

When we teach poetic terms, we have to remember to keep our priorities straight. The poem always comes first; terms and definitions are a useful support for the reading and writing of poetry, not material to be drilled and memorized for its own sake. What's important here is the use and understanding of poetic elements, not simply their names. That a child can spell and define *simile* or *alliteration* has little to do with being able to write, as Andrew did, lines like these: "snow as white as a wedding gown, / sleet as solid as sugar cubes."

POETIC FORMS

When I first attempted the Sunday *New York Times* crossword puzzle, my goal was just to finish it, and the rare occasions when that happened caused me great happiness. Years passed and I got better and pretty soon I was finishing most of the puzzles I started, so I set myself a rule: No word could be entered unless its space in the puzzle already contained a letter from another word (except for the top row; I had to get started somewhere). After a while this limitation lost some of its appeal and, looking for a new spur, I began to time myself. If I could finish in thirty minutes or less, the day was a success.

I think we do this in many of the endeavors that we repeat over long periods of time; we look for ways to challenge ourselves. Poetic forms may have come about in this way. Perhaps our prehistoric poet who earlier in this chapter invented rhyme got so good at making up and remembering his poems that one day he said to himself, "I bet I could make this rhyming thing even more interesting. Suppose I make up a rule, like the first two lines have to rhyme and then the next two have to have a new rhyme and then the next two...." And there he was, composing couplets.

"Grassroots" from *Good Morning, America*, copyright © 1928 and renewed 1956 by Carl Sandburg, reprinted by permission of Harcourt Brace & Company.

Children, however, haven't been writing poetry long enough to need rules to make it an interesting endeavor. They are beginners at the craft. If, in the early years when I was happy just to finish the crossword puzzle, someone had yanked it out of my hands and yelled, "Thirty minutes! Time's up!" I would have been extremely frustrated and annoyed. If it happened the next time I picked up the puzzle, and the next, I might well have quit doing puzzles. Certainly the pleasure would have left the process.

Imposing rigid poetic forms on children can have the same effect on their writing of poems. Many children will cheerfully follow our directions and turn out dozens of diamantes and cinquains, but if the focus is on following directions and completing a pattern rather than creating original images that express their unique visions of their lives, the results won't be poetry.

I wish it hadn't taken me so long to find that out. For more years than I care to admit, I embraced every new verse form that appeared in teachers' magazines and enthusiastically taught it to my students, who dutifully followed my instructions. Of course there were always one or two young writers whose poems transcended the forms. The recognition they received from me confirmed their status as classroom stars but did nothing for the rest of the class. The other kids, convinced they could never approach that level of achievement, were even less inspired to attempt writing poetry. I wasn't fooled; I knew those stars would have done as well if their teacher had been a rose bush. But even the natural-born writers were capable of producing lines that made me wince: "The lion is fierce / But his ears are not pierced."

Then I began teaching writing as a process and wondered why, if my kids could write authentic personal narratives, their poems were so unsuccessful. Eventually it occurred to me that all their models and past experience of specific poetic forms—couplets, limericks, haiku, rhymed stanzas, cinquains, and so on—might be hampering them instead of helping. Reflecting on my own experience was illuminating: Just writing a simple limerick took me a long time and taxed my brain. I hadn't realized that poems written according to formal rules can be wonderful to hear and read and yet not useful to most children as models of writing frameworks. Because it was simply too difficult to find words that expressed their original thoughts or observations and at the same time fit into the limits of a form, they picked words for their malleability instead of their meaning. As long as it rhymed and fit the formula, a word was in.

When I began to provide examples of unrhymed free verse, my kids and I found we could write authentic poems that gave us and our audience pleasure. Instead of satisfying the requirements of a poetic form, we worked to find the precise words and placement on the page that would best fit the images and experiences in our heads.

An Analogy for Poetic Forms

Some educators feel that children should be carefully taught to use poetic forms, beginning with the rhymed couplet and working their way up to the sonnet and other complicated structures, or else their writing will be frivolous and not worthy to be called poetry. Let's take as an analogy a master carpenter, an artisan whose natural ability and desires led him to this career and who has polished his skills to a high luster over time. In his shop is a fortune in tools of all kinds, which he uses with care and knowledge to produce work of high quality.

Now let's look at my tool kit. Maybe you have one something like it. In a small plastic carrier with a handle are a hammer, several screwdrivers, a drill, pliers, measuring tape, and level. With those few tools I've been able to hang pictures, speakers, and hooks, install simple shelves, and manage a few uncomplicated repairs. These small achievements gave me pleasure and a sense of accomplishment beyond their objective importance.

Just as I don't need to purchase and learn to use a shopful of costly, specialized tools to do small but satisfying tasks around the house, experience has convinced me that children don't need to master and use restrictive poetic forms in order to write poems that satisfy the writer and please the reader. My hope was that my students would write and read poetry all their lives, even if only sporadically. That way they would always have access to the pleasure of expressing in poems the bits of their lives that cried out for that expression. At the same time, they could read the works of published poets with the same delight and appreciation I feel when I run my hand over the shining wood of a carefully crafted piece of furniture.

Teaching Poetic Forms

What we do need to try to do, however, is identify those young poets in the making who are galloping ahead of the rest of us and provide them with guidance and opportunities to explore the forms they are ready for. I wish I could say that's what I did, but in the real world of the classroom I was as bedeviled by limits and obstacles as I suspect you are. So let's consider the ideal for a moment.

At Upper Utopia Elementary School, children learn to love the sound and sight of poetry in the primary grades. They're encouraged to say and write it in whatever form suggests itself to them. By early third grade they're reading and writing short unrhymed poems in a workshop setting and by the time they get to fourth grade are proficient. From this point through middle school and beyond, students who show the ability to handle more stringent formal demands are helped and encouraged to do so.

Well, until you and I are offered a contract by the Upper Utopia board of education, we'll have to keep on doing our best to help children learn to love writing poetry here in Lower Reality, where most of us teach. One way of doing that is to use poetic forms very carefully.

Rhyming Couplets

Probably the least demanding rhymed form (and possibly the most abused) is the couplet, or two lines ending in words that rhyme. "Questioning Faces" by Robert Frost, about an owl that almost flies into a window where children sit watching, captures a wonderfully rich image in a series of couplets that provide children with a clear example of the form.

Children with an affinity for rhyme can often use this form effectively. Beth was a third-grader in Carol Graham's class in Naples, Florida, when she wrote this poem.

A Day on Big Pine Key

One weekend we went to Key West,
And here is why it was the best:
My grandpa said, "Let's go for a ride,
I'll show you where the key deer hide . . . ."
We drove for a while, then saw a sign
And here's what it said line for line . . .
>   DRIVE WITH CAUTION
>   YOU ARE ENTERING
>   AN ENDANGERED SPECIES AREA.
>   PLEASE PROTECT THE KEY DEER.

My heart took a leap, we were finally here!
I was about to see my first key deer!
I looked out the window and what luck!
There ahead was a key deer buck!
Out of the car I climbed; he let us get near,
I couldn't believe it—a real key deer!
He was small, proud, and furry,
But away he ran—in such a hurry.
We walked through the woods, around each tree,
And yes, we found more—a thrill to see. ❖

Beth Dehnart
Grade 3

Because couplets seem to children such a natural way to use rhyme, very little instruction is needed. It's more likely that you'll need to encourage your students who choose this form to keep the idea of their poems firmly in mind, as Beth did, so as not to lose it in the service of the rhyme. Children who have had lots of experience writing unrhymed poems will be better equipped to deal with this than those who begin with rhyme. Invite them to experiment with other rhyme schemes, and keep your approach flexible.

Limericks

Some rhyming forms are firmly fixed and allow little latitude, such as the limerick. Edward Lear was the first and arguably the most famous writer to use this form extensively. His humor and irreverence appeal to us all, but especially to children.

> There was an old man of West Dumpet,
> Who possessed a large nose like a trumpet;
>   When he blew it aloud,
>   It astonished the crowd,
> And was heard through the whole of West Dumpet. ❖

When you read Lear's limericks to your kids, be sure to tell them a little about him as a person. Myra Cohn Livingston includes fascinating information about his life and the sources of some of his poems in her introduction to a selection of his works *How Pleasant to Know Mr. Lear!* He endured poor health, an uncertain income, an unprepossessing physical appearance, and lack of recognition in his chosen career as a painter of landscapes but never lost the desire or ability to express his sense of fun in writing.

The limerick form is said to have come from an Irish song in which the verses told about the escapades of people from different villages and were followed by the chorus, "Will you come up to Limerick?" The five-line form with its a-a-b-b-a rhyme scheme and shorter third and fourth lines looks deceptively simple. Be sure to try it yourself before you ask your kids to write one. Reading and hearing limericks is great fun, of course, and writing one collaboratively can ease the burden of composition.

Cinquains

Sometimes a verse form appeals to us because it is very clearly defined. Few teachers can resist forever the lure of a procedure that lets us say without exception, "This is the way you do it." The cinquain is this kind of form, a five-line unrhymed verse constructed by counting syllables. In one version of it, the first line contains two syllables, the next four, then six, then eight, and the last line, like the first, has two syllables. It was developed from an earlier verse form and named (from *cinq*, French for "five") by Adelaide Crapsey, a twentieth-century American poet. Here's one by a fourth-grader.

> Snow flakes
> Are bright as silk
> As they fall from the sky
> As they melt in the blazing sun
> Bye, snow. ❖

Although this is a very limiting form, the writer was able to meet its requirements and still create a vivid image with his use of simile and the intensity of "blazing" in line four. Many children, though, will find it difficult to juggle the demands of poetic expression and formal structure. If we have to choose between the two, poetic expression comes first.

As is true with rhyming poems, the difficulty of writing cinquains doesn't diminish the pleasure of reading them. Myra Cohn Livingston's *Sky Songs* is a cycle of poems in this form that your students will enjoy.

Haiku

Haiku, a lyric poem form popular in Japan for about five centuries, also requires syllable counting but, with fewer and longer lines, seems easier to deal with. The structure is deceptively simple: three unrhymed lines with five syllables in the first line, seven in the second, and five in the third. Kenneth Koch (1973) finds the form too restrictive and suggests we ignore syllable counting when teaching children to write haiku. Instead he offers contextual structures (e.g., ask a bird or animal an unusual question) and focuses on brevity and imagery, comparing the poem to a drawing.

Authentic Japanese haiku emerge from Zen, a way of living and thinking that is outside the experience of most Americans. This, however, does not prevent our enjoyment of the form. Perhaps because the poems come from a culture different from our own, they show us unexpected possibilities. These poems capture the image of a moment, usually having to do with the natural world, and sometimes include the poet's emotional response to it. They often surprise us with sharp contrasts or opposites.

> Bee, your pincushion
> body that looks so soft holds
> one pin pointing out. ❖

Children are fascinated by the natural world. They live in the here and now and are constantly being confronted with life's contradictions: a perfect fit with haiku. Before you ask your students to write haiku, share as many as you can with them, both visually and orally. Focus on the mood and content rather than the syllable count.

Cricket Songs, a collection of haiku translated by Harry Behn, is an excellent resource. Another book of verses in this form, *Haiku: The Mood of Earth* by Ann Atwood, is unusual in two ways. First, the author is not Asian; second, her haiku are accompanied and apparently were inspired by her spectacular nature photographs. The introduction gives a fine overview of this poetic form.

Narrative Poems

The narrative poem doesn't constitute a verse form as such, but because it, too, probably began with our poetic caveman, it deserves attention. Everyone loves to hear a story, and a story in poetic form is even better. What would Christmas be without "A Visit from St. Nicholas"? From "The Three Little Kittens" to Longfellow's "Paul Revere's Ride" and Poe's "Annabel Lee," narrative poetry pleases all ages. "The Owl and the Pussycat" by Edward Lear and Lewis Carroll's "Jabberwocky" are short enough to memorize and say to your class. Carroll's "The Walrus and the Carpenter" is great fun for you to read (use different voices for the two characters) and for the kids to hear. Shel Silverstein has written a great number of hilarious narrative poems.

By contrast, many of the narratives in *The Oxford Book of Story Poems* are about adventures, some of them spooky. Among the dozens of poems in this collection are Tennyson's "The Lady of Shalott," Robert Browning's "The Pied Piper of Hamelin," and "Switch on the Night" by Ray Bradbury. Some of them are perfect for Halloween, notably "The Hairy Toe."

Although making a story into a poem is too difficult to appeal to many kids, you never know when or where inspiration will strike. I wouldn't have expected Eric to write a forty-line narrative poem, but that's how he told his story of a beaver who made friends with a stream, endured adversity, discovered gold, and lived happily ever after. Sometimes children will choose personal rather than fictional narratives to write as poems, capturing in special words events they cherish, as Paolo did.

Horses

Every time I ride a horse I get a little scared
The horse gallops down the road
And its hoof almost smashes a rock.
On the way back
The horse trots on the hard and ugly rocks on the ground
We ride under bridges and over streams
And we never never stop.
When I get off, the horse is tired
And it needs a little rest.
As he kicks his hind legs up in the air
I take a brush
And I comb its soft beautiful fur. ❖

Paolo Mangonès
Grade 4

Michael's imagination produced a brief narrative with a metaphysical slant which is shown in the next poem.

The Special Carrier

Quack, quack!
  As a duck bathes his head in
    the glistening water,
      Suddenly a gun bursts
        the duck is shot it struggles
          like a butterfly trying to
            break out of a cocoon.
              The duck dies as a
                butterfly bursts out of
                  its cocoon and begins
                    to fly up bringing the
                      duck's spirit to heaven. ❖

Michael Hofmann
Grade 4

Forms That Play with Words

Some poetic forms that are used in elementary classrooms result in wordplay rather than poetry because their focus usually is so firmly on structure that poetic language seldom occurs. But there are many who say that poetry *is* wordplay, so decide for yourself whether the following forms can lead to poems in your classroom.

Acrostic poems are made by writing a name or word vertically and beginning each line of the poem with the letter thus provided. If a child's first name is used, it often (but not necessarily) occupies the first line as well:

Bill
Interested in everything
Looks for snakes and turtles
Loves lizards. ❖

The diamante is named for its shape: The first line has one word; the second, two; the third, three; the fourth, four. The fifth line goes back to three words, the sixth has two, and the last line has one word. The lines are spaced to form a diamond shape. Often diamantes are used to emphasize parts of speech. Here's an example of a diamante that uses numbers of words without requiring them to be certain parts of speech:

        Ball
      White sphere
   Flies through space
  Straight for the fence
      I run fast
       But it's
        Gone.
        ❖

The Shape of a Poem

Concrete poems, which are printed on the page in the shape of the thing they're about, are a lot of fun but very hard for children to pull off. The best known example is in *Alice in Wonderland* by Lewis Carroll and recounts a conversation between a cur named Fury and a mouse. It winds and curves down the page—a mouse's tale (in verse) in the shape of a mouse's tail.

A classroom example might look like this:

```
    A
GIRAFFE
   I
   S
     S
     O
       T
       A
       L
       L
         A
         N
         D
  HIS HEAD IS SO
  FAR ABOVE HIS LEGS
    HE PROBABLY CAN'T SEE
           H    T    E    K
           I    O    L    N
           S    E    S    E
                S    E    E
           A              S
           D    O    B
           O    R    E    A
           R         L    N
           A    A    O    D
           B    N    W
           L    Y         E
           E    T    H    L
                H    I    B
                I    S    O
                N         W
                G         S ❖
```

Handle with Care

Poetic forms are tricky in the elementary classroom. If they're too hard for children to use, they inhibit or even paralyze the process of writing. If they provide formulas that are usable but so restrictive that they shut out the child's poetic images, the process is again undermined. Most important, if forms are taught first as the right way to write poems, they will appear to be at the top of the teacher's priority list and may continue to enchain the children's original ideas even after the teacher proclaims that rules of rhyme and line patterns are flexible or even ignorable.

As a teacher (and as a parent, too), my basic impulse was always to make things easy for my children. It was a long time, longer than I care to remember, before I recognized that learning is inherently difficult and trying to pretend it isn't just gets in the way. Remember what it was like when you first began to play the piano or ski or play tennis or golf or do a new dance step? Being a learner means working hard and feeling inadequate. But the old adage "learning is its own reward" can be true for children. They're willing to struggle through a difficult learning task because doing something well and being recognized for it gives them tremendous pleasure.

Clearly, learning to write good poems is hard work. It's our job as teachers to help our children find their paths to learning and to clear away the stumbling blocks they find there so that the difficulty of the learning process seems manageable to them. Poetic forms will help some children along that path but put boulders in the way for others; we need to know our kids and our subject matter well enough to find the right fit. And we need to remember that, without the idea or image of the poem, form is a hollow shell. The poem comes first.

REFERENCES

All unreferenced quotes are from conversations with the author or observations of the author.

Atwood, Ann. *Haiku: The Mood of Earth.* New York: Charles Scribner's Sons, 1971.

Behn, Harry, trans. *Cricket Songs.* New York: Harcourt, Brace & World, 1964.

Carroll, Lewis. *Alice in Wonderland.* Reprint. Cutchogue, NY: Buccaneer Books, 1981.

cummings, e. e. *Hist Whist and Other Poems for Children.* New York: Liveright, 1983.

Frost, Robert. *The Poetry of Robert Frost.* New York: Henry Holt, 1969.

Harrison, M., and C. Stuart-Clark. *The Oxford Book of Story Poems.* Oxford: Oxford University Press, 1990.

Heard, Georgia. *For the Good of the Earth and Sun.* Portsmouth, NH: Heinemann Educational Books, 1989.

Hughes, Langston. *The Dream Keeper and Other Poems.* New York: Alfred A. Knopf, 1932.

———. *Selected Poems of Langston Hughes.* New York: Vintage Books, 1990.

Johnston, Tony. *I'm Gonna Tell Mama I Want an Iguana.* New York: G. P. Putnam's Sons, 1990.

Koch, Kenneth. *Rose, Where Did You Get That Red?* New York: Vintage Books, 1973.

———. *Wishes, Lies and Dreams: Teaching Children to Write Poetry.* New York: HarperCollins, 1980.

Lear, Edward. *How Pleasant to Know Mr. Lear!* New York: Holiday House, 1982.

Lewis, C. S. *The Lion, the Witch and the Wardrobe.* Illus. by Pauline Baynes. New York: Macmillan Child Group, 1986.

Livingston, Myra Cohn. *Sky Songs.* New York: Holiday House, 1984.

Merriam, Eve. *It Doesn't Always Have to Rhyme.* New York: Atheneum, 1964.

———. *Fresh Paint.* New York: Macmillan Child Group, 1986.

Moore, Lilian. *Something New Begins.* New York: Atheneum, 1982.

Nash, Ogden. *Parents Keep Out.* Boston: Little, Brown, 1951.

Prelutsky, Jack, ed. *Read-Aloud Rhymes for the Very Young.* New York: Alfred A. Knopf, 1986.

Rogers, Timothy, ed. *Those First Affections.* London: Routledge & Kegan Paul, 1979.

Sandburg, Carl. *Good Morning, America.* New York: Harcourt Brace & Company, 1928.

———. *Wind Song.* New York: Harcourt Brace & Company, 1960.

———. *The Complete Poems of Carl Sandburg.* New York: Harcourt Brace Jovanovich, 1970.

Sendak, Maurice. *Chicken Soup with Rice: A Book of Months.* New York: Harper & Row, 1962.

Silverstein, Shel. *Where the Sidewalk Ends.* New York: Harper & Row, 1974.

Worth, Valerie. *Small Poems.* New York: Farrar, Straus & Giroux, 1972.

———. *All the Small Poems.* New York: Farrar, Straus & Giroux, 1987.

Chapter 4

ORAL POETRY

SINGING, PERFORMING, AND DISCUSSING POEMS

The ice melts so sweetly off the rooftop,
Looks like a rhinestone dripping to the ground. ❖

When I say those two lines from the beginning of Jaime's poem "Ice," it's as if they insist I say them again, to let the rhythm catch hold: The *ice* melts so *sweet*ly off the *roof*top . . . and if I say them yet again, I could almost dance to them. If I were still a child, perhaps I would.

I can imagine a troubadour singing the first two lines of Danny's "Ocean Nights."

The moonlight shines on the sparkling ocean water.
It is night and the whole world is asleep. ❖

The words seem to ask for a melody, perhaps an old English folk tune. And not until I hear the poem spoken aloud am I aware of the sibilance that suggests the sound of rippling waves.

The images these poems create for the inner eye are vivid, but it is when the words gain voice that we hear the music hiding in them. Like small children of long ago, poems that are seen and not heard are unfulfilled. Yes, there is magic in the way a poem on the page meets our eyes, but poetry's roots are in the sound of the voice. I haven't yet found a poet who doesn't want her or his poems to be said as well as read.

Just as poetry began when language itself was young, so do very young children begin to make poems long before they can write. Of the poems in *Those First Affections*, approximately one-third of the pieces were spoken by children between the ages of two and six and had to be written down by an adult. So poetry still grows from its roots in the human voice.

THE MUSIC OF WORDS

Lee Bennett Hopkins says poetry gives children "quiet music." Melody and harmony are absent, though sometimes suggested, but rhythm is integral. Poems are verbal music, spoken songs. Stephen Spender, the British poet, writes, "The music of the words I am trying to shape takes me far beyond the words, I am aware of a rhythm, a dance, a fury, which is as yet empty of words" (Vernon 1970, 75).

Our concepts of classical poetry come from the ancient Greeks, who saw it as an indivisible combination of music, dance, and words (Murray 1957, 6). While a bard chanted the poem and accompanied himself on a lyre or harp, the chorus stepped and swayed in time to his words, perhaps on a threshing floor to celebrate the harvest or around an altar to worship their gods. The metric foot we use today to note poetic rhythm began as the measured steps of these ancient performers of poetry.

Rhythm appeals to us on a visceral level. Catch the sounds of a marching band in the distance and your step quickens to match the beat, your spirits lift a bit. Perhaps this affinity for rhythm begins in the prebirth infant, comforted by the steady pulse of the mother's nearby heart. The rhythm of a poem reaches our metaphorical hearts before the meaning of the words arrives in our minds.

On the page, white space, line breaks, and the rhythm of the words direct the reader's phrasing and thus help interpret the poem's meaning, just as Sinatra's famous timing interprets the meaning of a song. Some poems ask to be sung, particularly those with strong rhyme, rhythm, and repetition, and find a wider audience when set to music. Many of us think of Shel Silverstein's "The Unicorn" as a popular song of the 1970s and overlook its life as a poem in *Where the Sidewalk Ends*.

In *Near the Window Tree*, Karla Kuskin invites her reader to make up a tune to go with a poem she says is almost like a song, a lullaby. It begins, "Wordless words. / A tuneless tune," and if you repeat those two lines three or four times, then hum them wordlessly, a simple melody will obligingly attach itself to them.

You can help your students discover the music in poetry by singing it to and with them. One of the many acts of courage required of teachers is to stand before a class and sing; this can be particularly painful if one's voice is not notably musical, yet most of us do it. Poetry is a kinder vehicle than song because the amount and nature of the singing is up to us. We can choose to say most of the poem and sing just a few words or we can limit the melody to two or three notes. In a poem with a repeated refrain, we can sing just that part.

Of course, I'm speaking to the teachers whose singing voices are like mine. If you're at all musically talented, adding song to poetry will bring pleasure undiluted by embarrassment to you and your class. After you've read a particularly musical poem a couple of times, a melody might gradually suggest itself to you. Or you and your class might be able to think of a well-known melody that fits a poem's cadence. Making up a tune with your kids is even more fun and, depending on the age and talents of your class, can become an individual or small-group project for a poetry celebration.

Eloise Greenfield's "Way Down in the Music" from *Honey, I Love* doesn't need a melody; it's a rap song kind of poem. Read it aloud and you'll want to go out and find a percussion backup. You can turn songs back into poetry, too. At the Florida Reading Association 1992 Conference, Jacque Wuertenberg showed a book made by a primary class that uses the song "What a Wonderful World." The words are on the left side, just a few on each page, and on the right are photographs and drawings that fit the words. Children can read this simply as a poem, read the words silently while listening to a tape of the song, or sing along with Louis Armstrong's gravelly voice.

ORAL EXPERIENCE PROMOTES LEARNING

Recent classroom-based research shows that language learning is enhanced when oral and written language experiences are interrelated. In whole language primary classrooms, teachers read and reread beloved poems to their classes and the children don't have to be told to join in. They love the predictability of familiar lines and rhymes. The pleasure of saying the words blends with the sweet feeling of accomplishment as they remember more and more of the poem with each repetition.

Using big books and charts furnishes your students with the visual counterparts of the words they are hearing and saying. Repeated letter patterns in rhyming words show them letter-sound correspondences. Add poetry's emotional appeal and the social context in which you present it, and you have a powerful blend, a synergy, to promote the learning of reading and writing.

Discussion Furthers Comprehension

Oral poetry is probably most widely used in classrooms for the purpose of helping children understand and feel at home with the condensed language of poems. Sound is the soul of poetry; let your students hear the words before they see them. Just read the poem you want them to study, without preamble. If you're sure it needs some background to be appreciated, make it very brief. As Donald Graves says, "Poets write with the intention that their poems stand alone, without extensive introductions" (1992, 16).

After you read the poem twice, and assuming it's a good poem that matches the developmental level and interests of your kids (and of course you wouldn't choose it otherwise), a few open-ended questions are all you need for a discussion. Following are some possibilities; I'm sure you'll think of others on your own.

- What words stick in your mind?

  What did you see in your mind's eye?

  What did the poem make you think of?

Did it remind you of anything that's happened to you?

What do you think the poet was thinking?

Which questions you ask, and how many, will depend on the imponderables of the poem, your students, and everyone's frame of mind on that particular day. Most important is the way you listen: with an open mind, nonjudgmentally, ready to pick up on individual insights. Your kids need to know that it's safe to say what they're thinking, that you, but especially their peers, aren't poised to mock or shoot down their words. It's essential that you establish and maintain a classroom community in which everyone's ideas are respected.

Perhaps you'll find, as I did, that most of the responses come from two or three of your most verbal students. Try as I might to avoid it, I sometimes got caught in a waiting game: I waited for less-verbal students to volunteer while they waited for me to give up and nod in the direction of a frantically waving hand.

An effective way to overcome this is a strategy I first experienced in a workshop run by Lucy Calkins. After showing a piece of writing by a child, she said, "Now turn to your neighbor and share your ideas." She only allowed a minute or two and we still had plenty to say when she called our attention back; instead of passive listeners, we had become active participants.

When we do this with children, the ones who are dying to say something get to say it, and the ones who think they never have anything to say find themselves talking to a receptive partner. This makes it easier for them to respond in an ensuing whole-class discussion. Ask the class what they heard that was interesting (as well as what they said), and the comments of those who are still too shy to speak up can be repeated by their partners. Or you can repeat to the class what you heard as you circulated for the few minutes of "talk to your neighbor."

Middle-Grade Poetry Discussions

Talking about poems can develop understandings that go beyond the verses themselves. Pat Thomas-MacKinnon writes of an interesting use of nursery rhymes and conversation to develop social concepts in her fifth-grade classroom. The discussion began when Pat told her class she had attended an in-service session on multiculturalism. After establishing the meaning of the term and other applicable ones such as *bias* and *stereotype*, she and the children considered the images of women and men that are communicated by rhymes such as "Little Miss Muffet" and "Peter, Peter, Pumpkin Eater."

In the writing time that followed the conversation, some children wrote revised versions of the old rhymes. The King of Hearts became the baker and the queen, the thief; the old woman in the shoe turned into an old couple who kissed their children before they sent them to bed; and Little Miss Muffet fearlessly stepped on the spider.

Edie Ziegler isn't put off by responses of "I don't get it" when she reads a new poem to her class. She explains that sometimes poems have deeper meanings, messages that you have to dig under the top layers to find. After one or two guided journeys through poems to discover hidden meanings, her kids tackle works by cummings or Whitman, exploring like excavators to find what's buried there.

Edie encourages a free exchange of interpretations, emphasizing that there is no one "right answer." In a discussion of a line in which the poet wrote of being above the world, one student said, "I think she means she's up in heaven."

That was met with, "No, I think it means she wants people to look up to her."

A third member of the group said, "I don't know *what* it means!"

"She's really written a *deep* poem!" Edie said, allowing her students the freedom to express confusion as well as opinions and enabling them to progress along the bumpy path of understanding poetry.

Joanne Hammond believes that "poems have to be heard and tasted" and uses discussion to extend her children's understanding of particular poems and the nature of poetry as well. Poetry workshop begins with everyone seated on the floor in a circle. Continuing an earlier discussion, Joanne asks, "Why do you think poetry is harder to read and write than stories?"

"It has different kinds of words."

"It does weird things like, you know, personification and figurative language and stuff."

Joanne smiles and says, "A poem has to paint a picture in words."

"Like 'Annabel Lee!'" a girl exclaims and many others murmur agreement.

Joanne continues, "In a story, the writer can tell you all about the characters and setting, but in a poem the writer has to create the background with just a few words. That means you have to bring something to the poem yourself." After a little more discussion she tells the class she has chosen one of her favorite poems to read to them; it's "All But Blind" by Walter de la Mare. She asks the children to listen for what they think the poet's message is and then reads:

All but blind	All but blind
In his chambered hole	In the burning day
Gropes for worms	The Barn-Owl blunders
The four-clawed Mole.	On her way.
All but blind	And blind as are
In the evening sky,	These three to me,
The hooded Bat	So, blind to Some-one
Twirls softly by.	I must be. ❖

After a silent moment, Joanne reads the poem again, stopping after each stanza to clarify word meanings. At the end, several children begin to sort out their concepts of the poem's message.

From *Peacock Pie* by Walter de la Mare. Copyright © 1969 by The Literary Trustees of Walter de la Mare. Reprinted by permission of Henry Holt and Company, Inc.

"Ohh! He might not understand someone's feelings... or ignore someone."

"You can't see what they're thinking, someone you've never met before... someone different from you, a person from another country."

Joanne said, "Like countries where people are being killed by the thousands, but we're blind to them. How might *I* be blind to *you*?"

A boy hesitantly offered, "What we think... when we're outside."

"Sometimes our parents don't understand because they don't have the same problems," another student said.

"Think of other words for understanding," Joanne said. "Sometimes we say, 'They don't *see* it.'"

Several "Ooh"s were breathed out. "Blindness isn't only sight, it's also for feelings!"

A girl who had been quiet for most of the discussion said, "Telling what a poem says is like asking your parents what something tastes like and they can't explain it."

But Be Careful Not to Overdo It

Notice that Joanne's class worked out their own interpretations of the poem through open discussion. It's important that we as teachers don't get carried away with our erudition and take over this process. Jean Little's poem tells what happens then.

After English Class

I used to like "Stopping by Woods on a Snowy Evening."
I liked the coming darkness,
The jingle of harness bells, breaking—and adding to—the stillness,
The gentle drift of snow....

But today, the teacher told us what everything stood for.
The woods, the horse, the miles to go, the sleep—
They all have "hidden meanings."

It's grown so complicated now that,
Next time I drive by,
I don't think I'll bother to stop. ❖

Maybe you remember feeling the same way as a student; I know I do. We need to keep firmly in mind that there are no answer keys to poems: There is no single, set-in-concrete explanation of what a poem means. The condensed, evocative language of poetry is fertile ground for readers to discover their own meanings, led by their own experiences, mind-sets, and imaginations.

"After English Class" from *Hey World, Here I Am!* by Jean Little. Text copyright © 1986 by Jean Little. Reprinted by permission of HarperCollins Publishers.

Discussing a poem can be scary for kids; most school experience teaches them that there is a right answer out there and if they don't hit it or at least come close, they're going to look dumb. This is not to say that all ideas are correct and deserve approval. It does mean that you need to establish a classroom climate in which everyone's ideas are seen as evolutionary, as stepping stones on their individual learning paths, rather than as products to be judged.

In this climate, "correctness" is not a useful concept; children's responses and perceptions that show effort of thought and the spark of originality are valued instead because these are indicators of real learning. Poets themselves are often surprised by the meanings readers find in their poems. Their writing springs from intensely personal experiences, ideas, and emotions; it's not possible for the reader to know exactly what the poet was thinking and feeling.

Add Interest with Poets' Lives

Poets become real people when we tell children a little about their lives. You could tell your class, for example, that Dr. Seuss grew up in Springfield, Massachusetts, where his father's job included supervising the zoo. They'll be interested to know that young Theodor liked to go in the cages with small lions and tigers even though, as he said, he "got chewed up every once in a while." Finding out that Seuss was actually Dr. Seuss's middle name and that he was not a doctor could lead to a discussion of pen names.

Older kids will appreciate Langston Hughes's poems more deeply if they know that his parents were divorced when he was small, leaving him to be brought up by his grandmother. They were so poor that Hughes was ashamed to bring friends home from school. Unhappy and lonesome, he found comfort in books, where life was better. He was fourteen and graduating from grammar school in Lincoln, Illinois, when he was elected class poet—in spite of the fact that he had never written a poem (Berry 1983). Your kids could have a lively discussion about whether he might have become a poet if this hadn't happened.

Poets Reading Poems

Langston Hughes's poems were among the works Agnes Homan read as a visiting poet to classes in Highlands County, Florida, in the 1980s. She and her partner, Donna Thomas, found that kids from grade 1 through high school responded to the work of poets whose work is considered to belong in the adult domain.

Whether you're just beginning to introduce poetry in your classroom and feel a bit unsure or have been working with it for years, you and your kids will benefit from having real live poets come to read and talk about their own writing or that of others. An obvious benefit is the interest generated by a new face; another, less obvious, is the new perspective a practicing poet's voice can bring to the reading and writing of poetry.

Homan and Thomas began by talking with the students about what a poem is and what it consists of: imagery, form, and sound. Then they read one or two poems and discussed them with the kids. "Actually, *they* discussed them with *us*," Agnes Homan says. "We just asked pertinent questions and they took it from there." The questions, rather than being academic, had to do with how the children felt about the poems they heard.

William Carlos Williams's "The Red Wheelbarrow" was the major focus of each session. They pointed out the shape of the poem on the page, which slightly resembles a series of wheelbarrows, and went on to explore its meaning through the give-and-take of discussion. Sometimes Homan was startled by children's insights, particularly that of a fifth-grade boy who was enthralled by the idea that everything depended on the single wheel. "Yes, it does!" he said excitedly. "God's the big wheel that everything depends on!"

Audiocassettes can bring poets into your classroom anytime you want them, of course. They also can bring the voices of poets no longer alive, such as that of Carl Sandburg. His voice is a perfect match for his conversational yet evocative style of writing. If you like the late John Ciardi's poems for children, you'll welcome his recording.

Jack Prelutsky sing-speaks his poems, accompanied by guitar and the occasional kazoo. "Louder Than a Clap of Thunder" is enhanced by sound effects that add much to its humor. Even without music or special sounds, the poet delivers the poems with a dramatic gusto and a variety of voices that are irresistible.

"My Mother Says I'm Sickening," a hilarious protest by a kid overburdened by rules, will have your class laughing too loud to hear it all the first time. "When Dracula Went to the Blood Bank," spoken in a chilling Transylvanian accent, is perfect for Halloween, as is "Ah! A Monster's Life Is Merry." Prelutsky's recorded poems will add immeasurably to a poetry class, but also be ready to play one at any time of the classroom day for a breath of fresh air. It's a perfect way to break the doldrums or ease the tensions that sometimes accumulate like ants at a picnic.

Lively Parts of Speech

I haven't yet seen a curriculum guide that doesn't call for teaching parts of speech. Most worksheets and tests don't go beyond the simple identification of nouns, verbs, and so on, but the major purpose of children's being able to identify them is so that they can use them effectively in writing. "Use strong verbs!" we writing teachers cry.

Oral poetry provides excellent opportunities for "strong verb" minilessons. Imagine reading this poem (anonymous, from Hopkins's *Side by Side: Poems to Read Together*) to, say, second-graders:

Leap and Dance

> The lion walks on padded paws,
> The squirrel leaps from limb to limb,
> While flies can crawl straight up a wall,
> And seals can dive and swim.
> The worm, it wiggles all around,
> The monkey swings by its tail,
> And birds may hop upon the ground,
> Or spread their wings and sail.
> But boys and girls have much more fun;
> They leap and dance
> And walk
> And *run*. ❖

Ask them, "What does the lion do? The squirrel?" and write on the board the verbs they supply. If the poem is on a chart, ask them to say the verb or verbs in each line and try to perform the action. Then (carefully!) invite them to act out what boys and girls do. This will do more than any worksheet to impress on your kids what verbs are. Better than that, it will focus their attention on the power of verbs in their writing.

Those of us who teach older kids look constantly for ways to develop their vocabularies. "The Turkey Shot Out of the Oven" (Prelutsky 1990) is a treasure chestful of strong verbs like *ricocheted*, *splattered,* and *blanketed*. When you read it to your class, you'll find that giving vocal emphasis to the verbs not only focuses on that part of speech but fits perfectly with the content of the poem. The ending caps all those marvelous verbs with the kind of humor that endears a poem to all of us, but especially kids, when the narrator vows that he'd "never again stuff a turkey / with popcorn that hadn't been popped."

You can point out all parts of speech to your children by reading aloud poems that lend themselves to this. Be careful, though, to begin with the poem for its own sake, enjoying its music and images with your class before searching for its nouns or verbs. For example, William Carlos Williams's "The Red Wheelbarrow," ubiquitous in anthologies and famous for its ambiguity and sharp images, can illustrate nouns and adjectives more clearly than any textbook.

> so much depends
> upon
>
> a red wheel
> barrow
>
> glazed with rain
> water
>
> beside the white
> chickens ❖

When you read it aloud to your class, someone will probably say, "That's not a poem!" and this will give you an opportunity to discuss briefly just what a poem is. You might want to ask them to close their eyes for the second reading, which will help them identify the vivid image that is an element of poetry. Showing them the poem on a chart or the board and reading it a third time leads to the discovery of rhythm in the words.

Ask your kids to close their eyes again, imagine the poem, and tell what they see. Write their responses, which will surely include wheelbarrow and chickens, on the board and point out the strength and solidity of nouns: words that make us think of things we can easily visualize (intangible nouns can come later). Perhaps one of your intuitive students will state that this poem *depends* on nouns.

Ask them to imagine the wheelbarrow without the word *red* and the chickens without *white*; then put back those words to point out the importance of adjectives to make nouns clear and specific in our minds. You might take a minute or two for the familiar activity of adjective building: Begin with a noun (*tree, elephant, cookie*) and have a round-robin of adding adjectives to make the image of the noun very specific and, usually, very funny as well.

Notice that the focus is very clearly on the poem and not on a parts-of-speech exercise. Using poetry as the basis of a skill and drill activity is a perversion of this magic language and, unfortunately, still happens in too many classrooms. We must never commit the kind of vivisection that kills the poem in the name of skill instruction. But when we put such instruction where it belongs, which is subordinate to the understanding and appreciation of the poem itself, our children will learn, as readers and writers, the nature and function of nouns, verbs, and other parts of speech; and this is the kind of learning that stays with them because it continues to be useful to them.

From *William Carlos Williams: Collected Poems. 1909-1939.* Vol. I. Copyright © 1938 by New Directions Pub. Corp. Reprinted by permission of New Directions.

MEMORIZING POEMS

Another kind of magic happens when children hear poems straight from you without a book or chart in sight. If you're just beginning poetry with your class, reciting a poem from memory is a good way to start. It isn't as daunting as it sounds; all you need is one short poem that you can say to your kids while looking right at them. They will be enchanted by the sight and sound of their teacher saying a wonderful poem to them without looking at a book.

I'm sure your first response is, "Where am I going to find time to memorize a poem?" As members of a profession that requires us to be everywhere at once and have eyes in the backs of our heads, we're used to doing more than one thing at a time. Think of things you do every day that only require part of your mind: kitchen chores, driving to school and back, waiting in line, exercising. Copy a poem on an index card and keep it readily available so you can use those moments to memorize a line at a time. You'll be surprised how quickly you'll have made the poem your own.

When you're memorizing a poem, it's important to choose one you truly enjoy. For that matter, every poem you share with children should be one you enjoy, but the first one you memorize for your class needs to be special for you, one you like so much that you wish you'd written it. Ideally it should feel so right to your mouth and ears that you can almost hear your own voice as you read the poem silently. It should, of course, also be appealing to your kids. In addition to rhyme and rhythm, humor is a never-fail ingredient for success. When you find your poem and make a copy of it, carry it around with you until it's safe in your memory.

Reciting poetry, like much of teaching itself, is a performance art. If you're used to performing from memory, whether you're acting or storytelling or reciting poetry, rehearsing is second nature to you. But if you're a neophyte, it's important to practice at home the day before you perform your poem for your class. Use a mirror and a tape recorder to make sure you're using drama but not too much. Try it out on friends or family members. As chief role model, you want to provide the best possible example for your kids.

Poems Just for You

It's easy for us as teachers to focus so much of our attention on our classrooms that our out-of-school lives suffer from neglect during the school year. When you're out poetry hunting, don't limit yourself only to material you can use in school. Look for poems that speak to your heart and mind and save them for yourself. I know people for whom poetry is such an integral part of their lives that they can quote a line or two to fit almost every situation or event. One, a teacher who has read E. B. White's poems for adults as well as *Charlotte's Web*, can be counted on to greet a new parent with "Hold a baby to your ear / As you would a shell; / Sounds of centuries you hear / New centuries foretell" (1983, 100).

I envy that ability and hope to gradually expand my repertoire beyond Robert Frost's "Something there is that doesn't love a wall," which has been a perfect match for several situations. As you become a collector of poems, you might find yourself ready with "But children, remember Sarah Stout / And always take the garbage out!" (Silverstein 1974) the next time you want that job done at home, or, as summer vacation nears, "I must go down to the seas again, for the call of the running tide / Is a wild call and a clear call that may not be denied."

There are some small, unexpected benefits to memorizing poems. Reciting them in your mind when caught in traffic or doing hall duty can help to pass time pleasantly and reinforce them in your memory as well. If a difficult parent conference or learning-resistant student refuses to leave your mind at bedtime in spite of your need for a good night's sleep, repeat your favorite poems over and over; slumber will come.

Making Memorization Student-Friendly

The power of your position as role model in your classroom will motivate your kids to want to memorize poems themselves; capitalize on it. Tell them you wanted to do it because it was fun to learn a poem you loved and to share it with them. Explain how you went about it and be specific about what worked for you. Invite them to memorize poems and let you know when they're ready to say them to the class. Chances are very good that after a few days of encouraging reminders, someone will volunteer and become your class's first peer role model. This will stimulate those who might have been intimidated by the prospect of trying to do something you, the teacher (read "expert"), did well.

Because your children will learn this process mostly by imitating you, your responsibility looms large. Gregory Denman tells of a child who spent the days with her grandparents while her mother worked. The little girl's mother was midwestern; her paternal grandparents had migrated from the Deep South. The accent of her everyday speech echoed her mother's, but when she repeated the nursery rhymes taught to her by her grandmother, her "voice came straight from Dixie!" (1988, 46). You may be startled to hear echoes of your own voice as you listen to your students say poems they've memorized.

So your motivation to rehearse thoroughly before you recite a poem to your class goes beyond just wanting to put on a good performance. Your poetry accent includes phrasing with pauses and silences; inflection as pitch and tone change; emphasis that comes from variations in volume and speed; body language, including facial expression; and that singular quality that emanates from the feeling and understanding you as a person have for the poem. When you see bits of your performance mirrored by your kids, the time and care you took to prepare it will be more than worth the effort.

If you're a beginner at performing poetry, you'll have immediate empathy for the child who has chosen, learned, and volunteered to recite a poem in front of everyone. It is not an easy task and will seldom be performed with great success the first time. It's important to fend off discouragement and recognize that practice will produce, if not perfection, certainly improvement. Barbara Cullere's class has a poetry party every Friday. Children volunteer to perform poems that they found and loved during the week. "The first time we do it, it's always a bomb," Barbara says. "But I make a big fuss over the one or two who get it, and every week we're a little better."

The benefits of this process go far beyond the enjoyment of a performance. Repeated reading and saying of a poem is analogous to the progression of taking a piece of writing from first draft through to publication (Graves 1992, 9-15). Children as well as adults move through deeper levels of understanding as they grow increasingly familiar with a poem. The poetic language they internalize emerges later in the poems they write. Sometimes actual words or phrases from poems they've learned turn up in their poems, or you may note a developing awareness of rhythm and sound or an increased use of poetic conventions.

Some of us might shy away from engaging our classes in memorizing poems because of unpleasant recollections of forced recitations when we were in school. Let's turn those negative experiences around by examining them to discover what we want to avoid now that we're the teachers. Perhaps you had to learn a poem written a couple of centuries ago that was supposed to be in English but sounded like another language to you. Chances are you knew next to nothing about the poet and therefore cared even less. Maybe the poem's topic was so far outside your range of experience and interest that its meaning escaped you completely.

What does this tell us about helping our kids learn to memorize poems with enthusiasm instead of dread and loathing? To begin at the beginning, we have to collect a quantity of wonderful poems that we know will appeal to them. Most but not necessarily all will have been written in this century, many in the past couple of decades. Keep in mind, though, that Kenneth Koch's inner-city children in third through sixth grade related to poems by William Blake, Shakespeare, and John Donne; don't limit yourself to this century.

We need to bring these poems to our classes in a way that shows they are special; this is where careful rehearsal comes in, whether we plan to read or say the poems. Above all, we'll instruct our kids to choose among these poems for their own reasons by helping them to recognize images and ideas that speak to their own experiences. Memorizing poems like these, far from a boring chore, is a way to possess a treasure. Eloise Greenfield's poem "Things" touches on this and is one of my favorites for oral reading or memorizing:

Things

Went to the corner
Walked in the store
Bought me some candy
Ain't got it no more
Ain't got it no more

Went to the beach
Played on the shore
Built me a sandhouse
Ain't got it no more
Ain't got it no more

Went to the kitchen
Lay down on the floor
Made me a poem
Still got it
Still got it ❖

Fitting Poems In

Perhaps your children will build small repertoires of poems they can say by heart. Keep these collections alive by finding places in the day where a child can say a poem; it only takes a minute or two. You might start the day by asking, "Who can say a poem for us this morning?" Your enthusiastic appreciation will support the performer and encourage everyone else.

Gregory Denman's students enjoyed playing "poetry tag" (1988, 81) while their teacher dealt with the intricacies of the morning lunch count. One person stood and said a poem, then tagged the next one to recite, and so on, until Denman finished identifying the brown baggers, hot lunchers, and cold lunchers and tallied the payment column.

Sometimes the content of the poem will fit beautifully as an introduction to a theme or subject. If, for example, one of your kids or perhaps you have memorized Tony Johnston's "A Little Seed" (only five lines), you couldn't ask for a better lead-in to a seed-planting project. Ogden Nash wrote several poems about food with even fewer lines ("Celery," "The Parsnip," and "The Pig," for example) that will add welcome humor to a nutrition unit.

"Things" from *Honey, I Love* by Eloise Greenfield. Text copyright © 1978 by Eloise Greenfield. Selection reprinted by permission of HarperCollins Publishers.

CHORAL SPEAKING

For a long time, choral speaking has been out of favor in many classrooms, maybe because, as with memorization, its practice was artificial and uncomfortable for children. I suspect that teachers who love poetry have continued choral speaking with their kids because they know how much fun it can be. More and more teachers are discovering this; if you haven't already, consider giving it a try. It brings poetry and children together within a social context that fosters learning.

The crucial element in successful choral speaking is the poem itself. Just as with memorization, it must touch children's minds and experiences and, above all, it must be a good poem. So first of all, review your collection of favorites to find the one you think will sound best in your students' unison voices. The criteria for choosing a poem to memorize apply here as well, with the added one of avoiding polysyllabic challenges.

You, the Conductor

Saying a poem in a group offers children comforting insurance against the potential embarrassment of standing alone and speaking, yet there's enough tension left to sharpen their desire to do well. You, however, have to stand alone as the conductor, without a sheltering group of peers clustered around you. Conducting choral speaking is a little like conducting a piece of music: You ensure that everyone starts together and stays together.

Just as the conductor of an orchestra masters the score before approaching the musicians with baton in hand, you need to begin by becoming thoroughly familiar with the poem your class will learn. Read it several times until the sense of the poem is fully clear and real to you. Then go on reading it aloud until the sense merges with the sound and the poem is a spoken whole.

James Britton states that "poetry is not drama" in that "it never ceases to be essentially the voice of one man speaking his mind" (1982, 11), and therefore it requires a delivery that is more conversational than declamatory. At the same time, the music inherent in the words needs to be heard in the voices. Because your class will be learning how to speak poetry by listening to the way you do it and imitating you, it's important that your delivery be evocative but not hammy, natural but not humdrum.

By this time you will have become so familiar with the poem that it won't take you long to decide on the best phrasing and inflection. Gregory Denman (1988, 44-45) suggests that the reader of poetry choreograph the words by finding the correct poetic breaths, or natural groupings of words, that belong together.

When you've settled on your oral interpretation, it's time for you to stand in front of a mirror in the privacy of your own home and practice conducting your imagined class. Use whatever hand, arm, and body movements seem right to you, whether they suggest Leonard Bernstein on the podium or only involve your fingers. Most of us feel a little foolish or at least uncomfortable doing this at first.

But your only audience will be your class, and they'll be concentrating on their own performances; your self-consciousness will soon wear off.

Beginning Choral Speaking with Your Class

Before you engage your class in actual choral speaking, read the poem to them and help them get to know it well. Let's imagine a classroom scenario using the poem "Things." Go back to page 100 now and read it aloud a couple of times.

The message is simple but strong: Among life's ephemera, poems last and are worth keeping. Did you fit your voice to the rhythm of the words? Probably you noticed that the singsongy swing of the first three lines in each stanza breaks and forces a slight pause before the last two lines. This rhythm fits the sense: After the happy memory comes a shift with the recognition that the source of happiness didn't last. Then, in the third stanza, the mood changes to quiet triumph with the three firm beats of "Still got it."

You can't help but know the poem you've chosen by heart after so many repetitions, so introduce it to your class by saying it to them once or twice. Let the sound of the poem sink in before you present it to their eyes. Then you'll want to have the poem written large on chart paper so everyone can read it at once, or perhaps, depending on your kids' ages, you'll provide individual copies.

Next, with the words visible, talk about the poem for a few minutes. Some questions you could start with are

What did you think of when you were listening to the poem?

Did you ever do (or think) the same kinds of things as the poet?

Why do you think the poet said what she/he did?

Keep this part brief, just enough to establish for everyone the sense of the poem. Be careful, though, to focus on the children's interpretation and avoid the didactic urge to point out the message to them. If kids know they can count on you to tell them what to think, they'll wait for you to do it or perhaps resent you for kidnapping their autonomy and turn you off. Because learning takes place through the process of thinking, we need to give our students every possible chance to do that.

If your class hasn't yet experienced choral speaking, you'll want to tell them that it's like singing a song in a group but without music, and that you're going to help them stay together. Then say it to them again so that the rhythm and inflections of your voice are clearly in their minds before you ask them to speak it chorally. Notice that you don't have to tell them what to do with their voices or how to do it; showing them is enough. Have them speak it twice, tell them enthusiastically what was good, invite a few of their reactions to the experience, and go on to the next part of the day. It should only take half an hour to get from start to finish.

The next day, begin by recalling their successes, say the poem again to them, and perhaps point out an aspect of their delivery that needs attention. By the time they say the poem twice, you'll probably notice that several aren't looking at the words. Depending on your class's attention span and other exigencies of the day, this might be a good time to challenge them to put away their copies of the poem or the chart and say the poem from memory. This session will probably take about fifteen minutes.

If you don't get to saying the poem without looking at the words on the second day, you can start day three that way. The third session doesn't need to last longer than five minutes. From here on, you can enliven those minutes spent waiting in line or for a special visitor or teacher to arrive with a choral rendition of the poem. You might want to schedule a weekly choral-speaking time to refresh everyone's memories in case you're fortunate enough not to have those moments of downtime.

More Possibilities

If all has gone reasonably well, your class is now looking forward to learning another poem together, and some of them may have nominated their favorites for this honor. Fight the urge to shorten the first session when the next poem is introduced. Without your careful preparation and modeling and the discussion necessary to arrive at the sense of the poem, the level of performance might drop and cause disappointment instead of delight.

This is, of course, only one model for introducing choral speaking to your class and is intended mostly for the teacher who is new to the process. In *Writing: Teachers and Children at Work*, Graves describes the way a teacher of thirty seven-year-olds goes about it. She says a poem twice, then invites the children to join in, saying whatever words they remember. She doesn't show the poem on paper and waits until later to discuss it, letting the children begin by enjoying "the taste and beat of the words" (1992, 71). How you proceed in your class depends on the ages and characteristics of your kids, your own preferences and style, and the large collection of variables that exists in every school.

After their whole-class experience, perhaps your students will want to work up some choral speaking or reading of poems in small groups. By then, they will have internalized the necessary strategies and will be able to work on their own. Encourage them to discover for themselves the music in a poem by trying out various oral versions until they find one that best fits the poem they've chosen.

Beginning the Year with Chants

Marilyn London begins the school year by leading her fifth-graders in a chant, easing the first-day-of-school tension. She doesn't label it poetry at that point. "Poetry's a heavy word," she says. "Me" by Karla Kuskin (1980) is a wonderfully hilarious poem to use in this way. It begins "My nose is blue, / My teeth are green."

Marilyn repeats the poem, taking on the role of cheerleader. "Come on, say it with me," she says, and by the third time, the children are chiming in with whatever words they can recall. By the third day of school, just about everyone knows the whole poem. "This helps to set the tone for the year," Marilyn says. "It makes us a family."

On the second or third day, she divides her class into small groups and hands them packets of poems. Their authors range from Carl Sandburg to contemporary poets to schoolchildren; some are anonymous Navajo poems. Marilyn reads the poems aloud, then tells her kids they can decide, in groups, to chant one any way they like. They could say the poem backward or forward or start with the last line and go up while half the group starts at the top and reads down. She wants them to play with the way poems can sound so that any negative preconceptions of poetry and the resultant barriers are broken down.

Each group chooses one poem from the packet to perform and spends about fifteen minutes in rehearsal. When it's time to say their chants, Marilyn tells them, "If you give us 100 percent of your effort, we'll give 150 percent of our attention," encouraging groups to shift roles from performers to attentive listeners. Throughout the year, poetry is an integral part of these children's school day. Marilyn knows that, for some of them, it will remain an integral and well-loved part of their lives.

Chants in a Child's World

Chanting is just a way of saying poems with a rhythmic swing. Poems that make good chants have a strong rhythm and often repetition and rhyme, making them easy to remember. They're ubiquitous in popular culture, from jump-rope rhymes to rap songs, and hold special appeal for young children. You'll probably remember the rest of at least one of these childhood chants:

Engine, engine, number nine,
Runs on the Chicago line. . . . ❖

Sam, Sam, dirty old man,
Washed his face in a frying pan. . . . ❖

Teddy bear, teddy bear, turn around
Teddy bear, teddy bear, touch the ground. . . . ❖

When you're on the playground, keep your ears open for new variations of the old rhymes. You might want to have your class make a collection of their favorites; this could become a book to share with the rest of your school or an all-school program, or both. You won't need special costumes or a complicated script to put on a show of rope-jumping and hand-clapping games accompanied by chants, and it's sure to delight your audience.

Recess is a good time to listen also for scraps of children's rhythmic speech that you can catch and turn into a chant on the spot, or you could scribble it down and save it for a later class. This could become a living collection of original chants that is added to throughout the year. Anything you do to increase your kids' awareness of words and their sounds will add to their pleasure and skill in reading and writing poetry.

In *Living Between the Lines*, Lucy Calkins tells how chanting brought a child's poems acceptance where they were once looked down on by classmates. When Shelley Harwayne listened to Samantha read her simple, repetitive poem in a circle of unappreciative peers, she said, "It sounds like a jazz chant, doesn't it?" (1991, 289). As Shelley repeated the lines with a swinging beat, the once-bored children joined in; soon they were turning Samantha's other poems into jazz chants, too.

Benefits of Choral Speaking

Done well, choral speaking brings long-lasting benefits to children. In *Explore Poetry*, Graves tells of a teacher who starts her sixth-grade class on choral speaking the very first day of school (1992, 99). She finds that the experience of choral speaking quickly builds a sense of community and pride in achievement and at the same time enables her students to memorize two or three poems rapidly and enjoyably through the use of sound and rhythm.

Kids recognize the need for practice to make choral speaking sound good; repetition is a given part of the process and results in an increase in comprehension of language, accuracy of oral representation, and enjoyment of literature. Every member of the class, not just the ones with talent, has the chance to participate in successful performances; this builds a wonderful self-confidence.

You may discover also that your children's writing is strengthened and energized by experience with choral speaking in the same way that memorization enhances writing. Graves finds that increased attention to oral poetry encourages kids to "experiment with sound and sense" (1992, 58) when writing poems. Frequent repetition necessarily plants poetic language and rhythms in the mind; when the child's activity switches to writing, those structures are waiting to be built upon as the child creates new poetic expression.

With all the attention to vocal production in unison, you can expect to observe improved diction in your students' speech. Harder to verify is the fascinating possibility that by integrating the mental processes involving sight, sound, and concepts, we help to build neuronal networks in the brain that enhance the learning process.

Taking Choral Speaking to Larger Audiences

You'll find over time, of course, that some of your classes develop a talent and love for choral speaking and that others never seem to quite get it. Let's look at some ways to expand and extend the experiences of those who have a natural affinity for this method of exploring oral poetry.

Chances are that as your kids get better and better, they'll want to go public with their entertaining performances; or perhaps you'll suggest sharing a poem with the class next door, or the principal, or whatever audience presents itself. Choral speaking is perfect for all-school programs: It will be a refreshing novelty in most schools, and the massed voices produce enough volume to be heard in a large room.

"I Woke Up This Morning" by Karla Kuskin (1980) suggests an interesting treatment through choral speaking. The lines of the poem are printed in increasingly larger type, until the last line, "I'm Staying in Bed," seems to shout at the reader. The topic, rebellion at all the demands made by adults, is a sure winner with your kids. Have one child read the first two lines, add one or two voices for the next two, and so on until the entire group very loudly proclaims the last line.

Humor is a great encourager to kids when they're trying to learn a poem. "Laughing Time" by William Jay Smith consists of a series of couplets, each one followed by a line of laughter sounds: "Ha! Ha! Ha! Ha!" or "Hee! Hee! Hee! Hee!" If you like this poem, you can orchestrate it by having a different child or small group of children say each couplet and the whole class chant the laughing lines. This minimizes the amount of memorizing each child has to do and still adds up to a complete poem.

You can greatly widen your class's audience by videotaping them saying a poem; you'll find many highly effective uses of these audiovisual records. They're a welcome leavening at meetings of small groups of teachers and/or parents where kids can't be present, and ideal for back-to-school nights or open houses, giving you a chance to show instead of only tell about your program. Does your class have a pen pal arrangement with another school? Videocassettes of choral poetry are excellent for pen pal exchanges with classrooms in other parts of the country or world.

When you're videotaping, experiment with the camcorder: Imagine yourself taping a chorus for television, zooming in on individuals and zooming out to include the whole group; try taping from different angles. When you play the video for an audience, you might even want to tape their response to show your kids the next day, further encouraging their efforts.

POETRY READINGS

Have you ever had the experience of seeing on paper a wonderful poem written by one of your kids and then listening in dismay as the writer committed poetricide by reading it aloud at high speed and low volume? In a poetry workshop format, most children will have an opportunity to read their poems in a group sharing session. Even if they have had experience reading narratives in a similar setting, reading poems will seem different and possibly more difficult. Partly this is the result of the nature of poetry: It *is* different. A written narrative is much closer to everyday speech, making it a more familiar, less risky form.

This highlights the indispensability of immersing your children in oral poetry the very first chance you get. The more they hear poetry, the more familiar its forms become and the more comfortable they are with it. As you read with skill and enthusiasm poems you've chosen carefully, they learn to find pleasure in poetry.

Children Read the Poems They Write

As with everything, showing children how to read poems works better than just telling them. Children who have heard dozens of poems and memorized one or two or have spoken them with a group are well prepared to read their own effectively. A minilesson reviewing the components of effective reading followed by time for them to choose and rehearse a poem will give them what they need to read their poems well from that time on.

Students who haven't had those experiences but have heard much poetry will need a little more help in learning to read their own poems well. In your first minilesson, you might use a short poem you've read more than once to your class. Repeat it, using the phrasing and inflection you practiced. Then read it flatly, with none of the skill you've developed, and discuss the differences with the children. Tell them how you went about deciding how to read the poem so that it would sound good. Have them read it with you the wrong way—kids love it when the teacher tells them to do something the wrong way!—and then with the timing and expression that makes it come alive.

The next time, present a short poem that they haven't heard before and lead them through the decision-making process of preparing to read it aloud, inviting them to try out possibilities until you've cooperatively settled on an effective presentation. Read it chorally so that everyone has the experience of saying the words within the protection of group membership. They might demand to read it the wrong way, too, which will be fun. Encourage individuals to try it solo. It should be clear to everyone that there is no one right way to read a poem, but there are definitely good and bad ways.

Lisa Lenz writes of her first- and second-graders learning to be coaches so they could help each other improve their reading of poems. As active listeners, peer coaches celebrated successful readings and asked to hear them again. Think how effective that request for a repeat performance is. Every actor loves to hear cries of "Encore!"—the praise that goes beyond applause. For young children, the accolade also propels them into immediate, added practice.

Next, coach and reader identified parts that needed more practice and worked on them. When readers were ready to rehearse on their own, they found the privacy they needed by reading "to the wall." Lisa writes that a casual passerby might have thought it bizarre to see several children speaking earnestly to the wall just inches away from their faces, but it was a practice the children loved and used well.

These students also used audiotape recorders, which are invaluable tools to help children learn to read their poems effectively. Model the process for them so as to maximize its usefulness when they do it on their own. Choose a short poem that you haven't read aloud before and explain that it's hard to know how we sound to an audience, so you're going to record your practice reading.

When you play back the tape, pause at points where your reading could be improved and discuss them with your class. Tell them that they can use the tape recorder to hear how they sound when they read their poems so they can make them sound even better. Children can tuck themselves away in a quiet, private spot to record and listen to their first efforts or work in small groups if they prefer. With this experience, preparing for a full-scale poetry reading will go quickly and smoothly.

If you have access to a camcorder, use it as a rehearsal tool. The first viewing of the videotape you make will be a time for groans, laughter, and embarrassed excitement, so don't expect much productive evaluation until you play it again. Use it in the same way you would an audiotape, encouraging the readers to notice what's effective about their performances and what needs improvement. Of course, you'll want to tape the actual event, too.

Going Public with Poetry Readings

A public poetry reading, whether for adults or other children, can be an exciting occasion. It certainly was that for my class, as you read in chapter 1, and for the audience as well. It's also a wonderful way to motivate parents to come to evening meetings. Few mothers or fathers can resist the opportunity to see their children reading their own poems in public, even if it means giving up a favorite TV program and going out into the cold and windy night to sit on small chairs in your classroom.

It's possible to have your class read poems by other poets, but their own work will be far more appealing both to them and to their audience. Reading your own poem in public is a powerful validation, as perhaps you know from a similar experience. It highlights the essential part sound plays in poetry and motivates young writers to polish their work.

On a smaller scale, one or a few children could read their poems over the public address system in your school. In many schools, the principal broadcasts a morning greeting to start the school day. Following this with original poems read by your students will add interest and variety to the greeting as well as spread the word about the wonderful work your kids are doing.

More Ways to Perform Poetry

Professor Britton's dictum that poetry and drama are two different things notwithstanding, some dramatic embellishments can add interest to oral poetry for your class. Dramatic activities also increase children's direct involvement and thereby their learning. The social component inherent in these activities enhances learning in another mode.

Full-scale plays require lengthy preparations that can take over the greater part of every day for a couple of weeks; dramatizing poems is much simpler. Often a narrator will read the poem, eliminating the need for kids to memorize lines or for you to orchestrate a cast's words and actions. You don't have to have elaborate costumes; children can wear signs around their necks to identify their characters. Props can be kept at their simplest.

Kids who have been immersed in oral poetry can develop their own performances. Edie Ziegler divides her middle-grade classes into four or five groups and gives each group a copy of the same poem. She encourages the children to play with the words and rhythms, trying out various ways of performing the lines. They experiment, using voices and body movements, until they come up with a performable version. Even though every group uses the same poem, each interpretation is different from the next.

Impromptu performances like these are excellent preparation for presentations that require more rehearsal, such as pantomime or puppet shows. Sports poems are especially good for pantomiming and will increase poetry's appeal to kids who might not otherwise be vitally interested in poetry. Children who know the moves of a particular sport become deeply involved as they act out a poem. This is especially beneficial for kids who have difficulty reading aloud; this job is done for them by the narrator. *At the Crack of the Bat*, a collection of baseball poems, is excellent material for this treatment.

"Windshield Wiper" by Eve Merriam suggests an interesting presentation. The poem is written as two columns of phrases separated by a broad open space, and its appearance on the page resembles its topic. Some of the phrases are repeated, as in the first line: "fog smog   fog smog."

Imagine your class divided in half with each group standing in rows, Group A beside Group B. Group A says the line on the left as both groups lean to the left, then Group B says the one on the right as both groups lean to the right, as if they were all windshield wipers, and so on. Both groups say the last two lines in unison and sit down after the last word. Or perhaps you'd rather they act out the first few lines and start leaning with the words *rubber scraper*. The best approach is to share the poem visually with your class and cooperatively work out a way to perform it.

Act It Out

Narrative poems offer the most promise for dramatization. Catherine, in Karla Kuskin's poem of the same name (1980), makes a delicious chocolate cake from mud, weeds, bark, and gravel, then presents it to a friend. Although it would take only a couple of minutes to perform this poem, the sight of a child animatedly assembling those readily available ingredients and the recipient's reaction while a third child reads the poem can't fail to entertain.

"Mosquito" by J. Patrick Lewis tells the story of a treacherous skeeter who bites, promises to stop, and bites again. While one child narrates the poem, two others can speak the dialogue between the mosquito and his victim, and three more can act the nonspeaking parts of those who are bitten.

Stick puppets are just right for dramatizing a poem like "The House That Jack Built." The rat, cat, dog, cow, maiden, man, priest, rooster, and farmer can be drawn on and cut out of tagboard and attached to sticks that hidden puppeteers hold and use to manipulate the figures. A puppet stage (which is any kind of structure or arrangement that provides an opening where the puppets appear and a bottom and sides for the human actors to hide behind; large cardboard cartons can be made into one) can be transformed into Jack's house.

The poem that tells of the poor old lady who swallowed a fly is another good one for stick puppets. Find a very large piece of cardboard on which to draw the figure of the old lady. An artistically talented person (here's a good place to involve a parent) could draw her with a huge middle and suitable facial expression, adding to the humor of the poem. Cut an opening out of her middle big enough to accommodate in their turn all the creatures she swallowed. As the narrator reads the last line, "She died, of course," the puppeteer can cause the old lady to keel over on her back.

Aileen Fisher's "The Handiest Nose" is about all the wonderful things an elephant's trunk can do. A puppet stage and a few simple props are all you need to make this into a delightful presentation. The least simple, but still not difficult, of the props is a long, gray sleeve shaped like an elephant's trunk that will need to be sewn by you or a capable parent. This goes on the arm of a child who hides behind a cutout of an elephant's head and performs the actions described by the narrator. Usually the narrator reads without emoting, but he or she can give this poem an amusing finish by standing and reading the last line about the elephant's nose with feeling: "I'm glad it isn't *mine*."

Another stick puppet possibility is "Hippo's Hope" by Shel Silverstein, which can be found in *A Light in the Attic* complete with an illustration to guide the young artists who draw the hippopotamus puppet. This poem has three alternate endings, each of which can be read by a different narrator while the puppeteer maneuvers the hippo accordingly. Perhaps all three narrators could chant the two refrain lines in each verse, thus adding a touch of choral speaking to their performance.

If you can safely set up an elevated platform for kids to stand on, Shel Silverstein's "Dancing Pants" (1974) is great fun to perform. One pair of pants or as many as five can be dangled by the behind-the-scenes performers so that only the pants can be seen by the audience. As the narrator reads the poem, the pants "whirl, and twirl, and jiggle and prance." This poem ends by asking for applause from the audience, so it can serve as a good opening warm-up piece or a closing act for a full-length program; or it can stand alone.

Center on a Theme

Primary children will especially enjoy creating a poetry zoo or forest or jungle, whether for their own pleasure or that of a larger audience. The advantages of this kind of poetry program are many. First, the necessary resources are plentiful: animal costumes, from simple masks to head-to-toe suits, are often available, and every library is full of animal poems. Kids get a chance to dress up and act like animals while classmates read or recite the corresponding poems.

Begin by collecting poems about the kind of place you and your class choose to be the focus of your presentation. "At the Zoo" by Aileen Fisher is a good starting-off poem for a program on that topic. Jack Prelutsky's "I Know All the Sounds That the Animals Make," in which the narrator oinks like a bear and quacks like a frog, will delight young children and audiences alike. "The Zoo Was in an Uproar" by the same author contains a variety of unusual verbs and lots of alliteration, which will especially please third-graders. Poems from his book *Zoo Doings* are full of wordplay based on sound: "willy wally wallaby," "gallivanting gecko," and "widdly, waddly walrus" with "flippery, floppery feet" are just a few examples.

Karla Kuskin's "Fall" (1980) is told by a child walking in a forest who sees deer, rabbits, squirrels, and chipmunks and hears the black bears roar. The well-known "Stopping by Woods on a Snowy Evening" by Robert Frost can provide an interesting change of pace. Jane Yolen's "Grandpa Bear's Lullaby" is a good possibility for a poem to close a poetry forest program.

Poetry in Harmony

A uniquely effective form of oral poetry, devised by Paul Fleischman and presented in *I Am Phoenix* and *Joyful Noise* (winner of the 1989 Newbery Medal), calls for two voices to read a poem. The words for one reader are printed on the left side of the page, those for the other reader on the right. Sometimes one voice is heard alone, sometimes both in unison; sometimes both readers speak at the same time but read different words, creating a kind of spoken counterpoint.

This is clearly not the easiest kind of oral poetry to perform, but don't let that prevent you from exploring these truly remarkable poems. The form and imagery are strikingly appropriate to the topics, and the alternating voices create not only auditory interest but add to the sense of the writing as well. Use these poems with older, capable children or enlist another adult to perform them with you for your class. I was so captivated when I first read them that, book in hand, I corralled the first available person to read them aloud with me.

Another work for two voices is *Knots on a Counting Rope* by Bill Martin Jr., and John Archambault. If you've ever had the pleasure of hearing the authors recite this long, narrative poem, you know the enchantment that their spoken counterpoint weaves. Martin believes that reading poetry to children stores, indeed *locks,* language in their long-term memory, giving them a reservoir of language that is always theirs to draw from.

Don't forget the possibility, already mentioned, of including music in your presentations. Martin and Archambault use a drum to accompany their recitations; drums and tambourines are wonderful instruments for children to mark rhythms with. Just be careful that an enthusiastic drummer doesn't drown out the poem!

Music classes in some schools learn to play the recorder. A trio or quartet of this centuries-old wind instrument makes a charming background for a pastoral poem. If you or an available adult plays the guitar, its music is an appealing accompaniment for children's voices singing or speaking a poem. Note Jack Prelutsky's combining speaking and singing in the same poem as he accompanies himself on the guitar.

I'm not by any means pushing for full-scale musical productions, although schools occasionally put them on with great success, and poetry can have a valued part in them. On a classroom basis, we don't need the expertise of performers who have rehearsed to a fare-thee-well to bring joy and interest to poetry performances. The energy and enthusiasm of actors and audience will serve instead. The important thing is to share the magic of poetry in whatever ways work best for your particular class.

Visual Enchantment

The librarian of an elementary school where I taught made a practice of inviting all the classes once a year to a special program. We entered a darkened library, the once-familiar room made strange by its unaccustomed dimness, and settled on the floor. Then Sandy appeared in a small pool of lamplight and told us she was going to read some poems about colors.

Suddenly a large screen in front of us was flooded with shimmering, shivering light. A library aide, carefully rehearsed by Sandy, sat beside an overhead projector on which was a shallow glass bowl of water. Sandy's voice began, "What Is Red? Red is a sunset / Blazy and bright . . ." (O'Neill 1961) and before our eyes a drop of pure red appeared on the screen and spread, trembling, and then was joined by another as the aide dispensed food coloring carefully from a medicine dropper into the water.

Sandy went on to "What Is Purple? Time is purple / Just before night . . ." and the red changed magically to deep purple as the aide added drops of blue coloring to the water. In a new bowl of water, we saw yellow, ". . . the color of the sun / The feeling of fun," which was then mixed with blue to give us green, ". . . the smell / Of a country breeze." Several poems and bowls of water later when the program was over, we sat still, mesmerized by the blend of sight and sound we had just experienced.

More recently I saw the same technique used to illustrate different kinds of poems; the presenter added small plastic objects to the water—insects, a snake, a worm—according to the content of the poem. This is a procedure you can adapt to a large number of topics.

WRITING THE SOUND OF POEMS

"I write poetry for the same reason I read it: the sound of words, their taste on my tongue, is irresistible." So writes Bobbi Katz in *The Place My Words Are Looking For* (Janeczko 1990, 29). Help your kids learn to taste the sound of words by sharing with them poems that are especially rich with sound. Hearing and reading lots of such poems will lead readily to writing their own. Ree Young's ten-year-old son, David, understood that when he said to her, "Poetry is like listening to water and wanting to write down what you hear" (Janeczko 1990, 113).

Mother Goose verses are full of delightful nonsense sounds, from "Diddle diddle dumpling, my son John" to "Hickety, pickety, my black hen," but we've gotten so used to them that we take them for granted. Take your kids on a nostalgia trip through Mother Goose, reading and saying together the remembered verses of their early years (which will seem to them a distant past). Point out the fun and silliness of the nonsense rhymes and encourage them to think up variations, like "Flippety floppety, my fat frog."

If this meets with success and enthusiasm, your class could go on to write their own versions of Mother Goose and perhaps share them with your school's kindergarten. But if not, you've still reminded their ears of the fun we find in the sounds of words, and this is a big part of the joy of poetry.

Karla Kuskin asks her readers to "listen to the sound of words. There are light sounds and heavy ones" (1975, 38), and begins one poem with "'Cow' sounds heavy." Brainstorm with your children the sounds of words. You might start by reading Kuskin's cow poem and go on to ask for all the words they can think of that sound heavy, writing them on the board as fast as you can.

When they begin to slow down, ask for all the light words they can think of, and list those for a minute or two. Then invite them to write a poem about something that sounds heavy or light to them. Be sure to take time at the end of this class for a group sharing session so that everyone can hear the sounds of words and experience the tremendous variety of poems that has resulted in spite of everyone's having begun at the same point.

Kuskin also writes, "Some words look and sound like their meaning" (1975, 40) and illustrates this with her poem "Worm." Read Gertrude Stein's "Rose is a rose is a rose" to focus on the pure sound of an object's name. Explore the sound of words and phrases; repeat with your kids "weeping willow," "crackling," "bumpity bumpity," or whatever suggests itself until the sounds of the words have taken on lives of their own. Have your children make their own lists of words that sound beautiful or wet or sharp or noisy.

Notice all the hissing sounds in this poem by a fifth-grader, and the way they fit the feelings expressed.

Sisters

Sometimes sisters are so sassy,
Always snooping in your room.
Seldom smiling, seldom sweet,
Snapping at the little sisters,
Shouting orders out like queens,
Never sharing when they should,
But,
You can still love them. ❖

Pamela Keyes
Grade 5

Notice, too, the way the changed rhythm of the last line matches the shift in feeling.

Sounds for the Fun of It

X. J. Kennedy states that his poems start not with ideas but with "a promising blob of language" (Janeczko 1990, 36). A line pops into his head with "a bouncy beat," and another rhyming line sometimes joins it. In fact, he prefers to follow the rhymes and rhythms he discovers by fooling around with words over writing a poem centered on a single idea.

This will be true for some of your children, too. Encourage them to explore the sounds of words just for the fun of it. One of the poems I memorized is "Jabberwocky" by Lewis Carroll. I loved saying it to my kids from its famous beginning lines, "T'was brillig, and the slithy toves . . ." to the end as I watched their faces change from puzzled to delighted.

This fourth-grader's poem illustrates the pleasure of letting your imagination fly from the starting point of a funny-sounding word.

The Moozle

The Moozle eats people's noses
He has a big head and a one inch body
He weighs one thousand pounds
He is invisible to all humans
He walks on air
Then he falls on people
The Moozle is allergic to dirty socks.
He comes from the planet Bootoe. ❖

Michael Conti
Grade 4

Many words in our language began as sounds that later came to be represented by letters, such as *swish*, *murmur,* and *clang*. Although many children will happily roll the word *onomatopoeia* around in their mouths, knowledge of the term isn't necessary for them to enjoy the creation and use of words that represent sounds.

Read poems to them such as David McCord's "The Pickety Fence" with its "Give it a lick it's / A clickety fence." "Skeleton Train," in *I'm Gonna Tell Mama I Want an Iguana* by Tony Johnston, begins "Clackety-clack goes the skeleton train." It's ideal for Halloween week but will be just as much fun to say and hear at other times of the year.

In her poem "Boots" (see chapter 2), Helen found just the right words to make us think of the sound that boots, maybe slightly loose ones, make when worn by a small child. Clunk-a-da-pik, clunk-a-da-pik went her boots, as she clumped down the sidewalk.

Playing with Words and Sounds

Wordplay that juggles sounds and meanings has been a source of pleasure for centuries. Shakespeare is full of puns, of course, few of which are accessible to elementary school kids, but they can enjoy poems like "Green With Envy" by Eve Merriam, a conversation among vegetables in which the carrot "tops" what the asparagus said and lettuce "leaves" her comment for last.

Most young children find hilarity in jingles like "Fuzzy Wuzzy was a bear, / Fuzzy Wuzzy had no hair. / Fuzzy Wuzzy wasn't fuzzy, was he?" Ogden Nash is a master at this sort of wordplay, as in "The Panther":

> The panther is like a leopard,
> Except it hasn't been peppered.
> Should you behold a panther crouch,
> Prepare to say Ouch.
> Better yet, if called by a panther,
> Don't anther. ❖

Edward Lear, a master of fanciful verse, wrote poems that demand to be read out loud, and perhaps danced to. Say these lines from "The Jumblies" and you'll hear what I mean.

> And they bought a Pig, and some green Jackdaws,
> And a lovely Monkey with lollipop paws,
> And forty bottles of Ring-Bo-Ree. ❖

From *Verses from 1929 On* by Ogden Nash. Copyright © 1935, 1940, 1941 by Ogden Nash. By permission of Little, Brown and Company.

Verses like these not only charm us with their playfulness but teach children's ears and minds to use sound and sense in unexpected ways. Language is meant to express the entire range of human emotion and experience, and that includes delight in pure fun, especially for children.

CONCLUSION

Poets are virtually unanimous in asking that their works be read out loud, small children chant favorite verses or rhymes of their own making, and even twentieth-century lovers murmur poems in the ear of the beloved. Sound is the essence of poetry and needs to be integral to its use in the classroom. Give poetry the voice of children, and children will make poetry their own.

REFERENCES

All unreferenced quotes are from conversations with the author or observations of the author.

Berry, Faith. *Langston Hughes*. Westport, CT: Lawrence Hill, 1983.

Britton, James. "Reading and Writing Poetry." In Gordon M. Pradl (ed.), *Prospect and Retrospect*. Montclair, NJ: Boynton/Cook, 1982.

Calkins, Lucy McCormick, with Shelley Harwayne. *Living Between the Lines*. Portsmouth, NH: Heinemann Educational Books, 1991.

de la Mare, Walter. *Collected Poems 1901-1918*. New York: Henry Holt, 1920.

Denman, Gregory A. *When You've Made It Your Own . . . Teaching Poetry to Young People*. Portsmouth, NH: Heinemann Educational Books, 1988.

Fisher, Aileen. *Feathered Ones and Furry*. New York: Thomas Y. Crowell, 1971.

Fleischman, Paul. *I Am Phoenix*. New York: Harper & Row, 1985.

———. *Joyful Noise*. New York: Harper & Row, 1988.

Frost, Robert. *The Poetry of Robert Frost*. New York: Henry Holt, 1969.

Graves, Donald. *Writing: Teachers and Children at Work*. Portsmouth, NH: Heinemann Educational Books, 1983.

———. *Explore Poetry*. Portsmouth, NH: Heinemann Educational Books, 1992.

Greenfield, Eloise. *Honey, I Love*. New York: Thomas Y. Crowell, 1978.

Hopkins, Lee Bennett. *Side by Side: Poems to Read Together*. New York: Simon & Schuster, 1988.

Janeczko, Paul, ed. *The Place My Words Are Looking For*. New York: Bradbury Press, 1990.

Johnston, Tony. *I'm Gonna Tell Mama I Want an Iguana*. New York: G. P. Putnam's Sons, 1990.

Kuskin, Karla. *Near the Window Tree*. New York: Harper & Row, 1975.

———. *Dogs and Dragons, Trees and Dreams*. New York: Harper & Row, 1980.

Lear, Edward. *How Pleasant to Know Mr. Lear!* New York: Holiday House, 1982.

Lenz, Lisa. "Crossroads of Literacy and Orality: Reading Poetry Aloud." *Language Arts* 69 (1992): 597-603.

Lewis, J. Patrick. *A Hippopotamusn't and Other Animal Verses*. New York: Dial Press, 1990.

Little, Jean. *Hey World, Here I Am!* New York: Harper & Row, 1986.

Martin, Bill, Jr., and John Archambault. *Knots on a Counting Rope*. New York: Henry Holt, 1987.

Merriam, Eve. *Out Loud*. New York: Atheneum, 1973.

Morrison, Lillian, ed. *At the Crack of the Bat*. New York: Hyperion Books for Children, 1992.

Murray, Gilbert. *The Classical Tradition in Poetry*. New York: Vintage Books, 1957.

Nash, Ogden. *Verses from 1929 On*. New York: Little, Brown and Company, 1935.

———. *Parents Keep Out*. Boston: Little, Brown, 1951.

O'Neill, Mary. *Hailstones and Halibut Bones. Adventures in Color*. New York: Doubleday, 1961.

Prelutsky, Jack. *Zoo Doings*. New York: Greenwillow Books, 1983.

———. *Something BIG Has Been Here*. New York: Greenwillow Books, 1990.

Rogers, Timothy, ed. *Those First Affections*. London: Routledge & Kegan Paul, 1979.

Silverstein, Shel. *Where the Sidewalk Ends*. New York: Harper & Row, 1974.

———. *A Light in the Attic*. New York: Harper & Row, 1981.

Smith, William Jay. *Laughing Time*. New York: Farrar, Straus & Giroux, 1990.

Thomas-MacKinnon, Pat. "Conversations as Contexts for Poems, Stories, Questions." *Language Arts* 69 (1992): 588-96.

Vernon, P. E., ed. *Creativity*. New York: Penguin Books, 1970.

White, E. B. *Charlotte's Web*. Illus. by Garth Williams. New York: HarperCollins Children's Books, 1952.

———. *Poems and Sketches of E. B. White*. New York: Harper Colophon Books, 1983.

Williams, William Carlos. *The Collected Poems of William Carlos Williams*. New York: New Directions, 1986.

Chapter 5

GOING PUBLIC

REVISING, EVALUATING, EDITING, PRINTING, AND CELEBRATING POEMS

If you've seen your carefully chosen words in print, whether in a newsletter, magazine, or book, you know that publication is an earned reward to be savored and celebrated. Publication validates the writer by bestowing public recognition and creates a resource of energy ready to be tapped for future work. It can be an invaluable asset in your classroom.

Publishing a collection of students' writing is one of the best ways I know to wind up a unit of study. It provides for selecting and summarizing information and presenting it comprehensibly, all of which are invaluable study skills. Sculpting and assembling a body of materials into published form requires children to synthesize what they've learned in a way that appeals to them and is effective.

Unfortunately, publishing students' writing can also be a time-consuming hassle. I wince when I remember the times I delayed or even skipped publishing because the task of collecting, selecting, editing, typing, printing, collating, and binding the work of twenty-five or more young writers looked overwhelming. There are ways, however, to lighten that load. Poetry itself provides a tremendous advantage: It's short. A published poem that's four lines long can be as effective, both for the writer and reader, as a two-page story. Laura's "Sparkling Fields" (see chapter 3), a prizewinner in a children's magazine, is only two lines long.

The writing-process-workshop form of teaching poetry also helps ease the publication process. Ongoing sharing and conferring give children a clear sense of what's good and what needs revision in their poems so that the selection and polishing of a piece for publication happens smoothly and in a comparatively short amount of time. Reading commercially published poetry gives kids an awareness of the conventions of form and sharpens their editing skills. And of course publication is an accepted, often integral part of the writing process rather than the sometime thing it was in many classrooms of the past.

The easiest way to manage the publication process is to use a computer, word processor, and printer. The ease and clarity of on-screen revision and editing allow you and the children to focus on the content and not get bogged down in the pencil-paper-eraser mess. The word processor helps kids format their poems, allowing them to move and rearrange lines easily. Above all, it enables the printer to produce pages ready for the copying machine—no retyping! The ideal is to have enough computers available on a regular basis for your students to do much of their writing on a word processor, but even if your students can only use computers for their final copies, the brevity of poems eases the job of turning handwriting into print.

CHOOSING THE BEST POEMS TO PUBLISH

There are dozens of ways to "go public" with poetry (more about these later). My fourth-grade class and I decided the anthology, with a poem from each child, would work best for us. By the time we were ready to publish our book, the poems had been saved on computer disks and much revision had taken place. Next came the hard part: deciding which ones to publish. Experience has taught me that self-selection is the best way to go about this; a major benefit is not having to make the choices myself. Before I learned to teach writing as a process I thought that the teacher, who was, after all, the authority and final arbiter of everything, had to decide which poems to publish. So I agonized over my class's poems, more than 100 of them, and announced my choices to the kids, thinking the worst was over. Wrong. The writers didn't agree with the judge.

Faced with a publishing deadline, I didn't have time to sit down with each child and explain my choice by showing what was effective in the poem. In any case, the time when that would have been most useful to the writer had passed. The way I was teaching then, poetry and its rules and criteria existed "out there" in that teacher-dominated sphere that most kids struggled to figure out with varying degrees of success. A few, usually the very brightest or slowest, chucked the whole attempt as uninteresting or impossible and either waited it out or acted out, which was no fun for any of us.

Instructional materials for writing poetry focused on verses that rhymed and formulas that required certain numbers of syllables or lines. The more the kids followed the rules, the more stilted and artificial their efforts seemed to me. I hadn't the courage, confidence, or knowledge to strike out on my own and try to help my students find poetry in their own lives in their own ways. Although I praised successful attempts to follow the directions on the worksheets, the kids must have sensed that my approval wasn't as wholehearted as they wanted it to be.

Occasionally a child wrote a poem with striking images or a particularly original choice of words. My enthusiasm was welcome but puzzling to the kids because those poems often broke the rules. Without a variety of models to show us possibilities and the interaction of conferences to develop skill and standards, we were like hikers lost in a forest, going around in circles. No wonder my choices of best poems didn't always make sense to the kids.

Children Choose Their Own

When children choose from among their own poems the ones they want to publish, they develop the ability to evaluate their own work. We teachers have all been students at some time (many of us still are), and many of us have experienced the frustration of receiving what we felt to be unjust or mistaken evaluations of our writing. When we teach children how to evaluate their own work, we bypass this emotional quagmire.

As it was with everything we did, methods of self-evaluation varied among my fourth-graders. One or two strong-minded individuals knew immediately which poems they considered their best and had no interest in consultation. One or two children had written so little that choosing the best poem was easy: It was the one that was finished.

But most of the kids had written a dozen or more poems and took the selection process very seriously. Again I began the minilesson with a question: "What makes a poem really good?" The answers were varied, of course.

"It makes a picture in my head."

"It just sounds right."

"The poet put in just the right words."

"It's funny."

"I don't know, I just like it."

"Most of you have written a lot of poems," I went on, "but there's only room in our book for one from each of you. That means you have to choose the best one, the one you want to publish. Remember, when a book is published, it goes out there in the world and lots of different people can read it. What are some ways you could begin to choose your best poem?"

As we brainstormed possible strategies, I listed them quickly on the board.

Read all the poems over.

Ask a friend.

Ask Mrs. Armour.

Ask the principal.

Find the one I worked hardest on.

Choose three and then choose the best one.

"Go eenie, meenie, miney, mo," suggested Jason, who got good-natured sounds of derision from his classmates and a teacherly look from me. Pointing to our list on the board, I said, "These are good ideas. Go ahead now and start to look for your very best poem. Let me know if you want to have a conference with me."

The room was quiet at first; then a hum developed as children turned to neighbors for another opinion. I circulated, trying to keep conferences short so I could reach as many as possible. I had learned that by conferring with most of the students on the first day of a new part of the process I could save us all much time and wasted effort by catching misunderstandings early, showing a clear direction to head in, and especially by giving enthusiastic encouragement.

When a Student Chooses Less Than the Best

In the days that followed, a student would sometimes choose a poem that clearly was not one of the best available. When that happened, I wasn't above trying to influence the choice. We talked about why the writer had selected that poem and I explained why I liked one or two others better and then left the final decision up to the writer.

I often said something like, "I know you like this poem and I do, too, but remember, our book is going to be read by lots of people who don't know you. I really believe that for a wide audience like that, *this* poem will be better. And, of course, you'll always have your own favorite poem for you and your friends and family to read. Think it over."

I wasn't comfortable with this transaction and took it on only when a truly excellent poem was in danger of being bypassed in favor of one with a particularly personal appeal to the writer. Usually, but not always, the student changed the selection.

REVISION IN THE WORKSHOP

The prospect of seeing their work in print stimulates children to look at the selected poems with a refreshed eye and think about reworking their ideas into more effective forms. Sometimes publication-born inspiration produces brand new poems that go through varying amounts of revision before their authors pronounce them ready for publication. For us teachers, the prospect of putting out a class book sometimes sparks the commendable desire to produce the finest volume of poetry ever seen in our schools. This can push us toward taking over the revision process if we aren't careful.

As Gabriel Della-Piana has said, "Revision is not 'making a poem better,' it is making the poem more consonant or congruent with one's image of what the piece of writing is intended to accomplish" (1978, 106). Donald Graves put it this way: "Revision comes from burning questions writers have about their intentions" (1992, 69). Even the youngest writers have firm ideas about what they want to say. As teachers, we have to hold firmly to the role of guide or coach so that we can best help our children determine and achieve their intentions.

Revision was interwoven in the seamless fabric of our poetry workshop, impossible to see as a separate procedure. It grew out of all our activities. Minilessons led to it, whether by providing models of published poems or accounts of revision strategies individual children had found useful. Sometimes I resorted to thinly disguised exhortation, as in my shortest minilesson. I stood in front of the room at the beginning of class and said, "Do you know what I read yesterday? A poet's work was being published in a magazine and he called the printer and said, 'Stop! Stop the presses! I have to change a word in the third line!' Isn't that amazing? Poets never finish revising."

The children were familiar with the revision process as it applied to prose. They were used to searching for just the right words to express their ideas and have the maximum impact on the reader. Published poems showed us that one of the special qualities of poetic language was the use of unusual, striking words to make the reader see everyday objects and experiences in new ways.

We read and discussed these models in minilessons and I was always on the lookout for examples in the children's work. Jason's poem about fall helped us move beyond colorful leaves and showed us a more original way to see the weather and think about the passage of time:

October Winds

October winds fly
throughout the air, gracefully,
Restless trees waving in the winds,
and then,
at the turn
of your head,
suddenly,
the winds STOP!!
and you find out,
It's November. ❖

Jason Kates
Grade 4

Some lines were so striking that I had to share them with the class as soon as I read them, such as Jocie's "Bare trees turn white / When rooftops glitter / And the winds turn / Friends with the snow." We noted the repetition of "turn" and the unexpected shift of its meaning in line 3. We were delighted with the originality of Katie's "The wind is compared with / the world's sneeze" and Jill's "Wind gushes through the air / like a crowd of people." Those lines also gave me the opportunity to touch back on the idea of personification by remarking that the wind was written about as if it were a person and reminding the class that poets often did that.

The children's comments about their revision processes reflected their awareness of word choice. Jessica wrote, "I revised my poem by adding unusual words, putting in more information, and eliminating some words." Alan said, "I revised my poem by reading it over to myself and thinking if it was original or not." In her revision process, Sharon discovered a significant truth for all writers: "I revised my poem by leaving some words out. When I left the words out, I didn't need to use other words in their place."

Revision Conferences

Conferences were the vehicle for much revision, and it was hard to keep them short. Having to work within the framework of fifty-minute periods forced me to come to terms with the tyrannical nature of time. Instead of one long, leisurely conference, several miniconferences made it possible for more kids to get the help and encouragement they needed at that moment. I also had to recognize that time spent conferring with me was time taken away from writing. Again, the role of a writing-process teacher meant giving up the time-honored gratification of the captive audience. So I would flit like a bee around the room, crouching beside a child just long enough to deal with a single word, phrase, or problem before straightening up to move on to the next.

Keeping most conferences short also allowed enough time for a long one when it was necessary. As Donald Graves tells us, "Sometimes more listening is required" (1992, 62). After he asks the child to read the poem aloud, they talk about what sounds or parts seemed more important to the writer. Then Graves tells the child what he heard in the poem. A poem that is wandering or seems to be a jumble of interesting but disconnected possibilities needs this kind of extended conference. As the writer thinks about your questions, perhaps the direction of the poem will gradually become clear. Or the student might find the one strong idea that the poem really is about and can store the others away for possible future use.

That kind of conference can provide a richness and depth that short meetings don't allow. It helps children discover their intentions and often enables them to forge ahead on their own. Your knowledge of the kids in your class helps you decide who needs more of your time, who needs to be left alone, and who could benefit from a peer conference with a child who has had a similar experience.

Peer Conferences

At this point in the year, most of the kids in my class had learned how, when, and whom to ask for the help they needed. Experience had taught them that classmates were more accessible than I was for conferences both quantitatively (twenty-seven of them, one of me) and qualitatively. No matter how nonjudgmental and nonthreatening I attempted to be, I was still The Teacher. Seth's account of his revision process pointed that out: "The first draft of my poem was pretty dull. Then I had a revising conference with my friend. When I got to revise on the computer I changed some things to make it exciting. Then Mrs. Armour called me. Uh-oh! It was time to let her look at it. When she said she liked it, I was so happy."

When I first read that, I winced. This wasn't the role I wanted to fill. Was I fooling myself, thinking I had become the "guide on the side" while the kids still saw me as the "sage on the stage," the ultimate authority who must be accommodated? I reread my log of the previous month and then of the past year and thought about the events and experiences I had written about. I began to see them as signposts on the journey I was making. I certainly hadn't reached my destination—being the perfect teacher of the writing and reading processes—and realistically didn't expect to.

But progress was being made, and as long as I kept asking my kids for their ideas and observations and kept on learning from them, I was sure it would continue. Then, too, maybe there would always be a Seth, a child who saw the teacher as the final authority no matter how democratic the methods. On reflection, I decided that wasn't so terrible either.

So peer conferences were frequent and at least as valuable as teacher conferences. I had taught the basic procedures when writing workshop began, and the kids were used to approaching a friend, quietly asking for a conference, and finding a place where no one would be distracted by their conversation. If the writer wanted advice on shaping a poem by arranging lines or words, the conferees sat side by side at a table. Another commonplace sight was a pair of children facing each other, sitting cross-legged on the floor in a corner of the room, one reading and the other listening with greater concentration than I could always count on when I talked to the class.

Stephen's description of his process pointed out that, in revision, you have to know when to quit. "I started out by writing about rain. Then I added thunder, lightning, and sunshine. Then I had some other people look at it. I had a complaint, so I had a revision conference and changed some things. Then it came to me it was too long. I asked some people and they said it was all right so I kept looking. It just didn't come to me so I left it."

Are They Really Getting It?

Do you ever have anxiety attacks about whether your kids are really doing what all your carefully planned and executed actions are designed to get them to do? Sometimes it seemed as if all my minilessons, models, and conferences were like pebbles thrown in the ocean, leaving little ripples and then disappearing. I wanted to be a weather satellite in our classroom sky, able to look down and focus on each writer and see what was actually going on.

But in addition to the limitations of time and physical space, there was the constraint on the writer of my very presence. No matter how unobtrusively I tried to move around the room, when I stood beside a child, she or he stopped writing and looked up expectantly. I imagined wonderful words escaping from the writer's mind and dissolving in the air above his or her head, lost forever because I interrupted the process.

I also felt uncomfortable reading over a child's shoulder. I didn't like an observer reading along as I wrote and suspected the children felt the same. Occasionally I would have the good luck to happen upon a child who was using a strategy I had just suggested, or a child would call me over to show me a revision that had been inspired by the day's minilesson. Usually, though, I floundered along on faith that what I was doing was working, sustained and exhilarated by the wonderful words that I did get to see and hear in their authors' own good time.

It was encouraging to read what the kids wrote about their revision processes. Although most of them told of adding more or taking out what they didn't need or searching for words that were stronger or more original, Scott's account seemed to sum up exactly what happens when the poet's intentions are central to revision: "I revised my poem by traveling, in my mind, to where the poem would have taken place. Then I read the poem to myself. If anything sounded weird, I looked to see what was the matter, then revised the writing to how I saw it happen in my mind."

Revision Through the Grades

Although revision can and often does take place without publication, publication very seldom happens without revision coming first. Somewhere toward the end of the primary grades, the child who has been taking part in the writing process since entering school will have integrated the elements of the process so thoroughly that they will seem inextricable. The awareness of a potential audience will inform the writing from the beginning, if only indirectly.

First Attempts

For beginning writers, as Georgia Heard points out, revision is a matter of development from poem to poem rather than changing one poem. Kindergartners and first-graders embark on a new voyage of discovery every day; their poems are small, wonderful markers on the journey, such as this one cited in *For the Good of the Earth and Sun*:

> Angels sing
> Hearts go away
> Butterflies die❖
>
> *Barbara*
> *Grade 1*

Can you imagine a revision conference? It would either kill the poem or turn it into a story. Teachers' and classmates' responses to the feelings and thoughts expressed and the words used to express them in young children's poems will shape future efforts.

Invented spelling lets young writers express ideas and images that amaze us. Those of us who are fortunate enough to spend parts of our lives with preschool or primary-age children delight in repeating to others what we hear them say. Do we correct their unique, spoken views of the world? Very seldom, because we know their continued experience of reality will correct their misconceptions and errors in vocabulary and syntax. Further, we enjoy the freshness of their views.

Very young children can only approximate the written word in their attempts to record what they want to say. When Barbara, a first-grader, came to Georgia Heard to tell her the above poem, it existed in her mind and in a picture she had drawn. Heard asked Barbara if she was going to write some of the letters down and stayed with her as she sounded out the first couple of words. As Heard notes in her account of this incident, young children often need support in their early attempts to transform sound into writing. Here are the letters Barbara wrote:

eJs sc
H g g UW
BUTTERELY
DE ❖

Without the author to tell us her poem, we couldn't know what her written version said. Indeed, in a few days, Barbara might not be able to read it herself. Teachers often write down the conventional spelling of the words, perhaps on the back of the page, not as a model for the child to copy but as a backup, a guard against losing the poem to unreliable memory. Studies show that invented spelling gradually gives way to conventional orthography in the primary grades. Without it, young children's poems would be as ephemeral as their unique perceptions of the world.

Is It Right? Is It Right?

Somewhere in second grade the drive for correctness usually strikes. If you're teaching at this level and find that your class has had little experience writing poems, you'll probably have to work hard to encourage your kids' originality and calm their anxiety about making mistakes. Having them compose orally will help: Children can work in pairs, saying their poems to each other or composing one together. When they're sure of what they want to say, they can write it down. Emphasize to them that this is a first draft and doesn't have to be perfect.

Revision in this case will be mostly oral as they bounce their poems off each other. Teach minilessons in which you model this process with a child or another adult and use it in conferences. As you circulate around your classroom, be alert to discover children who are becoming particularly adept. Pair these individuals with others who are still developing revision skills.

The desire to be correct can intensify in third grade. Lucy Calkins finds that, despite children's reluctance to take risks, there are ways to rekindle in children the energy for writing that characterized their work in earlier grades. Poetry presents both the greatest risk and the greatest opportunity for children at this level because originality is required. Correctness is a virtue in prose; inventiveness is praised in poetry. As kids dare to write their own imaginings instead of relying on the safety of "doing it right," the rewards of satisfaction—theirs, their peers', and yours—will keep the creative fires burning.

Most of their experience in the earliest grades will have been with nursery rhymes and longish narrative poems. Shower your kids with a wide variety of published poems, especially short, vivid, unrhymed ones. Focus on originality as your students move from oral to written revision. In conferences and sharing sessions, celebrate striking syntax and effective rhythm whenever you find it; what you pay attention to is what your kids will try to incorporate in their writing.

Questions will help your students develop the awareness that leads to revision. When you ask, "How did you get your idea for this poem? What did you see? Can you close your eyes and see it now?" you encourage the seeing again that re-vision literally is. Some of the questions Georgia Heard asks are, "How's it going? How can I help? What do you think about your poem?"

Asking your students to read their poems aloud and reading them aloud yourself will help them hear the rhythm in their words. When you read, it also opens another avenue for reflecting on what they've written: hearing the poem in someone else's voice. Heard suggests to children that they keep a pencil handy in case they want to make any notes as they listen and, when she's finished reading, might ask, "What were you thinking as I read to you? How did it sound? Did you get any more ideas?" For many specific, inclusive suggestions to help your students revise their work, read the section called "'Someone Who Will Truly Listen': Conferring" in Heard's book *For the Good of the Earth and Sun*.

Revision at the Point of Utterance

Between second and fourth grades, revision seldom produces dramatic changes in children's poems. Teachers of the writing process think of revision as seeing again, rereading what we have written in order to find and structure words in ways that make our meaning clearer. In this way, draft follows draft until the writer is satisfied that no more changes are needed. But let's consider James Britton's concept of "shaping at the point of utterance" (1982, 139), the spontaneous expression in speech or writing of one's "interpreted experience." In this case, the writer's rereading leads to the next bit of writing rather than revision: "The act of writing becomes itself a contemplative act revealing further coherence and fresh pattern" (p. 143).

Britton notes the composing processes of young children and adult scholars as well who find clarification of their thinking in the act of writing rather than revising. "Once a writer's words appear on the page, I believe they act primarily as a stimulus to *continuing*—to further writing, that is—and not primarily as a stimulus to *re*-writing" (p. 140). Although Britton finds that this applies to writers of all ages, it is particularly pertinent for young children.

The concept also is in harmony with the nature of writing poetry, a more subjective process than writing prose. The purpose of a poem is to present experience, not explicate it. Although the audience can't be ignored (published poets who do this often lose their readers), it is farther away from writers of poetry, some of whom find their meaning at that point where thought meets paper for the first time.

Please don't think this means the whole idea of revision is out the window; of course not. It does mean we need to be aware that some children, especially in the early grades, can write wonderful first drafts of poems that won't get any better. Britton suggests that too much emphasis on drafting and revision can obstruct "shaping at the point of utterance." It's our task to help our kids achieve their own intentions in their poems and if that happens without revision, don't worry about it—celebrate it!

Older Children Revise

As children grow older, however, their work is more likely to benefit from revision. As we've seen, the uniqueness of the younger child's ways of seeing the world can be obscured by too much revision. But older kids often feel driven to conform to their concepts of external standards and requirements. From fourth grade on, more and more children will find it hard to craft personal experiences into authentic poems. It's a risky business, putting into words emotions and memories that come from deep inside you.

Kids' lives grow more complex every year. With so much happening and so much to think about, they can have trouble discovering or selecting the focus of their poems. First drafts might look like jumbled collections of clichés, and this is where revision is necessary. But revision is a difficult process for all writers, grown or growing, and in its complex forms not something we can reasonably expect from most elementary school children. If they continue from the early grades to write within the writing-process-workshop structure, however, we can expect children to develop revision skills that will produce remarkable results in the later elementary years.

Older children are becoming more aware of their emotions, are developing social consciousness, and are more able to reflect on their own actions and feelings. As a result, their poems are more likely to go beyond the portrayal of images to the consideration of issues. Fifth- and sixth-graders are beginning to think about the human condition as evidenced in their own lives or in the world at large. Many of them care deeply about justice and other ethical concerns. Poetry provides a natural vehicle for the expression of such highly charged content.

These are hardly what we could call easy topics. Big ideas and intense beliefs have a way of emerging in clichés the first time around and need to be wrestled into originality, in contrast to the spontaneity we often find in younger children's work. Talk is vital to the revision process here, keeping in mind the importance of first establishing an atmosphere of trust. In individual or small-group conferences, kids can explore their ideas and, by bouncing them off others, discover and clarify their own unique views.

Older children can benefit from straightforward responses to their work in terms of what does or doesn't work, but they still need positive recognition of the value of their effort (indeed, few of us outgrow that need). As peer influences become ever stronger, it's especially important to maintain a workshop atmosphere of professionalism where the standards of autonomy and hard work are understood, accepted, and valued by all.

You, the teacher, are paramount to the establishment of this atmosphere. It's essential that your students know they can trust and believe you. They will recognize genuine, honest responses to their work and will respond in kind, though perhaps not immediately. The time and effort you expend in the beginning to develop a relationship of trust and respect with and among your kids will result in writing above your highest hopes. If that relationship doesn't exist, children won't feel free to take the risks that authentic poetry requires.

Questions work best to aid the revision process but are most effective if you precede them with a nonevaluative restatement of what you understand the child to be saying in the poem. This does at least two things: It validates the writer's ideas, thereby bolstering authority and autonomy, and it tells the student whether the ideas are clear and true to the original intention.

You might find yourself acting as a kind of poets' introduction service. As you circulate around the classroom conferring, you probably will come upon more than one child who is grappling with the same theme. Pairing those students will give them an invaluable opportunity to develop the expression of their ideas. They can be each other's sounding boards, validators, and editors, benefiting themselves and you by allowing you more time to confer with other students.

Models Help Revision

Look for published poems dealing with topics that your kids care about. Whether you present them to the whole class in minilessons or share them with one child at a time, they will provide the models that every writer needs. If you keep a topic-indexed file of these poems as you discover them, within a year or two you'll have a resource that will enable you to locate poems quickly instead of racking your memory or spending precious time paging through anthologies.

An important connection that you can help your students make is tying images to concepts. If they have had experience writing poems in earlier grades, they'll be ready to do this; if not, help them learn first to create vivid word pictures. Then share with them poems that link images to ideas. This gives you a great opportunity to introduce poetry generally thought of as the province of adults. Certain works of Emily Dickinson, Robert Frost, Shakespeare, Marianne Moore, and many other renowned poets are accessible to children in the upper-elementary grades. Kenneth Koch read the poems of Donne and Blake to ten-year-olds and noted, "Though few had the critical skill to say much about the poems we read, they all could experience them" (1973, 24).

Treat yourself to an hour in your town library and browse through the poetry section; when you find a poem that you know will speak to your kids, make a copy on the spot. Three or four of these hours spread over the school year will furnish you with a collection tailor-made for the kids you teach. When you share one of these poems in a minilesson, tell your class that it is supposed to be for grown-ups but you know from their writing that they'll understand it and that it will help them with their own poems. You'll have pride and prestige working for you—both powerful motivators.

Some of Valerie Worth's poems connect images with a deeper meaning. In "Haunted House," a stiff-hinged door and empty jelly jars recall the house's owners who have grown old and died; the narrator in "Heron" says that fools pursue their prey, but he chooses to stand and reflect and let his prey come to him. You might ask your class to wonder about which came first to Worth, the image or the association, and extend that to their own poems.

When you confer, point out to your kids the effective images in their poems and ask if they evoke other ideas. If there seems to you to be a clear connection, you might say, "This line makes me think of . . .," but be careful to avoid steering in a direction that doesn't seem right to the student. If the poem is about a big idea but lacks images, ask the writer to think about what the poem is about and, with eyes closed, let objects or events swim up from memory or imagination. "That makes me think of . . ." can be a helpful response here, too, either from you or a classmate.

Critiquing Through Conferences

In *Sunrises and Songs*, Amy McClure describes how individual conferences combined with small-group and large-group critiquing helped fifth- and sixth-graders revise their poems. Here is a first draft:

People change with time
In the future, in the past
In the olden days
People just get older. ❖

After much discussion with the teacher and a classmate, the writer's final draft looked like this:

Time

People change with time
Like days grow into weeks
The past is grandfather to the future
And I am now. ❖

Johnny
Grade 5

Children in this class demonstrated the autonomy older children can develop with the help of talented teachers. They devised a strategy McClure calls "blackboard critiquing," which began when four girls used a small portable chalkboard to help in their revision process. They divided the board into quadrants, wrote one girl's poem in each, and worked on each in turn, making suggestions for changes.

Over time, more children adopted blackboard critiquing, developing their own styles and codes. Words were easy to see and easy to erase, leading to an increased willingness to experiment with possible changes. The teachers of the class, at first reluctant to use the technique for fear of displacing the children's ownership, eventually began to employ it in revision sessions and found their fears were groundless. In a community of poetry readers and writers, we are all learners and teachers.

The fundamentals of effective revision persist throughout the grades. Saturate your classes with fine poems of all kinds. The more poetry you read, the more you'll be able to find just the right poems to provide the models your students need. Listen closely to what they're saying in their poems and, when you confer, ask questions that will help the writer's meaning emerge. Establish a community of writers who trust and respect each other and show them how to help each other. Share your own poems and model your revision processes. Value original, genuine poetic expression and celebrate it whenever, wherever you find it.

EVALUATION

I remember a time when praising children's writing indiscriminately seemed the right thing to do. Fearing that a hint of criticism would discourage young writers to the point of giving up, we hoped to nurture their efforts by removing all pain. This ignored a law of physics that often applies to working with children: For every action, there's an equal and opposite reaction.

Wholesale approval unfortunately led many children to produce much facile, thoughtless writing; fortunately, this led us teachers to reconsider our practices. The truth that there is such a thing as bad writing and good writing came to the front of our consciousness. This brought with it, however, the same problem we were trying to avoid in the first place: the negative effects of evaluation.

The contradictory roles of encourager and evaluator have long been the two horns of the teacher's dilemma. We remember the red pen-slashed compositions of our youth and vow never to inflict that experience on our students. At the same time, it's our job to establish and uphold standards. The answer for me came, as so many answers did, from teaching writing as a process, where autonomy and ownership are essential. They led inevitably to shifting the major responsibility for evaluation to the writer instead of the teacher.

Self-Evaluation

Ownership and autonomy, essential elements of the writing process, lead naturally to self-evaluation. We need to teach our children as soon as possible how to evaluate their own work. Perhaps you've shared with me this uncomfortable experience of many teachers in the earliest stages of teaching writing as a process: Your class has written their first drafts and you know that revision comes next. You teach a minilesson about an attribute you notice needs improvement—strong verbs, perhaps, or telling details—and direct your class to revise their work accordingly.

But when you read their second drafts, you're dismayed to find that their revisions amount to little more than Band-Aids, inconsequential changes stuck onto their original drafts. Your kids, politely or halfheartedly, attempted to accommodate your request as they understood it, but the result was tinkering, not revision. When young writers revise for you, the teacher, they have the uphill job of having to read your mind. "What does she want?" they ask each other.

We can't blame them for this but we can't entirely blame ourselves either. The instructional model most of us experienced conferred authority on the teacher as the dispenser of information and directions. Our job as students was to do as we were told. Although the shortcomings of this model have led to the current emphasis on student autonomy and responsibility, old patterns don't depart without a struggle.

When we see glaring flaws in our students' writing, we naturally want to eradicate them as soon as possible. How? Why, point out their shortcomings and tell them not to do that anymore, of course. Does this work? Not very well. Too often it results in mindless conforming to partially understood, externally imposed rules. If you ask children why they made certain changes in their writing and they answer, "Because the teacher told me to," chances are slim that real revision is taking place.

As long as we allow children to hold us responsible for the quality of their writing by issuing broad rules for good writing and wielding the red pencil of correction, they will produce work that, although it may be technically admirable, is neither original nor authentic. Experience forces us to recognize that children need to work through the always difficult, sometimes painful process of revision for themselves, and the key to their success is the degree to which they can evaluate their own work.

A good way to help children develop self-evaluation skills is to ask questions about what they want their poems to say and whether they're satisfied with the way they've said it. We can model this in minilessons, using poems of our own. I began class one Monday morning by saying, "Last night we were driving back from the shore and it was really late. We stopped for coffee but I didn't want any so I stayed in the car. All of a sudden a bird began to sing in the little tree beside me. I couldn't believe it! A bird was singing in the middle of the night! It went on and on for about five minutes. It was so strange and beautiful that I kept thinking about it. When we got home I wrote this down." Then I wrote this draft on chart paper:

> In the middle of the night
> A bird sings its heart out
> To an audience of empty parked cars
> And me. ❖

"I was so tired by then that I just went to sleep, and I know I could make it better. What do I really want my poem to say? I think I want to show how strange and exciting it was to hear that beautiful birdsong so late at night in the middle of a parking lot on the Parkway. Maybe I could start with, 'The deep dark night is still. . . .' "

After a few suggestions from the kids, I said, "I'll work more on this later. When you're writing today, ask yourselves what you really want your poem to say." In another minilesson I asked the class to take out the poem they were writing and reread it. "What are the exciting, original, special words in your poem? What words could be better? Make a little mark beside them so you can work on them today."

Questions Are Crucial

Questions are the backbone of conferences. When I asked, "How did you get your idea?" or "What did you see in your mind when you wrote that part?" the writer came up with more information to put in the poem or a different angle to view it from. Questions often began with "Can you . . .": "Can you write that line so we can really see it? Can you think of more original words to use here?" My hope and intention was always that the children would make these questions their own and use them on themselves as they wrote and revised. As I walked around eavesdropping on peer conferences, I heard echoes of my questions as they shared and discussed their poems.

Lucy Calkins points out that "when we ask process and evaluation questions of children, the children teach us about themselves and their writing. These insights about our children provide the grounds for our teaching" (1986, 151). Indeed, isn't the highest function of evaluation to give us information about what we need to teach? Calkins goes on to list, among others, these evaluation questions (p. 150):

> How does this piece compare with the other pieces you've written this year? Which is the very best? Next best? What makes this one the best? Could you make it even better if you wanted to?
>
> What makes a piece of writing really good?
>
> What are the strengths of your writing? The weaknesses?

It's important that teachers recognize the difference between open-ended thinking questions and closed-ended testing questions. If we already know the answer, we're asking a question that will do little to encourage self-evaluation. We also need to realize that there's a subtle but crucial difference between the kind of judgment that says a child's poem is good or bad and can be summarized by a grade of A or C, and the kind of evaluation that asks how the child's poems have changed, what processes the child uses, or what potential needs to be developed further.

From *The Art of Teaching Writing* by Lucy Calkins. © 1986. Heinemann Educational Books.

Standards:
High Yet Attainable

This is not to say that every poem a child writes is as good as any other. When a teacher points out again and again the specific qualities of a poem that are wonderful, children learn standards. When we celebrate a particularly striking line or image in a student's poem, writers add knowledge of what works and the pleasure of success to their reservoir of ability.

I try to avoid referring to children as poets. A parent who applies first aid to a child is not a doctor, a babysitter who helps with homework is not a teacher and I, although I occasionally write poems, am certainly not a poet. It seems patronizing to call children members of an adult profession. Admittedly this is a personal position and not entirely defensible because I happily call them writers and authors, but these are more general terms.

Poets achieve their status through a combination of innate creative talent and a long-term devotion to their craft. Like all artists, they hold themselves to exacting standards and develop their skill through the expenditure of much time and effort. Sometimes their working drafts and notes are published and we get a rare glimpse of the intricacy of their composing and revising processes.

At the risk of sounding contradictory, I think that by not assigning to children the title of poet we can free them to experience the joy of writing poems. Teachers in writing workshops often say, "Oh, I could never write a poem!" yet their journals are salted with poetic ideas and images. They have picked up the belief that poetry is only for poets; how that deprives us all!

Years ago, paint-by-numbers kits abounded and the pictures that resulted were denigrated as worthless attempts by talentless pretenders to art. I'm sure no painter by numbers thought she or he was Rembrandt, but someone who painstakingly filled in tiny spaces with just the right colors and strokes had every right to be proud of the effort and the product.

Our children's poems, sometimes ordinary and sometimes sparkling with ingenuity, are worthy because writing and reading them gives delight and meaning to the lives of their writers and readers. Kids don't have to follow the forms and standards of published poets—indeed, they can't—for their work to be valuable; if we expect them to, we will produce students who believe they could never write poems, or, perhaps worse, those who feel their only road to success is plagiarism.

A tiny number of the children who pass through our classrooms will grow up to be professional poets. My fervent hope for the rest is that the great majority of them will become lifelong writers and readers of poems. If we help them learn that poetry is a joy and right of everyone that can shine in everyone's life and mind, they will.

Grades and Report Cards

I can think of no better way to kill most children's desire to write poems than to put a letter grade at the top of the page, unless, of course, it's an A. As portfolio assessment and other alternatives to traditional grading practices become more widespread, that danger diminishes. But because most teachers must assign grades to student writing, let's look for ways to minimize the negative effects.

A system that many teachers have found effective is based on the concept of allocating a certain number of points to each project, activity, or process. You can do this quantitatively (two points for each first draft, two for each revision, etc.) or qualitatively (one point for a short, fast, ordinary poem, up to five points for a thoughtful, painstaking work). The obvious pitfall inherent in this practice is that it encourages children to turn out poems for a grade and is likely therefore to result in inauthentic writing.

This hazard can be avoided or at least diminished by emphasizing self-evaluation throughout a marking period but putting off the actual assessment until the last week before marks are due. Rather than focus on product, criteria can more readily be applied to the process. For example, a teacher might select these criteria:

Originality

Evidence of revision

Effective editing

Growth; development of ability

Use of poetic devices and strategies taught

Body of work (number and length of poems)

You can continue to cultivate your students' self-evaluation ability by inviting them into the criteria-setting process. Teachers who are very comfortable with the democratic method of decision-making will involve their kids from the beginning. "You know you'll get a report card four times this year," they might say. "What standards do you think I should keep in mind when I evaluate your writing?" This method doesn't preclude the teacher from adding, "Another criterion I thought of is . . ." in case the class omits something the teacher considers significant.

Teachers who prefer a higher degree of control might present their own lists and say, "These are the criteria I think are important when I evaluate your writing. But it's still *your* writing, and your ideas about what makes it good are very important. Let's discuss these." If the students have become accustomed to acceptance and cooperation in their classroom, the discussion will further their understanding of evaluation as well as allow them to contribute other perspectives and possible additions to the list.

Next, a number of points can be assigned to each criterion. It's always tempting to divide the number of categories into 100 so that we'll end up with a familiar rating scale (95% = A, 85% = B, etc.), but it's just as acceptable to weight the score in any way that seems workable to you. Our earlier list might look like this:

Criteria	Points
Originality	7
Evidence of revision	5
Effective editing	3
Growth, development of ability	7
Use of poetic devices and strategies taught	6
Body of work (number and length of poems)	6

If a teacher prefers that every category have the same score, revision and editing could be combined and the points for each criterion changed to seven—or four or thirty, according to preference. If the number is low, however, the evaluator has less latitude in making fine distinctions; if it is very high, the quibble factor increases. You next need to match total scores to the marking system your school uses. The maximum score in the list above is 34; you (and perhaps your class) will decide how far below that the student can go and still get an A—and so on.

All teachers' lists will have some standards in common and some that are specific to the particular groups that will use them. The important thing is that the children know from the beginning what those standards are and understand their value. By putting off the actual computing of scores until the end of a marking period, you'll be better able in the meantime to focus on the children's intrinsic reasons for writing.

One of the criteria in the list deserves some clarification. At the beginning of this chapter I talked about brevity as an attribute of poems. How then can length be a criterion for evaluation? Usually it won't be, but occasionally you'll have a student who whips out one facile four-liner after another. In this case length is an indicator of less-than-optimum achievement.

Another evaluation practice that works well with older children is asking them to choose the poem or poems they want to be graded on. They should include all drafts of the poems, showing revisions that took place, and perhaps write a description of their composing processes. This offers an excellent opportunity for students to develop awareness of themselves as writers and also requires intensive self-evaluation.

Grades have a direct line to our self-esteem. The refusal of college students to accept less than an A or B has led to grade inflation in many institutions. Elementary school children don't get to evaluate their teachers, however, and therefore haven't the clout of college students. It's our responsibility to do whatever we can to preserve our students' self-esteem when report card time rolls around. The very involvement of the kids in the grading and evaluating process helps to defuse its negative aspect. Think of the times you've been graded, whether in classes or on the job. Were you included in establishing your grade or rating or was it handed down by an all-powerful professor or principal? If you've had both experiences, you know personally what a difference the first alternative can make if done well.

Part of doing it well is maintaining honesty between teacher and child. If you ask your kids to score themselves, make it very clear to them that you, as the teacher, have the final responsibility of determining the grades. Talk about why you're asking them to share in the process and just how you want them to go about it. Then allow classroom time—forty-five minutes could be enough—for them to review and evaluate their work before you meet with them individually.

Evaluation Conferences

Sitting down with each child and going over the work of two months or more may seem like an extravagant expenditure of classroom time. But consider everything that's going on in this process. Everyone has a chance to sit back and look at the big picture, a welcome change from daily detail. Everyone's attention focuses on the quality of achievement, guided by agreed-upon criteria. Both students and teacher have the satisfaction of reviewing an impressive body of work. A child who has produced little gains valuable information from seeing what others have done in the same amount of time. More specifically, the children reread their work as a whole with an evaluative eye, sharpened by the knowledge that a public rating is around the corner.

Given that both you and the student have already reviewed the poems and made your tentative ratings, the actual evaluative conferences can take from five to fifteen minutes each and might occupy a week of what would normally be writing time. Collect as many books of poems as you can find (be sure to include the ones you've been using in minilessons) so that before and after their conferences, the kids will have lots of poetry to read and reread and perhaps memorize. If you're planning a publication celebration, this is a perfect time for them to rehearse their part in it.

These suggestions apply mostly to the poetry workshop structure, where your children will have spent enough time writing poems so that a report card grade might be required. These evaluation procedures will also work in writing classes where poetry hasn't occupied the entire marking period. Many methods of evaluating and grading are in use; search out and develop one that works for you and the children in your classes.

EDITING

Most lists of evaluation criteria will include, as ours did, editing, which is the process of correcting errors of usage, conventions, and mechanics; mostly this means punctuation, capitalization, and spelling. Revision, however, deals with the content of the writing and is determined by the author. Editing is an objective process, as witnessed by the fact that it can be accomplished mechanically by a computer program that checks spelling and grammar.

Don't think for a minute that editing isn't important. Writers who think so little of their audience that they can't be bothered to polish their work in accord with prevailing rules sacrifice their audience's respect. Inadequate editing can wipe out the most striking content because the reader loses interest. If the writer doesn't care that much about the piece, why should the reader?

But we do need to recognize the place of editing. If we don't put it where it belongs, at the end of the process, it can interfere with the composition of content. Many of us were taught, unfortunately, that conventions and mechanics determined the value of our writing, and we have welcomed the acknowledgment that what we have to say is what matters first and most. Still, we sometimes have to fight the teacherly urge to attend to correctness too soon.

Editing is not every child's favorite part of the writing process, of course, but the prospect of publication makes it more attractive—or at least endurable. For my classes, poetry's attributes made editing seem less of a chore than it was when we wrote prose. The comparative lack of constraints regarding punctuation and capitalization still exhilarated them. Here was undreamed-of power: They could capitalize letters or omit periods because they chose to, not because the rules told them to.

With fewer rules, the kids seemed more interested in the ways published poets used mechanics and examined closely the poems I used in minilessons on editing. Those very brief minilessons were essentially reminders of what we had already discovered about the impact of line breaks, capitalization, and punctuation on the ideas and images the poet wanted to shape on paper. By now, the children had clear reasons for their use of mechanics as an integral part of their poems, and most had dealt with that in the revision process.

Spelling

Spelling, of course, was another matter. Early in the year, I taught the class to draw a line around words they thought might be misspelled, explaining that they could go back and correct them later. In minilessons, I showed them the resources available (dictionaries, books with lists of frequently used and often misspelled words, etc.). Although this worked for a few kids, I was startled by the number of correctly spelled words I saw circled in their writing, sometimes as many as the misspelled words that weren't circled. Apparently my belief that most fourth-graders have a sense of correct versus incorrect spelling was incorrect.

We came to rely more on peer conferences to catch misspelled words. I have no doubt at all that the ability to spell is somehow genetically established. Don't you know at least one person who is very bright but can't spell above a fifth-grade level? Dr. Edward A. White put the problem in perspective when he observed that spelling is a social skill. In today's culture, misspelling words in public is a source of embarrassment because correctness is objective and unarguable, available to all in the nearest dictionary. Write "I recieved a letter from my freind" and your reader will likely think the less of you: You're not as well educated as he or she thought.

Until the invention of the printing press made written language available to large numbers of people, spelling had a strongly subjective component. Shakespeare spelled his own name several different ways. Maybe a few conscientious printers, dissatisfied with variety and wanting to do things the *right* way, got together with some like-minded schoolteachers and agreed that certain words should be spelled certain ways, and people who didn't follow their rules were deemed to be poorly educated. Ben Johnson and other lexicographers continued the process.

Today, flexibility has just about disappeared from spelling for those of us above the age of reason, although there are differences between American and British spellings of some English words: Judgments are made on this side of the Atlantic, for example, but judgements are reached in the United Kingdom. Usage is still subject to slow change: *Ain't* was an acceptable contraction of *am not* at the beginning of the nineteenth century. If, when asked to identify yourself, you answer, "It is I," you will be technically correct but people might think you odd. Correct usage, to the dismay of traditionalists, is largely a matter of what we become most used to hearing.

Meanwhile, in the real world of the classroom, we teachers know the pain of inadvertently publishing children's work that contains errors. We feel that it reflects on our ability as teachers. Though most parents can learn to accept invented spelling in the primary years, from second or third grade on they justifiably expect their children to appear well educated in print. But most important is the significance of publication to the children. It presents the greatest risk and the greatest glory to young writers and as such deserves their best work. To permit less cheapens the experience for everyone, so careful editing before publication is a requirement.

Donald Graves (1983) suggests one rare exception, however, which is the child who resists all entreaties and arguments for close editing and refuses to make the effort to polish the final draft. This child may need the reality check of publication and an audience's response to printed errors to compel his recognition of the need to edit. But when young writers and their teachers are genuinely involved in the exacting, rewarding process of getting ready to publish, such an exception will be very rare indeed.

Editing Conferences

After the children edited their poems to a fare-thee-well, they signed up for an editing conference with me. Doing this at the word processor was fast and virtually painless. Spelling errors could be corrected with just a few keystrokes, and punctuation options were easy to view and select. If your software includes a spelling checker, this is the time to teach your class to use it; but until word processors become smart enough to choose between *to* and *too* or *there* and *their*, you'll still have to do the final check.

Perhaps computers aren't readily accessible to you. You might want to use an acetate overlay in revision and editing conferences. With the clear sheet over the poem and erasable markers, you and the writer can make corrections and try out possible changes with minimal damage to the handwritten draft. When the editing process is finished and the changes are agreed on, the student can incorporate them into the final draft.

Edie Ziegler's students compose on paper rather than computers, and she tells them always to write on every other line. She photocopies first drafts when she wants a record of "the way it used to be" before revision. At publication time, all copies of a piece are stapled together with the most recent on top. With revision and editing completed, Edie asks the children whether they want to copy their pieces in their own handwriting or have them typed. Often their pride of ownership kicks in and they painstakingly produce handwritten versions to send to the copying machine.

Several options exist for typing the remaining poems to ready them for publication. Some kids have computers and printers at home and, on their own or with parents' help, can produce final copies of their work. Parents often volunteer as typists either at home or school. Classrooms with teacher aides have built-in help. The last resort is, as always, us, the teachers. Before my school acquired computers, I spent numerous prepublication hours at home with my little Apple //c typing and printing out final copies, sustained by the memory of precomputer days and nights when I spent even more hours struggling with an old typewriter and every kind of error-corrector on the market.

WRITING AS REFLECTION

Make a practice of asking your kids to reflect in writing on their composing processes. As well as producing a wonderful addition to a published collection, this teaches children to be reflective, a practice too often neglected in our time-driven classrooms. They will discover aspects of their writing that they had been unaware of, and you will receive indispensable insights into their processes that will guide your teaching and responses in the future.

Almost always my students' commentaries added information that expanded our understanding and appreciation. Often their topics came from memory, but this wasn't always apparent in the poems. Tomoki, whose "Fireworks" begins chapter 1, wrote, "I got my idea of my poem because I remembered when I saw fireworks in New York. It was stuck in my mind, so I wrote it in a poem, and it came out to be a good poem." Fred's poem came from a specific memory, too, although we couldn't tell that from reading it:

Stars

When I look up at the night sky I see
The stars just sitting there peacefully.
They shimmer like flashlights in the night sky.
The moon is the biggest star that I see at night.
But they all go away when the sun rises,
And I'll wait until tonight to sit and gaze
At the shimmering stars again. ❖

Fred Drescher
Grade 4

His description of how his poem came to be also let me know that he connected a valued memory with our poetry workshop in a special way. "I got my idea for my poem when my family went to Maine. My cousin and I were sent to get wood for the fireplace. We sat on the beach and looked up at the stars. We saw the little dipper, a red star, and a shooting star. Then I thought of a poem about stars. I saved the poem for a school day to write it in writing class." I treasure that image of a little boy saving his poem for writing class!

Sometimes the commentary was richer than the poem. Jamie's "Night" begins with these three lines:

Night is like dark shadows everywhere
When I look anywhere I see my shadow
Night is beautiful! ❖

But her explanation tells us much more: " 'Night is like dark shadows everywhere,' I got that because one time I was at the beach and some men stopped to get ice cream. They stood so close together their shadows were touching. They were dark shadows and in that spot it looked like night." That remembered image, which was only one-fourth of her whole description, overflowed with possibilities for another poem. We didn't explore them then—I'm not sure she was ready for them—but I strongly hope she rereads her words after a few years and engages that memory again in writing.

Because her explanation was published beside her poem and parents have a tendency to save such things, there is at least a possibility of this happening. Publication carries children's writing into a future that is as remote and of as little concern to them now as the polar regions. But if you have remnants of your childhood writing, or perhaps that of your children, you know how precious they are made by the passage of time. When you publish your students' work, you make tangible a treasure that would otherwise be lost.

ILLUSTRATING POEMS

When children illustrate their poems, they tell you in yet another way what their writing is about. Amy McClure in *Sunrises and Songs* describes at length ways to help children create visual images to accompany their verbal ones. The fifth- and sixth-graders that McClure writes of used a wide range of media, from paints to charcoal to collage, when they illustrated their poems for bulletin board displays or books.

Illustration even became a part of revision as it revealed more of the poem's meaning to the child. Sometimes the writer changed or added to the poem after illustrating it; at other times the picture itself was revised or a second one was drawn. Picture books, covers as well as contents, were a rich source of ideas. Peggy Harrison, one of the class's teachers, made available materials and techniques and encouraged children to experiment. Illustration conferences resembled writing conferences, dealing with visual images as well as words.

Many of us have talents that apply here. Whether it's calligraphy, quilting, water colors, or cake decoration, these skills can be adapted to help kids find ways to illustrate their poems that go beyond felt tip markers. Don't be afraid to experiment along with your students.

When I visited schools in England, I was struck by the beauty and carefully wrought appearance of the children's work on display. In spite of spartan budgets, a variety of carefully chosen, eye-pleasing materials combined with painstaking penmanship in a wonderful blend of aesthetics and neatness. The children found pride and satisfaction in their accomplishment.

I wonder if we sometimes underrate our students' capacity to produce beautiful pieces of work for public view. It's humanly natural to do what's expected and no more, especially when we're young. I used to think that models of outstanding work would overwhelm and frustrate children but now I believe that, combined with support and encouragement, models can show what wonderful things are possible. If we don't provide this for children, it's almost as if we're cheating them of the satisfaction of exemplary achievement.

A certain amount of artistic talent in the teacher helps a lot, of course, and I'm still searching for mine. Because our fourth-grade anthologies were aimed at mass publication, our illustrations were limited to line drawings, fairly easy even for me to deal with.

In our cover contest, we discovered that children with a home computer and graphics software enjoyed a great advantage. This led to wonderful discussions of the aesthetic differences between handmade and computer-generated art. Over time, different classes worked out various attempts at balance between the artist and machine. Sometimes we used one cover on half the copies and another on the rest; after all, paperback book publishers do the same thing. Occasionally we inserted cover designs inside the book where they seemed appropriate. What I first thought was a wrench in the works turned into a rich stimulus to problem solving and consideration of values—aesthetic, social, and personal.

PRODUCTION

The first time we assembled a poetry anthology, I put out three folders, one for copier-ready poems, one for pictures, and one for explanations. The time I spent sorting seventy-five or so pieces of paper into sets of three by the same child taught me to use a separate folder for each writer, separate from the everyday writing folders that all other writing went into. We folded sheets of large, cheap drawing paper in half for this temporary use.

Writing the introduction was a privilege I kept for myself, though you might want to have your kids compose one, either individually or collectively. Here is part of the introduction to one of our anthologies:

> Poetry holds a special appeal for fourth graders; it lets them escape from the restrictions of logic and reality and fly free with words, enjoying them for their sounds, images and associations.
>
> The poems in this book are the result of a writing process that took place over many weeks as the children heard, read and wrote poetry every day. Finally each child chose one poem to publish, revised it until it was the best it could be, and then described that process so that you, our reader, can have an insight into the young poet's mind. [I know, I said "poet."]

The first poetry book we ever published was on a ditto machine, and compared with that, any copier is a miracle worker to me. If, however, your school has a copying machine that also collates and staples, you are truly blessed. A machine that turns out spiral-bound books is even better. Lacking these conveniences, a classful of kids can assemble a book very effectively, as described in chapter 1. If that isn't feasible, invite a handful of parents in for a collating party after school. They'll enjoy having a sneak preview of the book as well as the chance to help you and their children. And don't forget the refreshments!

DIFFERENT WAYS TO PUBLISH

Lucy Calkins points out the need to help children find real-world audiences for their writing. There are many ways to do this in addition to producing a class anthology. Publication in its simplest form is reading your poem to another person. Poems can be shared in small or large groups, orally or on paper. They can be printed in newsletters from a classroom, a school, or a local organization. Posting poems on school bulletin boards is publishing, too, because they can be read by other people, that is, the public. We have to remember to provide time and opportunity for children to read these poems. In many schools "reading the walls" is a regular and cherished part of the language program.

Nancie Atwell says, "A sense of audience—the knowledge that someone will read what they have written—is crucial to young writers. Kids write better when they know that people they care about will read their texts" (1987, 265). Her book *In the Middle* has six pages listing materials for and methods of publication that she has used with her middle school classes, most of which can be used for poetry in the elementary grades. It also lists contests and print media that offer the possibility of printing children's work.

Many opportunities exist locally for children's poems to be published in newspapers and magazines. If you live in a community with a hometown newspaper, call the features editor and ask about the possibility of doing a story on your class's poetry that would include some of their poems. Make your proposal as unique and appealing as possible to enhance the possibility that a busy editor will consider it. Shopper newspapers, often distributed free locally, are likely to welcome your proposal.

Children's magazines that are published nationally can present an avenue for getting your children's poems in print. You probably have some in your classroom, or you can survey them in your school library. A list of such sources is available in Suzanne Barchers's *Creating and Managing the Literate Classroom*.

A favored form of publication in the early grades is the individual book; its size, shape, and construction can be as creative as its contents. As a first-grade teacher in New Hampshire, Mary Ellen Giacobbe invited parents to her classroom before the school year began to construct books with sturdy, beautifully decorated cardboard covers for individual children to write in. Her clear directions, complete with diagrams, are given in Donald Graves's *Writing: Teachers and Children at Work*.

A book can also be as simple as a few pages stapled together by the young writer. Be on the lookout for teacher workshops where you can learn to make little blank books in delightful shapes and sizes by folding and cutting. You or your children can produce these in minutes.

Children can also publish collections of favorite poems written by others. In *Sunrises and Songs*, Amy McClure tells of personal anthologies fifth- and sixth-graders made of poems by John Ciardi, Ted Hughes, Robert Frost, and Langston Hughes, among many others, which they illustrated and organized thematically around topics such as holidays, animals, or nature. Think of what's involved in making such a collection: Children read widely to find poems they like and share them with each other; they evaluate them according to their own developing criteria; and by copying, rereading, and repeating the ones they select, they make the poems their own.

RECORD KEEPING

A minor benefit of publishing children's poems is that it provides you with a record of their work. Writing kept in a folder or a notebook does the same thing but in much bulkier form. My classes published one major anthology at the end of our poetry workshop; I think now a better idea would have been to use more of the forms of publication mentioned previously at more frequent intervals. By publishing more often you can more easily maintain momentum and attention to quality. It energizes both you and your kids.

Naturally, you don't want to do it so often or in such a routine way that it loses its significance. As students carefully choose and polish poems for a wider audience over time, they are demonstrating their progress. If you keep a folder for each child and drop in a copy of each published poem, you'll have a collection that can serve as a supplement to or, if necessary, a substitute for the evaluation conference procedure described earlier.

I also used record-keeping procedures that are standard in the writing workshop, such as Nancie Atwell's "status of the class" list. Two or three times a week at the beginning of class I stood in the front of the room with a list of names and asked the children what they would be working on that day, then quickly recorded their responses. The kids got very good at this and the process took less than five minutes. Consecutive lists showed me which poems they were working on, how long it took to finish a poem, how often they revised or edited, and so on.

For a more evaluative form of record keeping I used a pack of 5-x-8-inch index cards, one per child, kept together by a ring through a hole punched in the upper right corner of each card. After each conference and before going on to the next child, I noted the date and anything that seemed significant enough to record. At one time I tried carrying around a notebook with a page for each child, but found it too slow and awkward to use. The cards were easier to carry and manipulate.

One of the best ways to keep a record of what's happening is the one I used least, to my regret. A teacher's log (or journal or notebook), kept over time, is an invaluable source of information. Much as I tried to organize entry writing into my school day, something always interfered or took precedence so that my entries were usually a month or so apart. Even at those intervals they were useful, telling me what I was worried or excited or curious about last month and giving me the chance to reflect on the effects of my teaching. But how much more useful they would have been if I had written in my log every week! I hope you're more efficient with this process; the benefits can be tremendous.

Don't overlook the possibility of publishing your own writing. Writing articles containing your children's poems for local newspapers is an excellent way to start. Next, you might describe for a more specific audience what happens in your classroom when children write poetry. School newsletters welcome such articles. Professional journals, for example, the National Council of Teachers of English's *Language Arts*, or commercially published magazines for teachers offer a publishing potential. Think of the times you've been so excited about what your kids have written that you just had to tell someone about it. Put that excitement into writing and you'll inform and inspire hundreds, perhaps thousands, of teachers instead of just two or three.

PARTY TIME!

Publication and celebration go hand in hand. Children's excitement and delight are measureless when they hold their books in their hands and read their friends' and their own poems in print. The obvious, natural thing to do is have a party. Our poetry publication party, described in chapter 1, featured a reading by every poet, an audience of parents and school staff, the ceremonial handing out and autographing of books, and lots of food and drink.

Parties can be classroom-size or schoolwide. Poetry Day in an elementary school might include readings, recitations, or dramatic presentations in the auditorium. Children can dress as characters from favorite poems. Large, illustrated charts of published or original works can hang on the walls. Again, local news coverage will generate public interest and support for your program and school.

Celebrations can also be districtwide. In New Jersey's Northern Valley Regional District, two children from each classroom in third through eighth grade are selected to attend the annual poetry festival. They read their poems to an audience of peers, parents, and teachers in the high school auditorium, are treated to lunch in the cafeteria, and take home a book of their poems.

The small and large ways to celebrate children's poetry are virtually limitless. Find and use as many as you can. Like anything else, however, celebration can be misused or overdone. It's important not to cheapen it by praising work that's mediocre. We don't expect children to perform as adult poets, but we do have to set and maintain standards of excellence that match their stage of development. Kids know when we accept less than their best and will adjust their efforts accordingly. To celebrate such poems subverts the whole process.

Poetry parties that are too frequent can become just another ho-hum event; this is antithetical to the whole idea of celebration as a way of marking something special. Our aim is to make poetry an integral part of the day in every classroom. Celebrations should be like fireworks, rare enough that they don't lose their ability to thrill us and frequent enough that we look forward eagerly to the colors and sounds of their wonders.

POLISH, PUBLISH, AND CHERISH

Publishing is a little like putting the star on top of the Christmas tree. First you have to go out and choose the tree; back home, you retrieve the ornaments from the dark corner you stashed them in last year. Next you sort them out, test the lights, and decide just where each bauble and garland should go. Then, when all is done to everyone's satisfaction, on goes the star: the cap, the culmination of all that work. Everyone stands back and sighs with happiness and appreciation.

When children publish poetry, theirs or another's, there's the same selecting, testing, changing around. Writers evaluate, revise, and reevaluate with their potential audience sitting on their shoulders, invisible but real. Publication provides the concrete evidence of all that work, whether a book or a single poem on a bulletin board, and it delights and gratifies us as does the star on the tree. A published poem defies time and enriches us all.

REFERENCES

All unreferenced quotes are from conversations with the author or observations of the author.

Atwell, Nancie. *In the Middle: Writing, Reading, and Learning with Adolescents.* Portsmouth, NH: Boynton/Cook, 1987.

Barchers, Suzanne I. *Creating and Managing the Literate Classroom.* Englewood, CO: Teacher Ideas Press, 1990.

Britton, James. "Shaping at the Point of Utterance." In Gordon M. Pradl (ed.), *Prospect and Retrospect.* Montclair, NJ: Boynton/Cook, 1982.

Calkins, Lucy. *The Art of Teaching Writing.* Portsmouth, NH: Heinemann Educational Books, 1986.

Della-Piana, Gabriel. "Research Strategies for the Study of Revision Processes in Writing Poetry." In Charles R. Cooper and Lee Odell eds. *(Research on Composing: Points of Departure).* Urbana, IL: National Council of Teachers of English, 1978.

Graves, Donald. *Writing: Teachers and Children at Work.* Portsmouth, NH: Heinemann Educational Books, 1983.

———. *Explore Poetry.* Portsmouth, NH: Heinemann Educational Books, 1992.

Heard, Georgia. *For the Good of the Earth and Sun.* Portsmouth, NH: Heinemann Educational Books, 1989.

Koch, Kenneth. *Rose, Where Did You Get That Red?* New York: Random House, 1973.

McClure, Amy. *Sunrises and Songs.* Portsmouth, NH: Heinemann Educational Books, 1990.

White, Edward A. Address given at William Paterson College, Wayne, NJ, October 23, 1986.

Worth, Valerie. *All the Small Poems.* New York: Farrar, Straus & Giroux, 1987.

Chapter 6

POETRY ACROSS THE CURRICULUM

Just as adult poetry encompasses all of human thought, feeling, and behavior, poems can illuminate every part of your curriculum. When children are familiar with the unique pleasures of reading and writing poetry, including it in math, science, social studies, and themes takes only a few minutes a day and opens up a dimension of understanding and appreciation that isn't found in nonfiction prose.

Do you remember the "Learning can be fun" slogans that were everywhere a few years ago? They made me uneasy with the unspoken assumption that learning *right now* isn't fun and that somehow it's the teacher's job to entertain students. Both those statements held a bit of truth, however, and I wondered about and wrestled with the fun aspect of teaching and learning for a long time. It turned into an internal discussion I carried on with myself, a sort of "on the one hand . . . on the other" kind of dialogue.

Left hand: "Learning *isn't* fun; it's hard work!"

Right hand: "But if it isn't enjoyable, it isn't going to work in the long run. If kids aren't engaged in learning because they want to be, the learning doesn't really stick."

Left: "Then maybe *fun* can mean enjoyment of a learning activity instead of just fun and games."

Right: "Hmm . . . and then the teacher could collaborate in the enjoyment instead of being the entertainer on stage before an ever more demanding audience. . . ."

POETRY: BOTH FUN AND FACTS

Poetry is a made-to-order way of adding enjoyment to instruction in every subject area. Simply because it's different, it immediately introduces variety. We all know that children soon become inured to the "same old stuff," and we constantly search for ways to bring freshness to instruction. Poems can do that for us.

Humor is the seasoning that immediately awakens kids' mental appetites; it gets their attention, that first prerequisite for learning. Poems with their wonderful wordplay bring smiles and chuckles and put us in a receptive mood. Audiences soon tire of repeated jokes and one-liners, but poems are made to be repeated. Ogden Nash's rhymes, for example, are easy to store in your memory until a fitting situation arises—snack time, perhaps, for this one:

Celery

Celery, raw,
Develops the jaw,
But celery, stewed,
Is more quietly chewed. ❖

A more subtle advantage in using poetry when you're teaching a particular subject is its ability to present information in a different medium and in a way that goes beyond newness and variety. Poetry speaks to emotions and an aesthetic sense that are distinct from the logical side of our brains, the part that school instruction usually addresses. The more aspects or styles of thinking that we can appeal to, the more effective the learning.

Poems for Science

Poetry and science may seem to be an odd couple, unsuited to each other; actually, they complement each other beautifully. Science helps children understand the natural world, and poetry is a perfect way to express the wonder it inspires in them.

Just Think

Just think of the clouds
Being made of water.
Just think of a little seed
Making a big tree.
Just think of tape

From *Verses from 1929 On* by Ogden Nash. Copyright © 1935, 1940, 1941 by Ogden Nash. First appeared in the *Saturday Evening Post*. By permission of Little, Brown and Company.

Holding things together.
Just think of a bridge
Holding heavy cars.
Just think of Earth
Being round without us falling off.
Just stop a minute and think
Of all the things
That amaze and surprise you.
Just Think! ❖

> *Susan Flehinger*
> *Grade 3*

One of our chief aims when we teach science is to help children become careful observers; this is a role scientists and poets share. When you take your class on a nature field trip, you'll want them to look closely and make notes and sketches of what they see. Back in the classroom, those observations—droplets of dew on a spiderweb, the pattern of markings on an insect's back, the silvery track of a snail across the sidewalk—can be transmuted into poems.

Spiderweb

Round and round
the spider forms the web.
It looks like
a lace curtain.
Hanging down
down
down
down
Spiderweb. ❖

> *Christine Lee*
> *Grade 2*

Read Valerie Worth's "Magnifying Glass" to your class the first day you give them those lenses to use in their observations. Her "Amoeba," which starts to move with a "slow shrug," will delight older students who have seen that bit of life move under a microscope.

Tell your kids about scientists who also were poets. William Carlos Williams, for example, practiced medicine in Rutherford, New Jersey, all his life. At the same time, he was creating the body of poetry he is remembered for today. These accomplishments were noted by another poet, Carl Sandburg, in "Good Babies Make Good Poems."

When you're explaining the importance of precision in science, you might say or read Ogden Nash's "The Purist" to your class.

> I give you now Professor Twist,
> A conscientious scientist.
> Trustees exclaimed, "He never bungles!"
> And sent him off to distant jungles.
> Camped on a tropic riverside,
> One day he missed his loving bride.
> She had, the guide informed him later,
> Been eaten by an alligator.
> Professor Twist could not but smile.
> "You mean," he said, "a crocodile." ❖

Poems for Social Studies

Poetry anthologies are the most convenient source of poems for specific subject areas such as social studies; they're often organized into topical sections, letting you find what you're looking for at a glance. Whenever you pick up an anthology in the library, it's a good idea to take a minute to photocopy the contents page, making sure to add the author, title, and library call number. You'll have not only a record of scores of poems and where to find them but a place to note poems you've used successfully in the past.

One very useful anthology, *America Forever New*, compiled by Sara and John E. Brewton, contains more than 200 poems about our country, most of them from the twentieth century. In addition to sections about historical figures (both real and mythical) and events and the mountains, rivers, and cities of the United States, there's also one about transportation and one that shows the diversity of Americans. This remarkable collection includes poems you're not likely to find in standard anthologies.

Geography and Maps

Almost any anthology of poems for children will provide at least a few about places, whether countries, cities, or geographical regions. In *Favorite Poems Old and New*, for example, a section called "From All the World to Me" provides

---

From *Verses from 1929 On* by Ogden Nash. Copyright © 1935, 1940, 1941 by Ogden Nash. By permission of Little, Brown and Company.

a wide selection of poems from other countries. You can use them to introduce lessons or accompany displays of research, but you can also use them more directly in learning activities.

For example, consider using poems to enliven your study of maps; they're much more fun than worksheets. Share "Anna Banana" by Jack Prelutsky with your kids and invite them to investigate the unusual travels of the title character, who "walked on her hands from Montana to Maine."

You might have the children find Montana and Maine on a map of the United States and estimate the distance between them or determine the actual mileage. Encourage them to make up poems of their own using state names and various means of transportation for traveling between them. Some will be silly, some serious, and that's fine.

"Anna Banana" is only one of the many short, funny poems with city and state names in them that you'll find in Jack Prelutsky's *Beneath a Blue Umbrella*, and you'll be able to think of map activities for all of them. For example, Bonnie "lost three silver beads by the bay" in Baltimore and found them the next summer in a seashell in South Carolina. Your kids can figure out the mileage covered by the beads, as with "Anna Banana," but they will also need to consider geographical features such as coastlines and waterways, and all in the delightful context of fantasy.

In *Favorite Poems Old and New*, you'll find "Stately Verse," a long poem full of wordplay on state names that will make younger children chuckle. Here are the first two stanzas:

> If Mary goes far out to sea,
>   By wayward breezes fanned,
> I'd like to know—can you tell me?—
>   Just where would Maryland?
>
> If Tenny went high up in air
>   And looked o'er land and lea,
> Looked here and there and everywhere,
>   Pray what would Tennessee? ❖

Eve Merriam's poem about a peripatetic caterpillar-turned-butterfly in *Blackberry Ink* has that insect flying to a widely separated set of cities and states including Walla Walla, North Dakota, and Rome.

Lots of possibilities suggest themselves here. You could begin by copying the poem on chart paper and leading everyone in chanting it. Either the whole class or smaller groups might locate the various places; the butterfly's trip can be plotted on a world map with yarn and map pins; cooperative groups might find a more direct route for the butterfly to follow. Older kids would enjoy finding the butterfly's total mileage.

Carl Sandburg's "Localities" speaks of several little-known places (Red Horse Gulch and Cripple Creek, for example) and will provide older children with challenging map puzzles. Finding out which states the towns are in is a good cooperative-learning group activity. The first stanza of his "Work Gangs" contains several place names that groups can locate on maps.

Your class can make a striking wall display of poems written in the shapes of states. After they make large outlines of the states they are studying, the children compose poems that include what they've learned and print them on the lines that form the states' shapes. This is a good activity for children to work on in pairs.

Cities

Cities, with their improbably tall buildings, crowded streets, and atmosphere of excitement, have inspired poets over the centuries. *Something New Begins* by Lilian Moore contains a group of poems called "I Thought I Heard the City"; some of the titles are "Pigeons," "The Bridge," and "Foghorns." "Construction" describes a scene, familiar to city children across the nation, in which machines have giant mouths and arms but a tiny man has the power to tell them where to build a skyscraper.

In X. J. Kennedy's *The Forgetful Wishing Well*, a section called "In the City" holds eight poems that deal with the reality of the city, from street fights to taxi meters. Langston Hughes's poems, discussed in chapter 2, evoke the New York City of an earlier time but still ring true. They'll be best appreciated by middle-grade and older students.

Several poems in *Flashlight and Other Poems* by Judith Thurman speak to the experience of city children. "Hydrant," "Oil Slick," and "Blizzard" create vivid word pictures of scenes specific to city life. Particularly sharp is the image in "Zebra," created with only thirteen words.

Carl Sandburg's poetry is full of city images, from Chicago as "Hog Butcher for the World" to Broadway as a "Tall-walled river of rush and play." The poems "Slants at Buffalo, New York" and "Joliet" create vivid pictures of those cities, and "Good Morning, America" begins with a section about the skyscrapers that "fasten their perpendicular alphabets far across the changing silver triangles of stars and streets."

Native Americans

If your social studies curriculum includes Native Americans, Emerson Blackhorse "Barney" Mitchell's "Talking to His Drum" evokes a powerful image from the Navajo tradition. It's from Terry Allen's *The Whispering Wind* and creates a vivid portrait of an old man whose drumming is heard only by the Great Spirit of the Universe. *The Wind Has Wings*, a collection of poems from Canada, includes three Eskimo chants, one of which gives this book its title. They speak eloquently of the hardship of life in the frozen North and the joy of seeing the sun return in summer.

History

Its title notwithstanding, Carl Sandburg's "Open Letter to the Poet Archibald MacLeish Who Has Forsaken His Massachusetts Farm to Make Propaganda for Freedom" is about Thomas Jefferson and Ben Franklin. Sandburg's conversational style and unrhymed lines make readers feel they're listening to him chat companionably about those two remarkable men.

While you're examining that time in our country's history, don't disregard as archaic "Paul Revere's Ride," Longfellow's grand old story poem, particularly in a new setting illustrated by Nancy Winslow. It's ideal for reading aloud to a group. "Barbara Frietchie," by John Greenleaf Whittier, is available in a similar format for you and your class to enjoy when you study the Civil War.

If your social studies curriculum includes Canada or the Yukon gold rush, you can look forward to sharing with your class Robert Service's "The Cremation of Sam McGee." With its wonderful rhythm and tall-tale quality, it's perfect for a dramatic oral rendition. Your kids will love the humor, exaggeration, and surprise ending, even after it's no longer a surprise. The beautifully illustrated edition listed at the end of this chapter includes brief notes about the time, place, and customs of the miners.

Poems for Math Class

We're all familiar with counting rhymes for the youngest children, from "One, two, buckle my shoe" to "One little, two little, three little Indians." Poems for older kids that deal with numbers in any way, including counting and measuring, belong in math class; keep a small collection of them in or near your math plans.

There will surely be days when Carl Sandburg's "Arithmetic" speaks to everyone's feelings with its line "Arithmetic is where numbers fly like pigeons in and out of your head." "Counting" by Karla Kuskin begins with "To count myself / Is quickly done" and ends with trying to count the stars.

Take a Number by Mary O'Neill puts into rhyme every mathematical concept you're likely to encounter in the elementary curriculum, and then some. She begins with the Pebbler, the genius of ancient times who discovered one-to-one matching, moves through numbers, sets, arithmetical processes, measurement, and ends up with space and time. There's something here for every age and area of study.

When it's time to practice adding a column of one-digit numerals, put a copy of Shel Silverstein's "Band-Aids" on the overhead projector and enjoy reading it with your kids. Then have them record the number of Band-Aids that the poem's narrator is wearing on various parts of his body and add them up (the total is a satisfyingly outrageous thirty-five). Then you can segue neatly into two-digit numerals by adding this to the thirty-five he still has in the box to find out how many he started with. Consider how much more appealing and effective this lesson is than the usual worksheet!

Another poem good for addition practice is "Dragonflyer" by J. Patrick Lewis, in which a dragonfly tries to count twenty water spiders, fifteen frogs, seven sunfish, and thirteen "honeybees and bumble." You also might use this poem to tie math into a study of insects or water creatures.

Silverstein's "Smart" is perfect for studying the values of coins. The narrator of this poem, his dad's "smartest son," manages, through a series of steps, to swap a dollar for five pennies because each transaction gave him one more coin than he had before. Your kids will delight in figuring out how much he lost in each trade and in feeling deliciously smarter than the "smartest son."

You can follow it up with "Coins" by Valerie Worth, a poem short enough for easy memorization and a good model to use if you're encouraging your kids to write math poems as well as read them. Unrhymed and only six brief lines long, it's about how coins feel. Lest this seem mathematically irrelevant, think about teaching our youngest learners to differentiate among coins. Too often, children are expected to learn this via pictures of coins, two-dimensional representations removed from reality. Worth's poem focuses attention on the weight and shape of coins in the hand.

Edward Lear's well-known limerick about the old man with a beard can inject a little fun into early addition work if you ask your kids to add up the number of birds that made nests in his beard ("Two Owls and a Hen, / Four Larks and a Wren . . .").

When it's time to memorize number facts, make up rhyming couplets to help your students master the hard ones; for example,

> I know it, don't rush me, just wait.
> Yes! Seventeen minus nine equals eight! ❖

or

> Don't be gloomy, don't be blue,
> Nine times eight is seventy-two! ❖

Encourage your kids to make up their own rhymes for the combinations they have trouble memorizing. Silly ones seem to work best: They're fun, they defuse tension, and they're easy to remember.

When my class and I studied a theme, I had trouble finding math activities that fit both the theme and the math curriculum. Often math was unconnected with what we worked on the rest of the day. Poems can make the connection and provide literature experience at the same time.

When you're studying birds, for example, you might make up a poem something like this:

Feeding the Birds

My back yard is the birds' cafeteria
Chock full of bugs and sprinkled with seeds,
But when winter covers the ground with snow,
We have to open up Birder King
The fast food feeder for hungry birds.
It's a little glass house that holds eighty-two kinds
Of crispy and crackly crunchable seeds.
On Opening Day (you might not believe this)
Sixty-six chickadees, twenty-two cardinals,
Seventy-nine sparrows and twelve bluejays
Ate forty-seven million two hundred thousand
Five hundred thirty-two little seeds!❖

The possibilities here are numerous! Your students can practice numeral writing, addition, and division to find out how many birds came and how many seeds each one ate (if they shared fairly). For an entertaining and valuable research activity, challenge a group to list all the different kinds of seeds they can find that those birds might eat. As they carry on their research, the rest of the class can keep a running tally of the difference between their total and eighty-two.

For younger children you could make up a poem with smaller numbers. Then you could use a one-to-one correspondence to find out how many seeds there were for each bird and go on to illustrate the concept of division as repeated subtraction.

Older kids who are struggling with the intricacies of word problems will benefit from inventing their own based on the poem. This will give them a chance to identify an unneeded number (you don't have to know how many kinds of seeds there were to find out how many birds came, for example) as well as missing information (what do you have to know before you can find out how many seeds were left?). When you're working with place value, everyone can have fun making up and reading very big numbers of seeds that were put in the bird feeder for Opening Day.

If it seems an extravagant use of time to have your whole class make up math poems, look for one or two who are adept and invite them to write and solve number problem poems for homework instead of doing the usual computation practice. Their work can form a math poem anthology as well as provide day-to-day connections between numbers, poetry, and themes.

Spelling and Other Lessons

Probably you've asked your students to use spelling words in sentences or to make up a story with them. Depending on your class's affinity for writing poems, you might have them weave some of their spelling words into verse. If that's too difficult, let them work in small groups or as a whole class to create a collaborative poem. Or perhaps you'll find a poet laureate of the spelling list in your class, as did Pat Nix, who teaches second grade in Florida. When she asked her students to write poems using spelling words, this is what Stephanie wrote (spelling words are underlined):

What Should I Wear!

Heavens, I don't know what to wear!
You're a friend, you care.
I don't know which and I don't know where,
Therefore I'll look so silly at the fair.
The whole world will be there!
I'll feel silly while they stare.
You've got a voice, tell me so I don't have to go bare!
And what can I do with my hair?
Mom, buy your daughter a dress to wear!
Were you or weren't you there?
Tell me, am I talking to the air?
Can you loosen my bow so I can do my hair?
My head's not attached, please don't stare!
       Now what do I WEAR!❖

Stephanie Johnson
Grade 2

Homophones always caused the most anguish in my kids at spelling time. This old anonymous poem (you'll find it in *Favorite Poems Old and New*) will at least inject some humor into the task of sorting out various spellings of a sound, and at best might inspire your kids to write some poems of their own using homophones.

The Flea and the Fly

A flea and a fly got caught in a flue.
  Said the fly, "Let us flee."
  Said the flea, "Let us fly."
So together they flew through a flaw in the flue.❖

For parts-of-speech lessons, look up Ruth Heller's series of lushly illustrated books in rhyme that tell all about nouns, verbs, adjectives, adverbs, and even collective nouns. *Merry-Go-Round: A Book About Nouns* deals thoroughly with the various and sometimes confusing ways of forming plurals. Read it to your class a little at a time as a means of easing their difficulties with that process. The illustrations, brilliant double-page spreads, are even more entertaining than the clever, informative verse.

POETRY AND THEMES

Teachers who use an integrated curriculum or teach from a whole language perspective often organize instruction around themes. Poetry illuminates the topics our classes study and gives us a way to integrate literature. You probably have your own collection of favorite poems that you add to all the time.

Consider networking with other similarly minded teachers to pool your poetry resources. It's hard to find time for a project like this during the school year, but a couple of summer weeks at a computer could yield a database of themes and their corresponding poems. You might even be able to get a local grant to support the organizing and maintaining of this resource.

Food

The appeal of food as a theme is obvious, and the increasing importance of nutrition to maintaining good health over a lifetime makes it a worthwhile one for kids of all ages. Rose H. Agree's *How to Eat a Poem and Other Morsels* is a collection of verses about food and eating whose authors range from Mother Goose to contemporary poets, from Edward Lear to Carson McCullers.

Poems about food are everywhere. "Turtle Soup" is presented in *Alice in Wonderland* as a song but is delightfully readable as a poem with its chorus of "Soup of the evening, beautiful Soup!" Shel Silverstein's lentil soup is flavored with a piece of sky in "Sky Seasoning." In fact, Silverstein's *Where the Sidewalk Ends* is full of zany poems about food. In "Spaghetti" that favorite food ends up all over the room; in "Sleeping Sardines" the writer goes back to eating beans after opening the can and waking the sardines; and "Hungry Mungry," "Melinda Mae," and "I Must Remember" are all about a subject dear to children's imaginations: totally outrageous overeating.

Eve Merriam's poems in *Blackberry Ink* are about pizza, pancakes, witches' pudding, "Gooseberry, / Juice berry, / Loose berry jam," and other unusual foods. Their rhyme, rhythm, and humor will appeal especially to primary children.

For seasoning your study of nutrition, try silly poems about food such as Karla Kuskin's "The Meal." It's about Timothy Tompkins's breakfast, which included turnips, ketchup, and a prune, among other unusual items. "Happy Birthday, Mother Dearest," from Prelutsky's *Something BIG Has Been Here*, tells what kind of breakfast the kids made for Mom on her birthday; a watermelon omelet is just part of it. In the same book you'll find "Grasshopper Gumbo," which lists the dishes on the school cafeteria lunch menu, including "elephant gelatin / frog fricassee." J. Patrick Lewis in "How to Trick a Chicken" uses wordplay to make us chuckle. Because a chicken would rather "lay in a coop / Than lie in the soup," the farmer must politely offer to help her "get dressed."

Like all of Valerie Worth's poems, her "Raw Carrots" shows us how to turn experience into sharp images with just a few words. "Pie" is another of her poems that belongs in a food theme. Karla Kuskin's poem about a strawberry (in *Dogs and Dragons, Trees and Dreams*), told in the first person, is a good model to use if you want your kids to write poems about what it would be like to be a food.

Kids love to write about food in all kinds of ways and, when their subject is a particularly delicious favorite, can wax rhapsodic.

Watermelon

As the silver
sharp blade of
the knife slices
through the hard
green skin,
the knife gets
to the center
and juice starts to pour out
from both sides
and your mouth
starts to water.

> When you're done
> slicing, your mouth
> is soothed from
> hunger. And when
> your teeth sink
> into the pinkish
> fruit, the juice
> runs down your
> cheek and you think
> you're in heaven.❖
>
> *David Posamentier*
> *Grade 4*

Do you organize a good-for-you food feast as part of a nutrition study? Before you let them consume the beautiful, fresh fruits and vegetables, have your kids select just one and examine it very closely. Take a minute or two for them to talk about the special qualities they notice about their fruit or vegetable. What does its color make them think of? How does it feel to their fingers? Is it smooth or crinkly? What does it smell like? Then ask them to write a poem about their observations.

You can rely on them to come up with fresh, unexpected images such as these lines from Ariel's poem about an apple:

The shine of an apple's skin
Is like a sparkling crystal cave. ❖

If you have time and the inclination, they might write sequels later about the experience of eating what they had just described poetically. Ariel added,

So tender, luscious,
Oh, so good! ❖

Short poems written by kids make an entertaining addition to a food exhibit or bulletin board display. Ogden Nash's "Celery," given earlier in this chapter, is a good model to start from, with its simple form of four lines in rhyming couplets. Encourage humor as well as the incorporation of nutritional data; humor helps us remember information.

Your class might enjoy collaborating to compose a saga about the horrible fate of a character who ate all the wrong foods. Or, conversely, they could write of the adventures of a superhero who saves people from being overweight and high cholesterol counts. Remind them that they don't have to be as clever as Ogden Nash or Shel Silverstein, and that it's all right if some lines rhyme and others don't, or even if none of them do.

Weather

Poetry is a natural exploring ground for contrasts and surprises, and weather is full of both. It's a part of everyday life, familiar and common, yet has the power to destroy humankind's work and change not only the appearance but the very surface of the earth.

Wind

When you study the wind, you can choose among works by Christina Rossetti ("Who Has Seen the Wind?"), Vachel Lindsay ("The Moon's the North Wind's Cooky"), William Carlos Williams ("The Term"), Arnold Adoff ("Late Past Bedtime"), and Jack Prelutsky ("I Do Not Mind You, Winter Wind"), all of which, and others, you can find in Caroline Bauer's anthology *Windy Day*.

Wind by Mary O'Neill is a book full of rhyming poems about not only wind of all kinds but clouds, fog, the atmosphere, and other weather elements. The four poems about winds from the north, south, east, and west are accompanied by informational subpoems titled "This is your way of knowing." Use this book as a resource in the middle grades and above.

"Where Would You Be?" by Karla Kuskin evokes the excitement of a windstorm and invites the reader to brave being "whipped by the whine of the gale's wild cry." "Days That the Wind Takes Over," also from *Dogs and*

Dragons, Trees and Dreams, doesn't rhyme and is full of striking images: "Blowing cats around corners / Blowing my hair out."

Lilian Moore's poems look simple and spare, yet they contain strong, original images. "Go Wind," "Wind Song," and "While You Were Chasing a Hat" portray, with satisfying rhyme and rhythm, the sounds and sensations the wind brings to a child. "Hurricane" offers excellent opportunities for a poetry-writing minilesson in the midst of your weather study.

After reading and rereading the poem (which should be in everyone's view) to appreciate its power, draw your class's attention to the strength of the verbs in the first two stanzas, in which the wind "poured" and "roared," "tugged and tore." Ask what they notice about these words; someone is sure to say that the first two rhyme and the second two begin with the same sound. Talk about the personification of the "stunned trees" and the warlike imagery of twigs and branches as barbed wire and swords.

You won't have to assign these poetic devices; indeed, requiring them of young writers might produce forced, artificial poems. But if you tell your kids that these are the things that poets do and they can, too, and then celebrate the examples you find in the poems your students go on to write, you and they will be delighted by their success.

The mysteriousness of wind, invisible yet capable of tearing roofs off buildings, welcome in the heat of summer but fearful in winter's blizzards, makes it an ideal topic to write poems about. Here is something that all children have experienced directly, no matter where they live. If your kids are used to writing poems, a brief discussion pointed at recalling their thoughts and feelings about wind, or, better still, a quick trip outdoors for firsthand experience will be enough to start them composing.

If writing poems is still fairly new to them, read a poem or two a day while they collect information and impressions about the topic. On a more exotic level, the words associated with winds—*monsoon, mistral, sirocco, typhoon*—fairly cry out to have poems written around them, after the research that will identify them. Whether as an introduction or a summing up, poetry writing will carry learning into a deeper level than prose can reach.

Rain and Fog, Thunder and Lightning

Langston Hughes's poem "April Rain Song" with its wonderful opening line "Let the rain kiss you" always began our weather units, and soon after it came Carl Sandburg's "Fog" on its "little cat feet." More good choices for this theme are Lilian Moore's "Fog Lifting" and "In the Fog."

I encouraged my kids to begin writing their own weather poems as soon as we began the theme. The power and originality of children's poetry on this subject is remarkable. Notice the extended metaphor in this poem by a fifth-grader.

Rain

Rain is not really rain,
But cloud babies
who gulp water every day
   and drizzle when they spill it,
and cloud children
who drain the tub
through a broken pipe
which sprinkles lightly on earth,
   and cloud mothers
     who drop snow eggs
which break into flurries,
   and of course cloud fathers
    who build splendid ice castles
which,
  when broken,
    drop as hail.
Rain is not really rain,
but a slice of a cloud generation. ❖

Genevieve O'Donnell
Grade 5

The drama and danger of electrical storms is especially vivid for children. Although it's more common for teachers to ask children to write poems about a topic after they've acquired information, in the case of thunder and lightning, consider beginning with poem writing. All children have had experience with this frightening face of nature, and writing about it will spark their readiness to study this weather phenomenon. Notice how these poems reverberate with the force and menace of storms:

Thunder

In the dark dark sky,
the thunder flashes
it roars it sparkles and screams

The clouds are black and brown,
sometimes the rain tumbles down with the thunder
the ground gets wet and makes it all splashy ❖

Yasu Takei
Grade 4

Rain

Hills, valleys
all crying
all weeping
scared from
the constant
bash of thunder
scarred from
the constant
flash of lightning....❖

> *Daniel Forst*
> *Grade 5*

The storm that inspired the next poem was so fierce that two years later Andrew's memory of it was still strong: "I got my idea from an experience I had two years ago during a vacation when there was a really bad storm," he wrote. He went on to explain more of his composing process. "When I finished my first draft I reread it about nine times. Then I figured it needed something and guessed an ending. So I wrote four more stanzas that led up to when the storm was over."

Storm Night

The world shudders
at night before
the fury of
an angry storm.

With shrieks and howls
it dives on the earth,
With lightning and thunder
like a sword and a shield.

The earth is silenced
before the crying wind
and cold, wet rain.

The evil clouds with
horrible thoughts
hide the sky inside
and don't want to let it out.

The wind groans
as if in pain.
And no soul
understands it.

And then something changes.
The thunder crack
and lightning flash
do not seem as fearsome.

The clouds' grip on
the earth weakens.
The young rays of
sunlight start to
shine.

The clouds disappear.
The lightning and thunder
die with a flash.
The sun claims the sky. ❖

> *Andrew Zampieri*
> *Grade 4*

For contrast, Ogden Nash's "A Watched Example Never Boils" pokes good-natured fun at the scariness of thunderstorms. Its first six stanzas are about how delightful it is to watch the storm rage: "Oh happy you and happy me! / Isn't the lightning darling?" but it ends with telling the child, when diving under the blankets, to "leave room for Father."

Rainbows

Rainbows

Rainbows are like
colors in stained glass.
Sprinkled colored sugar,
Light feather-soft colors. ❖

> *Stephanie Witko*
> *Grade 2*

When you need published poems about rainbows, look for "Sun on Rain" by Lilian Moore. Its words flow down the page like a brilliant silk scarf and beautifully embody the glory of a rainbow. Barbara Esbensen's "Four Poems for Roy G Biv" (that name is a mnemonic for the order of prismatic colors) are about rainbows made in other places than the sky and are ideal to use when you teach about prisms. Carl Sandburg's tiny poem "Bubbles" (see chapter 3) carries a message that could spark a lively discussion.

It also reminds us that rainbows can happen in places other than the poststorm sky, as in this poem:

Rainbow

Under a sparkling
waterfall,
a running pool of water
creates
a new and gentle rainbow
which slowly
rises out of the gleaming water
like a color-sprinkled arc
with colors as
beautiful as
glistening crystals
sparkling in the
pinkish light of
dawn. ❖

Scott Rosenthal
Grade 4

Snow and Ice

We grown-ups, at least most of us, have lost the child's delight in the magic and mystery of snow. We see it as an impediment to traffic and something that must be plowed and shoveled away. Children see it as a collection of strange and beautiful properties to observe, investigate, and exploit.

Snow and its cousins, frost and ice, need to be acknowledged and celebrated when they appear, and poetry is a wonderful way to do that. If you choose to study them as part of a weather theme, you'll probably do it in the dead of winter in the hope that nature will cooperate with your plans. Some of us live in parts of the country that don't see snow and need poems to bring the experience into our children's imaginations.

Two poems in e. e. cummings's *Hist Whist and Other Poems for Children* capture a child's wonder and excitement in unusual but entirely effective ways. "Who(is?are)who" recreates the experience of a child and father who watch from indoors " . . . snowflakes / (falling & falling & falling)." The poem "blossoming are people" with its line "all the earth has turned to sky" joins reader and swirling snow in a dance of delight.

On cold mornings when your classroom's windows are laced with the extravagant patterns of frost, begin the day with Valerie Worth's poem by that name, in which she writes of "crystal forests." Her "Snow" with its "wide drifts / And heavy deeps" is good for reading after a major storm (or the imagining of one).

Robert Frost's "A Hillside Thaw" in *You Come Too* is good to read when the earth begins to warm, as is "Wet" by Lilian Moore. This poem vividly shows the water and mud that follows the spring thaw, ending with the brook "rushing / like a puppy loosed from its leash."

Children, of course, love to write their own poems about snow and ice. If you've been showering your class with poetry, it's unlikely that anyone will write something like "Snow is white, / Snow is cold, / I like snow." Should this happen, however, try to put the writer in touch with experience, whether of present snow, a memory of past snow, or other children's poems about it.

Snow

A white blurry sandstorm fills the air
It looks like white dirt on a lady's white dress
Or tiny white gulls landing on the ocean.
Blinding my eyes and heavying my feet
Cold as ice but soft as cotton that's what I think.
There are tiny little snowmen rapping on the window
Making it all snowy
Get out the hot chocolate!
Make the fire ablaze!
Let's talk by the window
Or sit there and gaze at the snow.
After it snows there are gigantic
Thick icicles that enclose and trap me in my house. ❖

Amy Bluestein
Grade 4

Snow

The snow falls from the sky.
It gently touches the grass.
Soon the grass is white.
Then it goes on some trees.
A branch breaks.
The branch falls and makes a hole.
You can see grass. ❖

Thomas Jarosky
Grade 2

These lines from Ben's poem "Ice" create a sense of gloom that is fitting for the darkness of winter:

> It sparkles in the sun
> And gets dimmer in the evening
> Ice, water that froze to death
> Because it was too cold❖
>
> *Ben Goodwin*
> *Grade 4*

Space and Time

Even young children can think and wonder about large subjects like these. Poetry is the ideal vehicle for expressing the sense of mystery we feel when contemplating the cosmos or the passage of time.

Space

When your theme is the universe, look in the library for *Space Songs* by Myra Cohn Livingston. Here are poems about virtually every aspect of the subject you and your class can think of, from the Milky Way to artificial satellites. The poems combine solid information with striking imagery, and the shape of the poems on their pages is varied and unusual, sometimes visually suggesting their subjects. Set on a black background and surrounded by vivid, dramatic illustrations, they're ideal for reading aloud to a group at the beginning of a science class.

Valerie Worth's "Stars" blends what we know scientifically, that stars are "Enormous suns," with the way stars look from here, like "Cold crystal / Sparks." Like all her small poems, it's a good size for writing on chart paper to display and share. When you study meteors, read Sara Teasdale's "The Falling Star" with its star that slid "down the sky, / Blinding the north as it went by."

Children squeeze space into a human dimension when they personalize it in their poems.

> A star is a fantastic flame.
> The night I look up,
> it winks an eye,
> and waves a hand.❖
>
> *Kyle Cummings*
> *Grade 2*

Little Star

Little star
who loves
to play
slides down
the crescent
moon then
dances around
rings of
Saturn then
floats in
the sky
twinkling
its bright
silver
color on
and off
waiting for
the sun to
come up so
it can sleep ❖

Carlos Molina
Grade 4

Alan set out to encompass the vastness of space but found himself thinking in human terms at the end.

Space

In space the world
is free.
The stars flashing
from lightyears away,
All of the planets
shining so bright that
your eyes get watery.
The beaming sun,
the bright moon,
it all makes your
eyes twinkle,
the comets diving
down into space
and the earth revolving
around and around
the sun.
The Milky Way,
the black holes,
they all stand out
And up above the
earth the Big Dipper
looks out for its little
brother
The Little Dipper. ❖

Alan Stegmayer
Grade 4

Clocks and Calendars

Time—the passing days, months, and seasons—is a topic you can use for a two-week theme or an ongoing part of other units throughout the year. Poems about the seasons and their accompanying holidays are numerous, and you probably have your own collection already. I hope your library has *Moments*, Lee Bennett Hopkins's anthology of poems about the seasons. It's not a thick book, but its poems are aptly chosen and varied in style and mood. This is a collection you might want to have on your desk year-round.

A Child's Calendar by John Updike contains a poem for each month of the year, describing peaceful scenes of small-town America in the mid-twentieth century. The poems consist of four to six stanzas of four lines each with a regular rhyme scheme that is used throughout the collection, creating an atmosphere of calm and order.

Marilyn Singer's *Turtle in July* is a wonderful series of animal poems in free verse that follows the months of the year and thereby the seasons. The poems inform with accurate information and poetically evoke the nature of the animals and their lives. For example, the rhythm of "Canada Goose" suggests the steady beat of geese's wings as they fly south. "Cow" tells in the voice of its subject, slow and ruminative, why she approves of June.

"Sniffing," in Aileen Fisher's *Feathered Ones and Furry*, is a good poem for primary children. It begins with the poet's beagle sniffing the ground, so it would be easy for you not to recognize that it's a poem to greet spring; but that's just what the poet sniffs in the last stanza.

Callooh! Callay! edited by Myra Cohn Livingston is a refreshingly original collection of contemporary poems about holidays by poets as diverse as Sandburg, Shakespeare, and Su Tung-P'o (who lived and wrote in eleventh-century China). Maurice Sendak's *Chicken Soup with Rice*, with a stanza for each month, can be used in a study of the calendar or throughout the year. Its whimsy appeals to a wide age range.

Poems about time itself aren't as easy to find. "Telling Time" by Lilian Moore blends clock sounds and the shadow on a sundial in a just-right evocation of time's passage. Barbara Esbensen's "Time" looks at the nature of time before clocks were invented. "The Gong of Time" by Carl Sandburg with its line "Hush yourself, noisy little man" invites thoughtful responses.

Here's a child's reflection on time-keeping:

Clock

The clock is always working.
The clock is telling time.
The clock is always moving,
It's the clock's life. ❖

Akiko Tsuda
Grade 4

The following poem expresses a child's view of the excruciating slowness of time's passage:

Time

Time   passing
s   l   o   w   l   y
like   molasses   slipping
       out
of   a   jar
silently   d r i b b l i n g
       by
Ticking
of a clock's hands
Telling us
Time has passed ❖

Caitlin Clark
Grade 4

The Animal Kingdom

We teachers know that a dependably fascinating subject for kids is the natural world's inhabitants, whether they run or fly, slither or swim. You and your class can choose to study one animal, such as the horse, or a family of animals, such as cats. Or a topic such as birds could become a subtheme in a larger unit such as the forest or the ocean. Whatever creature captures the interest and imaginations of your students, you'll find lots of related poems to read to them, and with help and encouragement, they'll find themselves writing their own.

Valerie Worth's *All the Small Poems* is a treasure house of poems that catch an animal in a small space of time and create its distinct appearance and movement. Her subjects are the horse, kitten and cat, dog, pig, cow, mouse, skunk, giraffe, lion, and anteater. "Tiger," about a caged wild creature, is especially effective.

Feathered Ones and Furry by Aileen Fisher is a collection of rhyming poems that deal with a variety of animals, including the badger and weasel as well as the more expected rabbits, cats, and horses. Don't miss "Squirrel" by Lilian Moore. It captures perfectly the frenzied activity of this common animal as he stores food in the fall. Jack Prelutsky's "Squirrels," from *Something BIG Has Been Here*, compares their tails to question marks.

Prelutsky's humorous poems in *Zoo Doings* are especially good for reading aloud; in "The Beaver" Prelutsky manages, while being entertaining, to include information about that animal. "A Hippopotamusn't," from the book of the same name by J. Patrick Lewis, also should be read aloud to your class if the river horse, or hippo, turns up in your study of wild animals. Flossing his hippopotamolars is just one of the unusual actions a hippopotamusn't forget to do.

The Enduring Beast, edited and illustrated by Miriam Beerman, is an anthology of poems for older children by poets who write for adults: Yvor Winters, Marianne Moore, and Pablo Neruda, for example. The variety of content and style provides much material for discussion and emulation. Jeanne Steig's poems in *Consider the Lemming* will appeal to older kids with their sophisticated humor and clever rhymes, often in limerick form. Her subjects are uncommon (manticore and sloth) as well as common (cat and dog) animals.

Prayers from the Ark by Carmen Bernos de Gasztold is a unique series of poems. Each one is written in the first person as a prayer from an animal and, even in translation, speaks in just the right voice. The dog is unquestioningly eager to please, the mountain goat quick and impatient. These poems readily suggest themselves as models for your students to use as starting points.

Perhaps you've read "The Runaway" by Robert Frost (1959), an account of finding a little Morgan colt left out in his mountain pasture as snow begins to fall and frightens him. Fourth-graders will appreciate the images of the colt and feel sympathy for his plight, although most of them will probably need a little background information about horses first. Older children can discuss the irregular rhyme pattern and compare the colt's predicament with that of young humans. For an interesting oral presentation, have one voice read the narration and another, the lines in quotation marks.

Pets

Even if you don't do a whole unit about pets, they're bound to call for attention in your classroom at one time or another. Poems about them are easy to locate in anthologies (for example, *Favorite Poems Old and New* has an entire section called "Animal Pets and Otherwise") and can be found in other poetry books as well. When you're talking about unusual pets, read "Lizard Longing," from Tony Johnston's *I'm Gonna Tell Mama I Want an Iguana*, to your class. The first two lines of this funny poem give the book its title.

Poems often suggest more possibilities for supplementary lessons than you'll have the time or inclination to explore. From this one, for example, you could branch out into a study of lizards, which might lead to reptiles or dinosaurs; or to fish, particularly dangerous ones; or to the meaning of the words *flora* and *fauna*.

Karla Kuskin's "I Have a Lion" in *Dogs and Dragons, Trees and Dreams* addresses the problem of losing pets with humor: A cat, a dog, and a bird all went away and didn't return, but the poet has a lion who will never leave because "He's stuffed."

Dogs

Most pets you'll find in poetry or your students' homes will be more common, such as dogs and puppies. *Feathered Ones and Furry* contains three puppy poems written from a child's point of view. "New Puppy" is sure to strike a chord with any youngster who has spent the day in school while "a bundle of wiggles" waited at home. At the other end of the dog's age range is "Old-Timer" (in *The Forgetful Wishing Well* by X. J. Kennedy), which tells about a "slow old hound" who won't move for cats or bark at strangers but is still loved.

E. B. White's "Fashions in Dogs" is a long, funny collection of vignettes about various breeds of dogs that older kids will enjoy. It includes this couplet: "My Christmas will be a whole lot wetter and merrier / If somebody sends me a six-weeks-old Boston terrier." Judith Viorst, in *If I Were in Charge of the World and Other Worries*, writes from the point of view of a child who wants a dog and knows how to get one. Her poem "Mother Doesn't Want a Dog" ends with " . . . more than a dog, I think / She will not want this snake."

Read poems like these to your class and discuss them briefly, and many of your kids will be eager to write poems of their own. Help them focus on the sensory impressions they get from their pets and the experiences that stick in their memories. If the poem you read to them rhymes, you might need to remind them that theirs don't have to. Megan found rhymes to begin and end her poem, but she wasn't confined by trying to continue the pattern.

My Old Dog

My old dog is my best friend
My old dog and I, our friendship will never end
My old dog is cute enough to charm Adolf Hitler
My old dog shakes hands like a lady
My old dog eats my liver and my brussels sprouts
My old dog eats anything on the floor
My old dog is playful and kind (except when she had the fleas)
My old dog swims in the pool with me
My old dog never lets me down
Me and my old dog will always be around. ❖

Megan Kelly
Grade 4

Cats

I know of at least two wonderful anthologies of cat poems. Nancy Larrick's collection of forty-three poems about cats of all kinds is called *Cats Are Cats*. The poems are of all kinds, too: short and long, rhymed and unrhymed, old and new. Myra Cohn Livingston's *Cat Poems* includes, among many other irresistible poems, "Catalog" by Rosalie Moore, which ends with this line: "Cats sleep fat and walk thin." If you have a group of kids who choose to study cats when you do a pet theme, find either or both of these books for them; they will be enchanted.

For a unit of study that extends to the wild members of the cat family, look for J. Patrick Lewis's "Tom Tigercat" in *A Hippopotamusn't*. This poem needs to be seen as well as heard because of its wordplay: Tom Tigercat "wouldn't think of lion, / no, he doesn't cheetah bit."

Karla Kuskin adds comments and suggestions for young writers to her poems in *Dogs and Dragons, Trees and Dreams*. Accompanying "This Cat," who "comes and goes / On invisible toes," is advice to use "a few special details arranged with care" to describe a pet rather than try to tell everything about it. In "Take a Word Like Cat," she invites children to "Draw with words. / Balance them like blocks." At the end, they'll find that they've built a "home / . . . of words around your word. / It is a poem."

Another good poem to use as a model is "My Cat" by Barbara Esbensen in *Who Shrank My Grandmother's House?* It's unrhymed and creates a picture of a sleeping cat who "has left / His motor running" that any owner of a feline will recognize.

T. S. Eliot's *Old Possum's Book of Practical Cats*, on which the musical "Cats" was loosely based, is a collection of longish poems said to have been inspired by Eliot's friends. With some explanation from you of the Britishisms (a larder shelf, the Flying Squad), middle-graders will enjoy "Macavity: The Mystery Cat" with its refrain, "*Macavity's not there!*" and "Mungojerrie and Rumpelteazer," who "had really a little more reputation than a couple of cats can very well bear." With a little practice, you'll have a wonderful time reading your favorites from this collection to your class; the rhythm of the lines is irresistible.

The death of a pet can be the most painful experience in a child's young life. Writing poems lets children express their feelings in a uniquely fitting way. The process of working the experience into poetic form and the resulting product, the poem that commemorates the event, help children understand and come to terms with this irrevocable loss.

My Kitten

I love my kitten
    But a week ago
        or two
We buried him
    in a tube
When I buried him
    Tears fell from
        my eyes
I tried to back up
    the tears
But all I could do
    was cry
I loved my kitten ❖

Krystal Darmanie
Grade 3

The emotion contained in those simple lines continues to move me, even after repeated readings. Let's look more objectively for a moment at two small aspects of the poem that help to create its impact. I wrote earlier of children's delight in being allowed to ignore punctuation when they write poetry. In this poem, the absence of punctuation contributes to the sound and sense of grief. Think of people's voices when they're very sad: Their sentences seem to trail off or hang incomplete in the air rather than end decisively with the lowering of pitch that stands for a period. Whether Krystal did this consciously, the fact that her teacher didn't insist on punctuation allowed its absence to extend the sense of the poem.

Notice the small but telling shift in verb tense in the first and last lines. Krystal begins with "I love my kitten" but ends with "I loved my kitten." Again, we can't know what her intention was, but I don't think it matters. Whether she meant us to or not, we feel that the small journey of this poem has brought her to an acceptance of the death of her pet.

Other Pets

Writing poems about their pets enables children to make tangible their strong feelings of affection through the simplicity of their description. Children, used to being small persons who are cared for by larger ones, find deep satisfaction in caring for small animals—hamsters, for example.

My Hamster

My hamster sleeps all day,
and is up all in the night.
In the night she likes to
play on her wheel, round and
round it goes, spinning very fast,
as if it was going as fast
as lightning. When I feed my
hamster she stuffs her cheeks
very wide, like a balloon being
filled with air.
Then she goes up to her little
bed and eats and drinks a lot. ❖

Douglas Zimmerman
Grade 4

Birds

I can't think of any other creature that has inspired as much poetry as birds have. The beauty of their song and plumage, the freedom of their flight, and the mystery of their instinct require more than prose alone can offer. From the Arctic tern to the penguins of the Antarctic, birds are everywhere and of an amazing variety; too great, in fact, to be confined in one theme. Your biggest problem will be deciding which ones to leave out.

If you narrow your theme to common woodland birds, you'll want to include hummingbirds. X. J. Kennedy's poem by that name in *The Forgetful Wishing Well* tells of a scientist who decided it was impossible for the hummingbird to fly on such small wings, but the hummingbird hadn't heard that, so it kept on flying. Eve Merriam in *Out Loud* calls her ruby-throated hummingbird a "scarlet needle-dart / skimming the air" in a poem with an unusual format. Jack Prelutsky's "The Hummingbird" sums this tiny creature up in just two humorous lines.

Several of Valerie Worth's small poems draw perfect pictures of familiar birds, from a robin's "ruddy / Rust" to the flamingo's "One / Pink / Leg." She defends the commonness of sparrows and evokes the atmosphere of a pigeon shed with simple but precisely chosen words. For a selection of poems about birds by a variety of writers, look for the section in *Favorite Poems Old and New* called "Bird-watcher."

Carl Sandburg wrote often about birds. In "Prairie" are nine lines about eggs in a mockingbird's nest, ending with this marvelous image: "Look at songs / Hidden in eggs." If I had to limit myself to just a few poems to include in a poetry unit, Sandburg's "Bluebird, What Do You Feed On?" would surely be one of them. In it the poet wonders how a bird whose "feathers have captured a piece of smooth sky" can change worms, bugs, and seeds into "lake-morning blue."

Crows are so big and loud that they're hard to miss in the landscape. As subjects for poems they offer contrast to the lyrical descriptions of more delicate birds. Kennedy's "Ten Billion Crows" is written from the point of view of a farmer's son who, after crows shamelessly devoured all the corn, says, "I hope their bellies ache for weeks. / I hope they crash and break their beaks." David McCord's "Crows" takes a more positive view of this bird.

Robert Frost in "The Last Word of a Bluebird" chooses a crow to be the narrator of this message for a little girl at the beginning of winter. Kids in primary grades will love to hear this read to them as part of their bird study.

Not all poets agree that crows say "caw." Valerie Worth hears them call "Thaw, thaw, thaw!" as they fly over the meadow at the end of winter. E. B. White in "The Answer Is 'No'" claims their consistently negative calls sound like "no" or "naw." His "A Listener's Guide to the Birds" supplies verbal representations of a variety of birdcalls with his customary humor and off-beat rhyme. After explaining that a male chickadee "Whistles, 'Fee-bee,' to express desire," he observes, "Our gay deceiver may fancy-free be / But he never does fool a female phoebe."

"Woodpecker" by Lilian Moore is a short, very effective poem based on sound information about what lies behind the noise that bird makes. You can achieve a three-way integration of subjects with Tony Johnston's "Aerial Sheet Music": birds, poetry, and music.

Every study of birds should include Alfred Tennyson's "The Eagle," (found in Jack Prelutsky's *The Random House Book of Poetry for Children*). Even young kids will respond to the majesty of these words, helped by a little interpretation from you.

He clasps the crag with crooked hands;
Close to the sun in lonely lands,
Ringed with the azure world, he stands.

The wrinkled sea beneath him crawls;
He watches from his mountain walls,
And like a thunderbolt he falls. ❖

Lead your class to speculate about what kind of countryside Tennyson's eagle might have lived in (don't forget to point out that the poet was British) and go on from there to find out through research the different eagle species and their habitats, including that of our national bird, the American bald eagle.

I Am Phoenix, the book of poems for two voices discussed in chapter 4, is all about birds. The poems combine beauty with accurate information about their topics. "Owls" and "Sparrows" name many members of those two bird families, and "Morning" counts a wide variety of birds from the awakening of one waxwing to 100 chickadees. The title poem recounts the legend of the mythical phoenix, which burned but rose from its ashes to live again. Reading these poems aloud to catch their magic is truly worth the effort.

J. Patrick Lewis, in *A Hippopotamusn't*, has written poems full of wordplay about owls, pelicans, woodpeckers, hummingbirds, peacocks, vultures, grackles, and robins, as well as a delightful shape poem that looks like a flamingo. His "Penguins" is a good model to use when your kids are ready to write their own bird poems. It doesn't rhyme, it includes information as well as imagery, and it sounds almost conversational.

Probably one of your kids (or you) will bring an abandoned bird's nest to the classroom. Show them "Nest" by Arnold Adoff from his book *Birds* and compare your nest with the "bowl of grass and twigs" he writes about. Discuss with them the poem's unusual format and encourage them to write their own nest poems.

Robert Frost's poetry often has a narrative content. "The Exposed Nest" tells a story of "a nest full of young birds on the ground" that a child tried to safely cover up again when it was exposed by farm machinery. Read this and others of his poems about birds ("A Nature Note," "A Minor Bird," "Come In") to your class so that they become familiar with this American poet's work early. It will help them when they meet it again in later grades.

Insects (and Spiders and Worms, Too)

Insects and spiders don't deserve the bad reputation they have with some of us. You might begin to address that situation with Karla Kuskin's "Bugs," to which the poet gives hugs. Ants are special favorites for study because of their intricate social structure and general availability. As a variation on the practice of beginning research by formulating questions about what the children want to know, have your class write question poems.

Ants

How big is an ant's brain?
Do ants fight together?
How strong are ants?
How much smaller are ants
 than me?
Do ants have teeth? ❖

> Daniel La Barbera
> Grade 2

After a day or two of collecting information about ants, read Ogden Nash's "The Ant" to your class.

The ant has made himself illustrious
Through constant industry industrious.
So what?

Would you be calm and placid
If you were full of formic acid? ❖

Grasshoppers are easy to find in the fall when school begins, whether in open fields or weedy city lots. "Boing!" from *I'm Gonna Tell Mama I Want an Iguana* is a natural choice to put on chart paper so your kids can read it in unison. It's also a good lead-in to learning about the sounds insects make, both real and imaginary.

Spiders are easy to find too but are likely to inspire sounds of disgust among your students and attempts at extermination. This can lead to research that will disclose the rarity and reclusiveness of poisonous spiders, the valuable work arachnids do, and the wonders of their web-spinning.

Two poems that connect the spiderweb with its natural purpose and exhibit a sly wit that kids will enjoy are "The Spider" by Jack Prelutsky (in *Something BIG Has Been Here*) and "Spider" by Lilian Moore. Begin a literature lesson for older children with Carl Sandburg's "Webs," which weaves a connection between spiders' work and that of people.

Also by Moore is "Move Over," a poem about a "Big / burly / bumblebee." Prelutsky's "Bees" in *Zoo Doings* is short and funny, fine for your class to memorize and chant together. "Bee Song" by Sandburg also asks to be said aloud. A unison reading of this short poem with three or four voices producing a background buzz at different pitches would be delightful. While you're exploring Sandburg's poems, look for "Cricket March" and "Bug Spots," about a bug "With a domino design over his wings."

From *Verses from 1929 On* by Ogden Nash. Copyright © 1935, 1940, 1941 by Ogden Nash. First appeared in the *Saturday Evening Post*. By permission of Little, Brown and Company.

Joyful Noise, mentioned in chapter 4, is a collection of poems for two voices entirely about insects. All children, but especially those in the primary grades, will love hearing you and a partner read "Grasshoppers," a poem that seems to bound off the page with its subjects. The humor in "Water Striders" will probably be better appreciated by older listeners. In that poem, two water walkers explain matter-of-factly how to practice their apparently miraculous skill but end by stating that their students usually sink before they can finish instructing them.

"Mayflies," also written in the first person, shapes information about the one-day life cycle of that insect in a way that evokes wonder and sympathy and could lead to interesting discussions about time, especially among older kids. "Honeybees" transmits information but would probably be most appreciated by your kids after they've learned a bit about those busy insects. One of the speakers is a worker ("Being a bee . . . is a pain.") and the other is a queen ("Being a bee . . . is a joy."). With a little practice, two groups of two or three kids (low voices for the worker, high ones for the queen) could regale an audience by performing this poem.

You'll have a hard time choosing among the poems in this Newbery Medal-winning book; if you can find time, you'll probably want to use every one that suits your grade level. Kids will love to chant the rhythmic "Water Boatmen" with its repeated call of "Stroke!" "The Digger Wasp" begins, "I will never / see my children," blending poignancy with fact. The last poem in *Joyful Noise*, "Chrysalis Diary," must not be missed if you plan to hatch butterflies in your classroom. Its first-person narrative begins on November 13 and ends on March 28 as the emerging butterfly recalls that "last night / I dreamt of flying."

Lilian Moore's "Message from a Caterpillar" tells the same story but in just sixteen very short lines. Another brief poem, Valerie Worth's "Caterpillar," brings to life the rippling movement of a caterpillar's "caravan / Of bristles." Also in Worth's *All the Small Poems* is "Mosquito," which shows us unusual aspects of that unpopular insect: her see-through wings and the way she looks at the swatter.

In a poem about another unwelcome flyer, Worth writes "Flies wear / Their bones / On the outside." These small, mostly unrhymed poems are just right for displaying on chart paper to accompany research. Read them to kids in the middle grades who are studying actual specimens of insects, and the poems they write from their observations will astound you.

Worth's "Mantis" begins seriously and then dances into a pair of puns that question the insect's piety. "Mrs. Praying Mantis" by J. Patrick Lewis manages to sound almost light hearted while describing that insect's eating habits, which include devouring her mate.

Frost's "Fireflies in the Garden" is short (just six lines) compared with most of his poems and is ideal for integrating literature into a theme in the middle grades and above. Read it to your class, then hand out copies and encourage your kids to talk about it. Remember that the richest appreciation of a poem comes from one's own responses to it rather than the deduction of its one true meaning. This work is full of words and phrases that kids will love to play with conversationally.

Some poems are rooted in a small fact and move from there to humor, always a welcome ingredient of the school day. "A Bug Sat in a Silver Flower" by Karla Kuskin (in *Dogs and Dragons, Trees and Dreams*) speaks of the injustice of little bugs being eaten by big bugs and ends with this wonderfully ridiculous line: "He also ate his underwear."

Dinosaurs

If you teach in the primary grades, you know that dinosaurs are an undying source of interest for your kids. A wonderful way to begin a theme on these extinct creatures is to read to them "Fossils" by Lilian Moore. One of the books you can find this poem in is Lee Bennett Hopkins's *Dinosaurs*, a collection of eighteen poems that range from humorous to informational to philosophical. *Tyrannosaurus Was a Beast* by Jack Prelutsky has poems about fourteen different dinosaurs that shine with his usual humor but also contain factual information and a challenging vocabulary. The highly motivational setting will inspire kids to relish the sight, sound, and meaning of words such as *prodigious*, *stupendous*, and *titanic*. The table of contents includes the time period, geographical habitat, and size of each dinosaur; at the end of the book is a simple timeline.

Mountains and Volcanoes

"March of the Hungry Mountains" by Carl Sandburg can be presented in part or as a whole to young children or middle-schoolers. Myra Cohn Livingston's *Earth Songs* is a collection of poems about mountains and other geologic phenomena. This poet's "Mount St. Helens" in *There Was a Place and Other Poems* provides a fine model for writing poems in this area of study. It's unrhymed and describes a clear, simple image.

Sometimes studying mountains gives rise to an interest in rocks and minerals. Geodes, those hollow balls of rock that contain crystal treasures, are especially fascinating to kids. Barbara Esbensen in her poem "Geode" writes of cracking a "stone egg" and finding "chiseled towers" and "vaulted glass rooms."

Ocean

Poets have been writing about the ocean for thousands of years and show no sign of stopping. In "Leaves of Grass," Walt Whitman wrote of "The boundless blue on every side expanding, / With whistling winds and music of the waves, the large imperious waves." In "Long Trip," Langston Hughes calls the sea ". . . a wilderness of waves, / A desert of water." Add to this richness the subtopics your class will suggest and you'll have more poems for an ocean theme than you can fit into the school year.

Many poetry anthologies have groups of poems about the sea that contain the classics and provide a good starting place when you're planning your ocean theme. *The Sea Is Calling Me,* edited by Lee Bennett Hopkins is a varied collection of poems by modern writers that seem to have been selected for their special appeal to children's senses.

For fun, share Jack Prelutsky's "Electric Eels," "Fish," and "Oysters" (from *Zoo Doings*) with your class. For drama, try "The Shark" by E. J. Pratt (in Downie and Robertson's *The Wind Has Wings*), a realistic yet poetic account of watching a shark swim into a harbor. It creates a chilling atmosphere that's exactly suited to its subject, "Tubular, tapered, smoke-blue, / Part vulture, part wolf."

You'll find gentler poems about beach and ocean dwellers such as the starfish and octopus in Valerie Worth's *All the Small Poems*, though her "Crab" is dead and "keeps a shape / Of old anger" in his claws.

Lilian Moore's "Until I Saw the Sea" (from *Something New Begins*) evokes perfectly the wonder of a child who sees the sea for the first time. To integrate reading and literature into an ocean theme, write this poem on the board or a chart, read and reread it to your class, and invite them to share the thoughts it produces. They'll probably want to talk about their first impressions and feelings of wonder about the ocean. Encourage them to explore how wind can "wrinkle water" and the sun can splinter the sea. Ask what they think the poet meant by the sea breathing in and out.

Don't worry if similar phrases turn up in your students' own poems later. Say something like "Oh, you remembered Lilian Moore's poem about the sea!" and keep in mind that it's a time-honored tradition for writers to learn from each other.

Also in *Something New Begins* are "Beach Stones" and "Mine," in which the sea takes back the sand castles and sand tunnels the child has built but is prevented from stealing the child's sand pail, too. Karla Kuskin remembers clearly what it's like to be a child at the beach, to "have a sip of ocean." That line is from "Sitting in the Sand," in *Dogs and Dragons, Trees and Dreams*; this book includes "Beaches," which begins, "There are reaches of beaches."

Perhaps you have a shell collection in your classroom that your kids add to (or lend to) when you study the ocean. You'll find lots of poems about the usual shells in anthologies; "Sand Dollar" by Barbara Esbensen from *Who Shrank My Grandmother's House?* tells about a less common souvenir from the sea, "loose money" from the ocean's "green silk pocket."

At the bottom of the page, the poet explains in prose what a sand dollar is and that if you break it open, you'll find five dove-shaped pieces that were the sand dollar's teeth when it was alive. "Souvenir" by Eve Merriam (1973) tells in a series of rhyming couplets how a shell can remind our senses of what it was like to be by the ocean.

Whales fit into several themes: ecology, history (whaling in New England), the ocean, or, more specifically, sea-dwelling mammals. They will capture the imagination of midwestern children as well as coast dwellers. Play a recording of the whale's song in the background when you read "Bluest Whale" by J. Patrick Lewis to your class, about a whale who swims alone and "blues the ocean."

If your children have spent time near the ocean, help them tap into their recalled experiences as sources of poems. Zachary remembered waking up on Cape Cod to the sound of the gulls.

Seagulls

In the morning you awake
with the cry of the gulls.
Sometimes they will swoop
down to catch their morning prey.
On a windy morning you
might see a gray and white
streak gliding by.
Sometimes you see them with
a clam or a fish in their
bright yellow beaks.
As the clam or the fish hits
the rocks you hear a loud
crack on the rocks below. ❖

Zachary DiMotta
Grade 4

Trees

Even in the cities, children will find trees to watch and wonder at:

Trees

No voices
No sound
They wave their arms
and greet us
They stretch hard
and point to the sky
having a race
to see
who's taller ❖

Sunny Im
Grade 3

When my third-grade class and I were working on an Arbor Day project, we decided to begin our study by looking very closely at a tree and then writing a poem about our perceptions. Fortunately, several large specimens grew on the school grounds, so out we went on a sunny afternoon to choose our special trees.

Our plan was to lie on the ground with our heads at the base of the trunks and look up into the branches and leaves above. Before we went outdoors, we talked about paying attention to how the sunlight looked, whether we could see bits of sky, the way the leaves moved, and what colors we saw. We also talked about noticing sounds and smells.

When I proposed this project, I was secretly doubtful that a classful of eight-year-olds would willingly lie on the ground and stare up into a tree for very long, but they quickly arranged themselves like wheelspokes around six different trees and lay there in near silence for some minutes. Then they got up and hugged their trees to feel the size and solidness of the trunks and the texture of the bark. They had brought with them pencils and notebooks so they could jot down their impressions instead of trying to remember so much. Back in the classroom, the notes and memories became poems.

Trees

Trees, you are so beautiful, as beautiful as can be.
Your bark feels rough and it feels strange.
You sound like a wave splashing on some rocks,
And you sound like a light breeze.
You smell like a mint leaf.
Oh trees, you all look different.
Oh trees, come live with me.
Oh trees, you make so many useful things.
Oh trees, you all are beautiful. ❖

Tara Jannucci
Grade 3

Arbor Day Poem

If you want to
Listen to the trees
You have to go
Outside to any
Tree you want
And you put your
Ear next to the tree
And listen to what
Is inside the tree. ❖

Eric Vesta
Grade 3

A couple of years later, I was teaching a fourth-grade class, and trees were part of our ecology theme. A student who arrived in the fall speaking almost no English wrote this:

Tree

The tree is green.
The leaf is green.
It's so beautiful.
Sometimes it plays music with the wind.
It's pleasant like a lullaby. ❖

> *Ayako Yamamoto*
> *Grade 4*

If you live where acorns are plentiful, enlist your class in collecting them until there are enough for each child to have one. After these oak trees in the making have been closely examined and commented on, hand out copies of "Acorn" by Valerie Worth and read it with your class. They will enjoy discussing her careful description of its shape and clear statement of its uniqueness in the last stanza.

A poem by Karla Kuskin (in *Dogs and Dragons, Trees and Dreams*) could inspire your kids to try shape poems about trees. It begins, "If you stood with your feet in the earth," and the arrangement of its lines are in the shape of a tree. A series of long lines of different lengths form the top, and single words, one beneath the other, make the trunk. Two poems by Robert Frost (1959), "Tree at My Window" and "Gathering Leaves," are good for integrating poetry into a tree theme, as is Sandburg's "Elm Buds."

Frost's poem "Birches" is available in a beautiful picture book format, illustrated by Ed Young, and is perfect for reading aloud to a group and then for pairs of children to read on their own. The images of this poem will please nearly all ages, but older children will be able to discuss the deeper meaning of being "a swinger of birches."

An irresistible bulletin board display for a tree theme across the grades is a brown paper or cardboard or papier-mâché tree with many branches. Students copy their revised poems on leaf-shaped pieces of paper and hang them on the branches, making a poet tree. If you're lucky enough to have a treelike collection of branches in your room, you can use that instead of a flat display. However it's done, wonderful poems about trees such as the next one need to be out where everyone can read and enjoy them.

Trees

Trees stand still
as giant statues.
The wind crashes on them.
And the rainy sky smashes on them.
They wave and wave
their little branches. ❖

> *Roded Bahat*
> *Grade 2*

Families

Teachers, more than anyone, are aware that the traditional family structure of mother at home, father at work, and two or three children at school and play, institutionalized in basal readers a generation ago, is no longer the norm. Poetry can help children in nontraditional families understand that others share their experiences and problems. At the same time, it addresses their emotions in ways that prose can't do.

There Was a Place and Other Poems by Myra Cohn Livingston is a collection of poems that speak to the experience of children in nontraditional families. Written from the point of view of the child, they're about what it's like to miss a mother or a father, to welcome or reject a new mom or dad, to be in the middle of adults' quarrels, or to live in a place the child longs to escape from. "The Secret" treats the painful knowledge that a family member has gone to jail and begins, "We don't mention where he went."

Poems in the first section of Kennedy's *The Forgetful Wishing Well*, called "Growing Pains," will be meaningful to older kids. They deal with such potential problems as little brothers, time spent watching television, and thank-you letters. "Family Matters" holds eight poems that look at the lighter side of family life, including the sadness of the dog that encountered a skunk and advice on how to stay up later than you're supposed to. Judith Viorst's poem "Night Fun" (in *If I Were in Charge of the World and Other Worries*) tells what it's like to have to go to bed and listen to the grown-ups having fun.

Having a new baby brother or sister can have its dark side, as Jack Prelutsky's "Life's Not Been the Same in My Family" (*Something BIG Has Been Here*) explains with humor. Shel Silverstein's "For Sale" puts into rhyme an older brother's attempt to auction off a "crying and spying young sister." When children write their own poems, composing a poem about feelings toward siblings can both validate and defuse those emotions.

Angry

When I'm angry
I go to my brother.
I hit him.
He laughs.
I say,
"You're nothing but junk!"
And I go away.❖

Sung Kim
Grade 2

Kids are constantly being told what not to do, and they enjoy writing poems about this fact of family life from their own perspective.

Bad Manners

Don't throw your food!
Don't think about burping.
You have bad manners.

Don't bite your nails
Don't put your feet on the table.
Don't smell your socks.
You have bad manners! ❖

George Puso
Grade 4

Sometimes the words that shape what kids feel about family life are easier or more acceptable to write in a poem than they are to say any other way.

He Said She Said

He said, eat dinner.
  She said, go to bed.
He said, clean up your room.
  I said

        Stop it!!! ❖

Amanda
Grade 3

Stop Working

Mom and Dad, I call
Stop going to work I say
You spend all your time and all day there
I never have time to play or talk to you anymore
I need you to talk to me, when I'm feeling down
I need you to help me to do things
I need you to be right by me so I can reach out and hug
        you
I need you in my heart
I need you in my soul
I need you to be with me

And I need you to tuck me in bed at night
I need you in my life!
Mom and Dad, I call
Everyone else, I say
Has a Mom and Dad for all day.
    So Stop Working! ❖

    Tally Rabinowitz
    Grade 4

Teachers sometimes include the topic of feelings in a family theme or, depending on students' needs, might treat it as a unit of study on its own. If you teach older kids, look for Mercer Mayer's *A Poison Tree*, an atypical collection of serious poems about feelings. Several of the authors aren't often represented in children's books, such as Theodore Roethke and Stephen Spender.

Writing poetry can unlock children's abilities to express emotions that otherwise would find no outlet. Children wonder and worry about many of the same things that grown-ups do, and some of their concerns are accentuated by their youth: identity, for example.

Two of Me

Sometimes
I feel
like I'm two people
one of me
loves ghost stories
the other me
is afraid of the dark
one of me
loves to wear skirts
the other me
prefers jeans
one of me
loves to climb trees
the other me
is afraid of heights
one of me
gets embarrassed easily
the other me
doesn't care what other people think. ❖

    Tiffany La Barbera

We who work with children know they're more reflective about life's deeper questions than most adults give them credit for.

Life

Life is like a candle.
When a candle burns
It will finish pretty soon
It will not stay forever and ever
Our job is to do in our lives
Good things not bad things
Like stealing, killing or taking a baby from his mother
                and father
And his family....
We want to go clean from this world
And let the evils take care of themselves. ❖

Rafiq Sarwari
Grade 5

Life and Death

Life is a wonderful thing
Laughing, playing, working
Before you die

Life is marvelous to me
But when you die you're shadows lurking
Life is a wonderful thing

So many things in life to see
It almost makes you want to sing
Before you die

And you will see
The true meaning of everything
Life is a wonderful thing

You wonder how it can be
Everything together and working
Before you die

And now you can see
With talking, learning, working
Life is a wonderful thing
Before you die ❖

Alison Amico
Grade 5

The latitude that poetry allows in arranging words on the page adds another dimension to the expression of feelings about life.

Roller Coaster

Life
is a roller coaster
all full of
     s,
  p   d
u   o
     w
      n
        s, t
          w
            i
          s
        t
      s, t
        u
            r
          n
      s,
      d
      r
      o
      p   oo
      s,   l p
        s,

<u>DARK TUNNELS</u> /\ and

D O O R S.❖

George Fainsilber
Grade 5

Poetry lets children give words to their hopes and fears in ways that adults need to attend to. It opens a window into the idealism of childhood that many of us have forgotten.

I Dream

I dream I'm in a world
where flowers never die,
and people can join hands
no matter what color they are,
I dream I'm in a world
where no one knows what war is,
but then I know it's all a dream. ❖

> Jessica Fazekas
> Grade 3

Ecology

The preservation of our biosphere also inspires children's idealism. Ecology is a comparatively new field for poetry, but a poem from long ago by Christina Rossetti (found in Jack Prelutsky's *The Random House Book of Poetry for Children*) catches its spirit:

Hurt no living thing:
   Ladybird, nor butterfly,
Nor moth with dusty wing,
   Nor cricket chirping cheerily,
Nor grasshopper so light of leap,
   Nor dancing gnat, nor beetle fat,
Nor harmless worms that creep. ❖

A poem that is more specific to today's problems is "Quest" from *Fresh Paint*, in which Eve Merriam asks where we will put our garbage when all the landfills are full and imagines the implicit abomination of "Dead batteries in the stars." Myra Cohn Livingston's "Smog" in *Sky Songs* creates even more graphic images of pollution's evils.

Lilian Moore's "Ecology" tells in just a few perfectly chosen words the story of a pond that's dying because humans killed off its resident muskrats. "The Whale Ghost" asks if we'll hear the "sad song" of the last whale to inhabit the sea. In *I Am Phoenix*, "The Passenger Pigeon" evokes poignantly the sad history of that vanished bird.

Because many children care deeply about the natural world they live in, they express their concerns about its survival in eloquent poems. Michael protested the careless starting of forest fires in this poem:

Fire

Blue and yellow it reaches its point
but when it stops it has reached everything in sight
the animals are gone too
trees are dying as everything is.
They have died because people were stupid. ❖

Michael Engle
Grade 4

When older children study the ecology of a specific region, they can collect enough information to carry them through the writing of long poems. This not only integrates subject matter with the writing of poetry but gives the child the satisfaction of completing an ambitious project such as this poem:

Amazon River

Picture paddling down the Amazon River.
Look, monkeys
Swinging rambunctiously on the branches.
Birds standing out in the daylight like a picture Aunt Teresa might make.

Scenery camouflaging itself with nature.
Plants, like bunches of cotton balls,
Packed together in a tiny box.
Everything all ties together.

It's a life web, all parts interacting.
If plants and trees were not there
Monkeys wouldn't swing
No birds to enjoy their canopy.

No place of hiding for panthers and jaguars.
No orchids clinging to limbs.
Now only we are
Paddling down the Amazon with no interest! ❖

Annamaria Zampogna
Grade 4

Poems that are written as part of an ecology theme can often find a wider audience. Encourage your children to submit their work to children's magazines or local newspapers. The following poems, for example, would be fine additions to an Earth Day section in a local paper or newsletter.

> The environment, our earth, the birds and the bees,
> We're destroying it, all of it, the flowers and trees!
> Why is it, I ask, that we must do this to it?
> Why must we kill, destroy and ruin our earth?
> "But we're not," they all say, but they are, yes they are.
> Why can't we save it, is there a real reason?
> "We are," they say and "We are" or "We will,"
> They've said it for years, they will till its gone.
> But our earth won't be here to say "We will" much longer. ❖
>
> Katie Reynolds
Grade 5

Earth Day

> Earth Day was meant
>   for saving the earth,
> For some don't know
>   what it's worth.
>
> Saving the earth is
>   what it's all about,
> People don't think
>   and they pave the route.
>
> Destroying trees, land and
>   water,
> Destroy the ozone, and
>   it'll get hotter.
>
> Trash! Honest! Use your
>   waste.
> If you don't, I'll disappear
>   in a haste.
>
> Earth Day was meant
>   for saving the earth,
> For some don't know
>   what it's worth. ❖
>
> Kristi Kief
Grade 4

CONCLUSION

We teachers, faced with the crowded curriculum and the public's demand that we correct the problems our culture confers on children, feel justifiably overburdened. We wish for more time and resources to spend on what really matters. Poetry is as close as we can come to Aladdin's lamp: It relates to every topic of study, it connects literature to all parts of the curriculum, it's short and quick yet worthy, and best of all—it's fun!

REFERENCES

All unreferenced quotes are from conversations with the author or observations of the author.

Adoff, Arnold. *Birds*. New York: HarperCollins Children Books, 1982.

Agree, Rose H., ed. *How to Eat a Poem and Other Morsels*. New York: Random House, 1967.

Allen, Terry, ed. *The Whispering Wind*. Garden City, New York: Doubleday, 1972.

Bauer, Caroline Feller. *Windy Day: Stories and Poems*. New York: J. B. Lippincott, 1988.

Beerman, Miriam, ed. *The Enduring Beast*. Garden City, NY: Doubleday, 1972.

Brewton, Sara, and John E. Brewton. *America Forever New*. New York: Thomas Y. Crowell, 1968.

Carroll, Lewis. *Alice in Wonderland*. Reprint. Cutchogue, NY: Buccaneer Books, 1981.

cummings, e. e. *Hist Whist and Other Poems for Children*. New York: Liveright, 1983.

de Gasztold, Carmen Bernos. *Prayers from the Ark*. Translated by Rumer Godden. New York: Viking Press, 1962.

Downie, Mary A., and Barbara Robertson, comp. *The Wind Has Wings*. New York: H. Z. Walck, 1968.

Eliot, T. S. *Old Possum's Book of Practical Cats*. New York: Harcourt Brace Jovanovich, 1939.

Eliot, T. S. *The Complete Poems and Plays*. New York: Harcourt, Brace, 1952.

Esbensen, Barbara. *Who Shrank My Grandmother's House?: Poems of Discovery*. New York: HarperCollins, 1992.

Farber, Norma, and Myra Cohn Livingston. *These Small Stones*. New York: Harper & Row, 1987.

Ferris, Helen. *Favorite Poems Old and New*. New York: Doubleday, 1957.

Fisher, Aileen. *Feathered Ones and Furry*. New York: Crowell, 1971.

Fleischman, Paul. *I Am Phoenix*. New York: Harper & Row, 1985.

Frost, Robert. *You Come Too*. New York: Henry Holt, 1959.

———. *Birches*. New York: Henry Holt, 1988.

Heller, Ruth. *Merry-Go-Round: A Book About Nouns*. New York: Grosset & Dunlap, 1990.

Hopkins, Lee Bennett, ed. *Moments*. New York: Harcourt Brace Jovanovich, 1980.

———. *The Sea is Calling Me*. New York: Harcourt Brace Jovanovich, 1986.

———. *Dinosaurs*. Illus. by Murray Tinklemann. New York: Harcourt Brace Jovanovich, 1987.

Hughes, Langston. *Selected Poems of Langston Hughes*. New York: Vintage Books, 1990.

Johnston, Tony. *I'm Gonna Tell Mama I Want an Iguana*. New York: G. P. Putnam's Sons, 1990.

Kennedy, X. J. *The Forgetful Wishing Well*. New York: Atheneum, 1985.

Kuskin, Karla. *Dogs and Dragons, Trees and Dreams*. New York: Harper & Row, 1980.

Larrick, Nancy, comp. *Cats Are Cats*. New York: Philomel Books, 1988.

Lear, Edward. *How Pleasant to Know Mr. Lear!* New York: Holiday House, 1984.

Lewis, J. Patrick. *A Hippopotamusn't and Other Animal Verses*. New York: Dial Books for Young Readers, 1990.

Livingston, Myra Cohn. *Callooh! Callay!* New York: Atheneum, 1980.

———. *Sky Songs*. New York: Holiday House, 1984.

———. *Earth Songs*. New York: Holiday House, 1986.

———. *Cat Poems*. New York: Holiday House, 1987.

———. *Space Songs*. New York: Holiday House, 1988.

———. *There Was a Place and Other Poems*. New York: Macmillan, 1988.

Longfellow, Henry Wadsworth. *Paul Revere's Ride*. New York: Greenwillow Books, 1985.

Mayer, Mercer. *A Poison Tree and Other Poems*. New York: Scribner, 1977.

McCord, David. *Far and Few*. Boston: Little, Brown, 1952.

Merriam, Eve. *Out Loud*. New York: Atheneum, 1973.

———. Blackberry Ink. New York: William Morrow, 1985.

———. Fresh Paint. New York: Macmillan Children's Book Group, 1986.

Moore, Lilian. *Something New Begins*. New York: Atheneum, 1982.

Nash, Ogden. *Verses from 1929 On*. Boston: Little, Brown, 1935.

———. *Parents Keep Out*. Boston: Little, Brown, 1951.

O'Neill, Mary. *Take a Number*. New York: Doubleday, 1968.

———. *Wind*. New York: Doubleday, 1970.

Prelutsky, Jack, ed. *The Random House Book of Poetry for Children*. New York: Random House, 1983.

———. *Zoo Doings*. New York: Greenwillow Books, 1983.

———. *Tyrannosaurus Was a Beast*. New York: Greenwillow Books, 1988.

———. *Beneath a Blue Umbrella*. New York: Greenwillow Books, 1990.

———. *Something BIG Has Been Here*. New York: Greenwillow Books, 1990.

Sandburg, Carl. *The Complete Poems of Carl Sandburg*. New York: Harcourt Brace Jovanovich, 1970.

———. *Breathing Tokens*. New York: Harcourt Brace Jovanovich, 1978.

Sendak, Maurice. *Chicken Soup with Rice*. New York: Harper & Row, 1962.

Service, Robert W. *The Cremation of Sam McGee*. New York: Greenwillow Books, 1986.

Silverstein, Shel. *Where the Sidewalk Ends*. New York: Harper & Row, 1974.

Singer, Marilyn. *Turtle in July*. New York: Macmillan, 1989.

Steig, Jeanne. *Consider the Lemming*. New York: Farrar, Straus & Giroux, 1988.

Thurman, Judith. *Flashlight and Other Poems*. New York: Atheneum, 1976.

Updike, John. *A Child's Calendar*. New York: Alfred A. Knopf, 1965.

Viorst, Judith. *If I Were in Charge of the World and Other Worries*. New York: Atheneum Children's Books, 1981.

Whitman, Walt. *Leaves of Grass*. New York: Doubleday, 1954.

Whittier, John Greenleaf. *Barbara Frietchie*. New York: Greenwillow Books, 1992.

Worth, Valerie. *All the Small Poems*. New York: Farrar, Straus & Giroux, 1987.

AFTERWORD
POETRY BEYOND THE CURRICULUM

Can you recognize new faces after one meeting, learn your way around a new environment quickly, and draw beautiful pictures? Then it's possible you had trouble with spelling and seldom found yourself in the top reading group as a child. And it's possible the right side of your brain overshadows the left. There's no question that my left brain is dominant. I won a regional spelling bee in sixth grade but, as a teacher, took more than a week to learn the faces and names of each new class and was known to get lost in my own school building.

Probably you've read about the selective differences in the way the two hemispheres of the brain process information. The left side of the brain is occupied with linear functions: language, logic, rationality, sequential processes, and mathematics; the right side deals with spatial relationships and dimensional interactions: perception of shapes and patterns, nonlinear connections, music, and art.

It's easy to see which side of the brain you need to do well in school. Instruction focuses almost entirely on left-brain functions as it proceeds step-by-step through one subject at a time, almost exclusively by using words. As a result, children whose right hemispheres are dominant—dyslexia is an extreme evidence—are at a great disadvantage in school. In a culture that prizes literacy less than ours does, right-brain thinkers would be high achievers with their ability to manipulate objects in space, interact socially, and move with grace and efficiency.

We teachers need to look for ways to foster right-brain connections in our students and in ourselves, to strive for "right brain and left brain in intimate collaboration" (Britton 1982, 141). Poetry is a way to do it: Its logic is allusive and nonlinear, its purpose is often to create images, its shape on the page shares value with the content of the words, and its sound has much in common with music. Yet its medium is language, the province of the left hemisphere.

John Archambault believes that the rhythm and song of poetry open right-brain channels, and his audiences agree, enchanted by the music of the poems he recites with Bill Martin Jr. Even without the talent and skill of that pair of modern-day minstrels, we can help this happen for our students by opening the world of poetry to them. Again and again I saw kids read and write poems with pleasure and success who, later in the day, left the room for remedial reading instruction. Their polar opposites were the students who, used to achieving success by learning the rules and following them, began by looking only for literal meanings in poetry and writing stilted, lifeless verses.

The more experiences children have with activities that require both sides of the brain to act in "intimate collaboration," the greater their overall achievement will be, and, just as important, the greater will be their opportunity to experience the aesthetic side of life.

It's easy to dismiss aesthetic experience as peripheral, but if we look at it more closely we see that it matters a great deal to us human beings in the way we live our lives. First of all, it's based in the emotions. The root of that word is "to move," and indeed, it is our emotions that move us, more forcefully than facts can.

When we share with children poetry that speaks to their emotions, we open doors that schooling too often keeps locked. We encourage them to know more than cold facts, to feel and wonder, and to reflect. This is the kind of learning that defines us as human beings and counterbalances the mechanization that threatens to dominate our lives.

Reflection, although it's a process that's essential to higher-level thinking and learning, doesn't happen enough in school. Indeed, because it requires a student to sit still and think, it often looks like time-wasting. We've been trained to equate overt activity with learning; this connection holds true if students are learning motor skills, but not if they're reflecting on ideas.

Poetry, however, *demands* reflection, whether we're reading or writing it. We frame mental images in response to the words on a page, wonder what the poet was seeing, or recall an experience we're reminded of. Writing a poem requires even more intense and prolonged reflection because we reexperience an emotion or event and shape it into a collection of words that expresses and transforms it.

When children read poems, they reflect on the vital experiences and emotions that poets share with their readers. When children reflect on their own vital experiences and emotions and write poems to express them beautifully in words, they share in the spirit and craft of an art that is uniquely human. What could be more basically educational than that?

But let's come down to earth, where our classrooms are. This is where we spend the minutes of our days, in the real world of bits of chalk, pencil stubs, and misspelled words on crumpled pages. It can seem to be a less than magical place until we stop and do some reflecting ourselves.

When we stop and think of the small events of the day, something a child did or said or wrote will shine in our memories and remind us of tomorrow's possibilities. Lucy McCormick Calkins asks teachers to start with a "precious particle," a small, shining event, and to "find miracles in the mundane." This is exactly what poetry does. Poetry finds and celebrates small miracles in the ordinariness of life and presents us with "precious particles" to share with the children in our care.

REFERENCES

Archambault, John. Talk given at the annual meeting of the International Reading Association, Las Vegas, NV, May 8, 1991.

Britton, James. "Shaping at the Point of Utterance." In Gordon M. Pradl (ed.), *Prospect and Retrospect*. Montclair, NJ: Boynton/Cook, 1982.

Calkins, Lucy McCormick. Talk given at the annual meeting of the International Reading Association, Orlando, FL, May 4, 1992.

INDEX

Aardema, V., *Bringing the Rain to Kapiti Plain*, 43
"Acorn," (Worth), 3, 184
Acrostic poems, 83
Adjectives, 95, 96, 158
Adoff, Arnold
  Birds, 177
  Flamboyan, 52
  "Late Past Bedtime," 161
  "Nest," 177
  Today We Are Brother and Sister, 52
Adverbs, 158
"Aerial Sheet Music" (Johnston), 176
Aesthetic experience, 198
African Americans, poetry by, 51, 52
"After English Class" (Little), 92
"Afternoon and His Unfinished Poem" (O'John), 50
Agree, Rose H., *How to Eat a Poem and Other Morsels*, 159
"Ah! A Monster's Life Is Merry" (Prelutsky), 94
Aldis, Dorothy, 32
Alice in Wonderland (Carroll), 84, 159
Aliki, *Feelings*, 35
"All But Blind" (de la Mare), 91
All the Small Poems (Worth), 3, 171, 179
Allen, Terry, *The Whispering Wind: Poetry by Young American Indians*, 49, 154
Alliteration, 6, 36, 70, 75, 76
Ambiguity, 95
America Forever New, 152
American bald eagle, 177
"Amoeba" (Worth), 151
Angelou, Maya
  "Life Doesn't Frighten Me," 52
  "On Aging," 52
  "Woman Work," 52
Animal poems, 170-75
"Anna Banana" (Prelutsky), 153
"Annabel Lee" (Poe), 82
"Answer Is 'No', The," (White), 176
Ant poems, 177
"Ant, The," (Nash), 178

Anthologies
  assembling, 144
  Native American, 51
  personal, 145
  pet poems in, 172
  of poetry, 29, 152, 170
  on the sea, 180
"April Rain Song" (Hughes), 162
Arbor Day, 182
Archambault, John, 197
  Knots on a Counting Rope, 112
Arctic tern, 175
"Arithmetic," (Sandburg), 155
Armstrong, Louis, "What a Wonderful World," 89
Arroz con Leche, 52
Art, computer-generated vs handmade, 143
Artificial satellites, 168
Art of Teaching Writing, The (Calkins), 45
At the Crack of the Bat (Morrison), 109
"At the Zoo" (Fisher), 111
Atwell, Nancie, 144, 146
  In the Middle: Writing, Reading, and Learning with Adolescents, 148
Atwood, Ann, *Haiku: The Mood of Earth*, 81
Audiotapes, of poems, 9, 94, 108

"Band-Aids" (Silverstein), 155
Bank Street Writer, 9, 12
"Barbara Frietchie" (Whittier), 155
Barchers, Suzanne, *Creating and Managing the Literate Classroom*, 145
Baseball poems, 109
Bat Poet, The (Jarrell), 4, 8, 11
Bauer, Caroline, *Windy Day*, 161
Beach poems, 181, 182
"Beach Stones" (Moore), 181
"Beaches" (Kuskin), 181
"Beaver, The" (Prelutsky), 171
"Bee Song" (Sandburg), 178
Beerman, Miriam, *The Enduring Beast*, 172

Behn, Harry, *Cricket Songs*, 81
Beneath a Blue Umbrella (Prelutsky), 153
Bernstein, Leonard, 101
Berra, Yogi, 64
Bias, 90
Big books, 31, 43
Bilingual collections, 52, 53
"Birches" (Frost), 184
Bird poems, 175-77
Birds (Adoff), 177
Blackberry Ink (Merriam), 153, 159
Blackboard critiquing, 131
Blake, William, 24, 99, 130
"Bluebird, What Do You Feed On?" (Sandburg), 176
"Bluest Whale" (Lewis), 181
Bradbury, Ray, "Switch on the Night," 82
Brain processes, and learning, 197, 198
Brewton, John E., *America Forever New*, 152
Brewton, Sara, *America Forever New*, 152
Bringing the Rain to Kapiti Plain (Aardema), 43
Britton, James, 36, 101, 109, 128, 129
Brother Eagle, Sister Sky (Chief Seattle), 51
Brown Bear, Brown Bear, What Do You See? (Martin), 31
Browning, Robert, "The Pied Piper of Hamelin," 82
"Bubbles" (Sandburg), 69, 165
"Bug Sat in a Silver Flower" (Kuskin), 180
"Bug Spots" (Sandburg), 178
Bulletin board displays, 143, 144, 161, 184

Calkins, Lucy McCormick, 26, 90, 127, 134, 144, 198
   The Art of Teaching Writing, 45
   Living Between the Lines, 105
Calooh! Callay! (Livingston), 170
Canada, poems from, 154, 155
Capitalization, 37, 139
Caribbean poetry, 53
Carroll, Lewis
   Alice in Wonderland, 84, 159
   "Jabberwocky," 82
   "The Walrus and the Carpenter," 82
"Catalog" (Moore), 173
Cat in the Hat, The (Seuss), 33
Cat poems, 172-75
Cat Poems, 173
"Catherine" (Kuskin), 110
"Cats," 174

Cats Are Cats (Larrick), 173
Celebration
   guest list for, 20
   poetry publication, 16, 19, 138
"Celery" (Nash), 100, 161
Cerf, Bennett, 33
Chants, 104, 105
Charcoal, to illustrate poems, 143
Charlotte's Web (White), 97
Chaucer, Geoffrey, 32
Chicken Soup with Rice: A Book of Months (Sendak), 31, 66, 170
Children's magazines, 145
Child's Calendar, A (Updike), 170
Chinese poems, 53
Choral reading, 44
Choral speaking, 101
   beginning, 102, 103
   benefits of, 105
   for larger audiences, 106
   videotaping, 106
Christelow, Eileen, *Five Little Monkeys Jumping on the Bed*, 45
"Chrysalis Diary," 179
Ciardi, John, 94, 145
Cinquains, 77, 80
City poems, 53, 154
Civil War poems, 155
Class anthology, 144
Classical poetry, 88
Clifton, Lucille, *Some of the Days of Everett Anderson*, 51
Clock and calendar poems, 170-71
Coconut Kind of Day (Joseph), 53
"Coins" (Worth), 156
Collaborative poems, 22, 158
Collage, to illustrate poems, 143
"Come In" (Frost), 177
Computers
   art generated with, 143
   creating graphics with, 18
   editing with, 120
   and spelling checkers, 141
   writing poems on, 9, 12, 37, 60
Concrete poems, 84
Conferences, 8, 9, 22
   critiquing through, 131-32
   editing, 16, 141
   evaluation, 138
   illustration, 143
   peer, 10, 124, 125, 134, 140
   planning, 26-27
   questions for, 134
   revision, 124, 126
   teacher, 125
Conkling, Hilda, "Dandelion," 73

Consider the Lemming (Steig), 172
Consonants, 75
Content
   and form, 60
   organizing, 62
"Counting" (Kuskin), 155
Counting rhymes, 29
Couplets, 39, 76, 77, 106
   rhyming, 31, 78, 79, 156, 161, 181
"Cow" (Kuskin), 113
Cowley, Joy, *Mrs. Wishy Washy*, 31
"Crab" (Worth), 181
Crapsey, Adelaide, 80
Creating and Managing the Literate Classroom (Barchers), 145
"Cremation of Sam McGee, The" (Service), 155
"Cricket March" (Sandburg), 178
Cricket Songs (Behn), 81
Critiquing conferences, 131
"Crows" (McCord), 176
Cullere, Barbara, 34, 36, 39, 99
cummings, e. e., 9, 91
   Hist Whist and Other Poems for Children, 69, 166
Curriculum, poetry across, 149-55

"Dancing Pants" (Silverstein), 110
Dancing Tepees (Sneve), 51
"Dandelion" (Conkling), 73
Daniels, Jim, 43
"Days That the Wind Takes Over" (Kuskin), 161
de Gasztold, Carmen Bernos, *Prayers from the Ark*, 172
de la Mare, Walter, "All But Blind," 91
Della-Piana, Gabriel, 122
Denman, Gregory, 23, 98, 100, 101
Diamantes, 77, 83
Dickinson, Emily, 130
Diction, 105
Dinosaur poems, 172, 180
Dinosaurs (Hopkins), 180
Discussions, middle-grade poetry, 90
Dog poems, 172-73
Dogs and Dragons, Trees and Dreams, (Kuskin), 160, 172, 173, 180, 181, 184
Donne, John, 99, 130
Downie, Mary A., *The Wind Has Wings*, 181
"Dragon Flyer" (Lewis) 156
Dramatic presentations, 44
Duthie, Christine, 30, 38

"Eagle, The" (Tennyson), 176
Earth, Native Americans' respect for, 51
Earth Day, 192
Earth Songs (Livingston), 180
"Ecology" (Moore), 190
Ecology poems, 181, 183-84, 190-92
Editing
   on computer, 120
   conferences, 16, 141
   evaluation and, 139, 140
   poetry, 11, 12
   student poems, 119, 120
"Electric Eels" (Prelutsky), 181
Eliot, T. S., 53
   "Macavity: The Mystery Cat," 174
   "Mungojerrie and Rumpelteazer," 174
   Old Possum's Book of Practical Cats, 174
"Elm Buds" (Sandburg), 184
Emotion. *See also* Feelings
   implied, 41
Enduring Beast, The (Beerman), 172
English as a second language learners. *See* ESL learners
Esbensen, Barbara
   "Four Poems for Roy G Biv," 165
   "Geode," 180
   "Sand Dollar," 181
   "Time," 170
   Who Shrank My Grandmother's House?: Poems of Discovery, 174, 181
Escher, Maurits Cornelis, 17
Eskimo chants, 154
ESL learners, poetry and, 43-49
Evaluating
   conferences, 138
   student poems, 132-35
Experimentation with poetry, 49
Explore Poetry (Graves), 105
"Exposed Nest, The" (Frost), 177

"Fall" (Kuskin), 111
"Falling Star, The" (Teasdale), 168
Family life
   in poems, 53, 185, 186, 187
   nontraditional, 185
"Fashions in Dogs" (White), 173
Favorite Poems Old and New (Ferris), 152, 153, 158, 172
Feathered Ones and Furry (Fisher), 170, 171, 172
Feelings, in children's poems, 9, 41, 185, 187, 189
Feelings (Aliki), 35

Feet, 11
Ferris, Helen, *Favorite Poems Old and New*, 152, 153, 158, 172
Figures of speech, poetic, 39
"Fireflies in the Garden" (Frost), 179
"Fish" (Prelutsky), 181
Fish poems, 172
Fisher, Aileen, "At the Zoo," 111
  Feathered Ones and Furry, 170, 171, 172
"Fishing" (Pratt), 51
Five Little Monkeys Jumping on the Bed (Christelow), 45
Flamboyan (Adoff), 52
Flashlight and Other Poems (Thurman), 154
Fleischman, Paul, *I Am Phoenix*, 111, 177, 190
Florida Reading Association Conference (1992), 89
"Fog" (Sandburg), 162
Follow Me (Nelson), 45
Food
  exhibits, 161
  poems about, 100, 159-61
  for poetry publication celebration, 21
"For Sale" (Silverstein), 185
For the Good of the Earth and the Sun (Heard), 126, 128
Forgetful Wishing Well, The (Kennedy), 53, 154, 173, 176, 185
Forms and conventions, 58, 60, 83
"Fossils" (Moore), 180
"Four Poems for Roy G Biv" (Esbensen), 165
Franklin, Ben, 155
Free verse, 77, 170
Fresh Paint (Merriam), 69, 190
Frost, Robert, 9, 79, 130, 145
  "Birches," 184
  "Come In," 177
  "Fireflies in the Garden," 179
  "Gathering Leaves," 184
  "A Hillside Thaw," 167
  "The Last Word of a Bluebird," 176
  "A Minor Bird," 177
  "A Nature Note," 177
  "The Runaway," 172
  "Something there is that doesn't love a wall," 98
  "Stopping by Woods on a Snowy Evening," 111
  "Tree at My Window," 184
  You Come Too, 167

"Garbage" (Worth), 3
"Gathering Leaves" (Frost), 184
Geisel, Theodor Seuss (pseud. Dr. Seuss), 93
  The Cat in the Hat, 33
  Green Eggs and Ham, 33
"Geode" (Esbensen), 180
Geode poems, 180
Geography poems, 152-53
Getting from Here to There: Writing and Reading Poetry (Grossman), 23
Giacobbe, Mary Ellen, 145
Gilchrist, Jan Spivey, 51
Global awareness, developing, 53
"Go Wind" (Moore), 162
"Gong of Time, The" (Sandburg), 170
"Good Babies Make Good Poems" (Sandburg), 152
"Good Morning, America" (Sandburg), 154
Grades
  and self-evaluation, 136
  and self-esteem, 138
"Grandpa Bear's Lullaby" (Yolen), 111
Grandparents' Houses; Poems About Grandparents, 53
Graphics. *See also* Illustrating for poems, 18
"Grasshopper Gumbo" (Prelutsky), 159
"Grasshoppers," 179
Grasshopper poems, 178
Graves, Donald, 10, 23, 36, 89, 122, 140
  Explore Poetry, 105
  Writing: Teachers and Children at Work, 103, 145
Green Eggs and Ham (Seuss), 33
Greenfield, Eloise
  Honey I Love, 89
  Nathaniel Talking, 51
  Night on Neighborhood Street, 51
  "Things," 99, 100
  "Way Down in the Music," 89
"Green with Envy" (Merriam), 115
Grief, in children's poems, 174
Grossman, Florence, *Getting from Here to There: Writing and Reading Poetry*, 23

Haiku, 77, 81
Haiku: The Mood of the Earth, 81
"Hairy Toe, The," 82
Hammond, Joanne, 24, 91
Hamster poems, 175
Hand-clapping games, 104

"Happy Birthday, Mother Dearest" (Prelutsky), 159
Harlem poems, 52
Harmony, performing poetry in, 111-12
Harrison, Peggy, 143
Harwayne, Shelley, 105
"Haunted House" (Worth), 130
Heard, Georgia, 38, 127, 128
   For the Good of the Earth and the Sun, 126, 128
Heller, Ruth, *Merry-Go-Round: A Book About Nouns*, 158
Hippopotamusn't and Other Animal Verses, A (Lewis), 171, 177
"Hippo's Hope" (Silverstein), 110
Hispanic Americans, poetry by, 52
Hist Whist and Other Poems for Children (cummings), 69, 166
History poems, 155, 181
"Hog Butcher for the World" (Sandburg), 154
Holiday poems, 170
Homan, Agnes, 93, 94
Homophones, 158
"Honeybees," 179
Honey I Love (Greenfield), 89
Hopkins, Lee Bennett
   Dinosaurs, 180
   Me!, 32
   Moments, 170
   The Sea is Calling Me, 181
   Side by Side: Poems to Read Together, 29, 95
"House That Jack Built, The," 110
How Pleasant to Know Mr. Lear! (Lear), 80
How to Eat a Poem and Other Morsels (Agree), 159
"How to Trick a Chicken" (Lewis), 159
Hughes, Gillian, 9
Hughes, Langston, 9, 52, 67, 71, 93, 145, 154
   "April Rain Song," 162
   "Long Trip," 180
   metaphor in poems of, 70, 71, 73
Hughes, Ted, 145
"Hummingbird, The" (Prelutsky), 176
Hummingbirds, 176
"Hummingbirds" (Kennedy), 176
Humor, in poems, 94, 100, 106, 150, 155, 158, 159, 161, 172, 179
"Hungry Mungry" (Silverstein), 159
"Hurricane" (Moore), 162

"I Am Crying from Thirst" (Lopez), 49
I Am Phoenix (Fleischman), 111, 177, 190
"I Do Not Mind You, Winter Wind" (Prelutsky), 161
"I Have a Lion" (Kuskin), 172
I Heard a Scream in the Street (Larrick), 53
"I Know All the Sounds That the Animals Make" (Prelutsky), 111
"I Know an Old Lady," 31
"I Must Remember" (Silverstein), 159
"I Speak, I Say, I Talk" (Shapiro), 74
"I Woke Up This Morning" (Kuskin), 106
Identity poems, 187
If I Had a Paka: Poems in Eleven Languages, 53
If I Were in Charge of the World and Other Worries (Viorst), 173, 185
Illustrating
   conferences, 143
   poems, 17, 143
Images
   creating visual, 143
   focusing on, 38
   in harmonic poetry, 112
   in poems, 9, 10, 85, 94, 95, 96
   and simile, 71
   tied to concepts, 130
I'm Gonna Tell Mama I Want an Iguana (Johnston), 115, 178
"I'm Staying in Bed" (Kuskin), 106
Insect poems, 156, 177-80
Internal rhyme, 41
"In the Fog" (Moore), 162
In the Middle: Writing, Reading, and Learning with Adolescents, 144
In the Trail of the Wind: American Indian Poems and Ritual Orations, 51
Invented spelling, 36, 37, 46, 126, 127, 140
It Doesn't Always Have to Rhyme (Merriam), 73

"Jabberwocky" (Carroll), 82, 114
Japanese poems, 53
Jarrell, Randall, *The Bat Poet*, 4, 11
Jeffers, Susan, 51
Jefferson, Thomas, 155
"Jellyfish Walk" (Johnston), 74
Johnson, Ben, 140

Johnston, Tony
"Aerial Sheet Music," 176
I'm Gonna Tell Mama I Want an Iguana, 115, 172, 178
"Jellyfish Walk," 74
"A Little Seed," 100
"Lizard Longing," 172
"Skeleton Train," 115
"Joliet" (Sandburg), 154
Joseph, Lynn, *Coconut Kind of Day*, 53
Joyful Noise (Fleischman), 111, 179
Jump-rope rhymes, 104
"Just Before April Came" (Sandburg), 67

Katz, Bobbi, *The Place My Words Are Looking For*, 113
Kennedy, X. J.
The Forgetful Wishing Well, 53, 154, 173, 176, 185
"Hummingbirds," 176
"Old-Timer," 173
"Ten Billion Crows," 176
Keyboarding, 37
King of Hearts, The, 90
Knots on a Counting Rope (Martin, Jr. and Archambault), 112
Koch, Kenneth, 9, 24, 66, 81, 99, 130
Rose, Where Did You Get That Red?, 24, 47
Kuskin Karla
"Bugs," 177
"Catherine," 110
"Counting," 155
"Cow," 113
Dogs and Dragons, Trees and Dreams, 160, 161, 162, 172, 173, 180, 181, 184
"Fall," 111
"I Have a Lion," 172
"I Woke Up This Morning," 106
"I'm Staying in Bed," 106
"Me," 103
"The Meal," 159
Near the Window Tree, 88
"Sitting in the Sand," 181
"Take a Word Like Cat," 174
"This Cat," 173
"Where Would You Be?," 161

"Lady of Shalott, The" (Tennyson), 82
Language Arts, 146

Larrick, Nancy, 29
I Heard a Scream in the Street, 53
Cats Are Cats, 173
On City Streets, 53
"Last Word of a Bluebird, The" (Frost), 176
"Late Past Bedtime" (Adoff), 161
"Laughing Time" (Smith), 106
Lear, Edward, 80, 115, 156, 159
How Pleasant to Know Mr. Lear!, 80
"The Owl and the Pussycat," 82
Learning, and oral experience, 89, 105
"Leaves of Grass" (Whitman), 180
Lenz, Lisa, 36, 108
Letter-sound correspondence, 43, 45, 89
Lewis, J. Patrick
"Bluest Whale," 181
"Dragonflyer," 156
A Hippopotamustn't and Other Animal Verses, 171, 173, 177
"How to Trick a Chicken," 159
"Mosquito," 110
"Mrs Praying Mantis," 179
"Penguins," 177
"Tom Tigercat," 173
Lewis, Richard
Miracles: Poems by Children of the English-Speaking World, 8
"Life Doesn't Frighten Me" (Angelou), 52
"Life's Not Been the Same in My Family" (Prelutsky), 185
Light in the Attic, A (Silverstein), 110
Limericks, 77, 80, 156, 172
Lindsay, Vachel, "The Moon's the North Wind's Cooky," 161
Line breaks, 12, 22, 58, 59, 61, 62, 88
editing, 139
Lion, the Witch and the Wardrobe, The, 58
List poems, 23
"Listener's Guide to the Birds, A" (White), 176
Little, Jean, "After English Class," 92
Little Miss Muffet, 90
"Little Seed, A" (Johnston), 100
Living Between the Lines (Calkins), 105
Livingston, Myra Cohn, 80
Calooh! Callay!, 170
Cat Poems, 173
"Mount St. Helens," 180
"The Secret," 185
Sky Songs, 81, 190
Space Songs, 168
"Smog," 190
There Was a Place and Other Poems, 180, 185

"Lizard Longing" (Johnston), 172
Lizard poems, 172
"Localities" (Sandburg), 153
London, Marilyn, 23, 103, 104
Longfellow, Henry Wadsworth, "Paul Revere's Ride," 82, 155
"Long Trip" (Hughes), 180
Lopez, Alonzo, "I Am Crying from Thirst," 49
Lorca, Federico García, 47
"Louder Than a Clap of Thunder" (Prelutsky), 94
Lullabies, 53

"Macavity: The Mystery Cat" (Eliot), 174
"Magnifying Glass" (Worth), 151
Manticore, 172
Map puzzles, 153
Maps, and poetry, 152-53
"March of the Hungry Mountains" (Sandburg), 180
Martin, Bill Jr., 197
  "Brown Bear, Brown Bear, What Do You See?," 31
  Knots on a Counting Rope, 112
Masell, Karen, 35
Math poems, 155-57
"May Flies," 179
Mayer, Mercer, *A Poison Tree*, 187
McClure, Amy, *Sunrises and Songs*, 131, 143, 145
McCord, David
  "Crows," 176
  "The Pickety Fence," 115
McCullers, Carson, 159
Me! (Hopkins) 32
"Me" (Kuskin), 103
"Meal, The" (Kuskin), 159
Meaning, in poems, 90-91
"Melinda Mae" (Silverstein), 159
Memorizing
  enhancing writing, 105
  poetry, 97-99
Merriam, Eve, 53
  Blackberry Ink, 153, 159
  Fresh Paint, 69, 190
  "Green with Envy," 115
  It Doesn't Always Have to Rhyme, 73
  Out Loud, 176
  "Places to Hide a Secret Message," 69
  "Souvenir," 181
  "Windshield Wiper," 109
Merry-Go-Round: A Book About Nouns, (Heller), 158

"Message from a Caterpiller" (Moore), 179
Metaphor, 9, 29, 70-72, 162, 163
Metapoetic, 73
Meter, 11
Metric foot, 88
Mexican-Americans, poetry of, 52
Milky Way, 168
"Mine" (Moore), 181
"Minor Bird, A" (Frost), 179
Miracles: Poems by Children of the English-Speaking World (Lewis), 8
Mitchell, Emerson Blackhorse "Barney", "Talking to the Drum," 154
Moffett, James, 30
Moments (Hopkins), 170
"Moon's the North Wind's Cooky, The" (Lindsay), 161
Moore, Lilian
  "Beach Stones," 181
  "Ecology," 190
  "Fog Lifting," 162
  "Fossils," 180
  "Go Wind," 162
  "Hurricane," 162
  "In the Fog," 162
  "Message from a Caterpillar," 179
  "Mine," 181
  "Move Over," 178
  "Something New Begins," 154, 181
  "Squirrel," 171
  "Sun on Rain," 165
  "Telling Time," 74, 170
  "Until I Saw the Sea," 181
  "The Whale Ghost," 190
  "While You Were Chasing a Hat," 162
  "Wind Song," 162
  "Woodpecker," 176
Moore, Marianne, 130, 172
Moore, Rosalie, "Catalog," 173
Morninghouse, Sundaira, *Nightfeathers*, 52
"Mosquito" (Lewis), 110
"Mosquito" (Worth), 179
"Mother Doesn't Want a Dog" (Viorst), 173
Mother Goose, 29, 33, 36, 46, 113, 159
Mountains and volcanoe poems, 180
"Mount St. Helens" (Livingston), 180
"Move Over" (Moore), 178
"Mrs. Praying Mantis" (Lewis), 179
"Mrs. Wishy Washy" (Cowley), 31
Multilingual books, 53
Multicultural poetry, 49-54
Multiculturalism, 90

"Mungojerrie and Rumpelteazer" (Eliot), 174
Music. *See also* Choral speaking
  poetry set to, 88, 112
"My Cat" (Esbensen), 174
"My Mother Says I'm Sickening" (Prelutsky), 94

Narrative poems, 31, 82, 128
  dramatizing, 110
  harmonizing, 112
Nash, Ogden, 64, 161
  "The Ant," 178
  "Celery," 100, 150, 161
  "The Panther," 115
  "The Parsnip," 100
  "The Pig," 100
  "The Purist," 152
  rhymes of, 150
  "A Watched Example Never Boils," 165
Nathaniel Talking (Greenfield), 51
National Council of Teachers of English, 146
Native Americans, poetry by, 49, 154
"Nature Note, A" (Frost), 177
Navajo poems, 104, 154
Near the Window Tree (Kuskin), 88
Neighborhood Odes (Soto), 52
Nelson, Joanne, *Follow Me*, 45
Neruda, Pablo, 172
"Nest" (Adoff), 177
Newspapers, children's poems in, 145
Nightfeathers (Morninghouse), 52
"Night Fun" (Viorst), 185
Night on Neighborhood Street (Greenfield), 51
Nix, Pat, 158
Northern Valley Regional District—New Jersey, 147
Nouns, 94-96, 158
Nursery rhymes, 90, 128
Nutrition poems, 159-60

Ocean poems, 180-82
Octopus poem, 181
O'John, Calvin, "Afternoon and His Unfinished Poem," 50
Old Possum's Book of Practical Cats (Eliot), 174
"Old-Timer" (Kennedy), 173
"On Aging" (Angelou), 52
On City Streets (Larrick), 53

O'Neill, Mary
  Take a Number, 155
  Wind, 161
Onomatopoeia, 74, 75, 115
"Open Letter to the Poet Archibald MacLeish Who Has Forsaken His Massachusetts Farm to Make Propaganda for Freedom" (Sandburg), 155
Oral poetry, 87-88
  and choral speaking, 101-106
  harmony with, 111-12
  and memorization, 97-99
  music of words and, 88-89
  performing, 109-11
  promoting learning, 89-93, 95-96
Orleans, Ilo, 66
Outdoors poems, 3. *See also* Ecology; Ocean; Tree poems
Out Loud (Merriam), 176
"Owl and the Pussycat, The" (Lear), 82
Oxford Book of Story Poems, The, 82
"Oysters" (Prelutsky), 181

Paints, for poetry illustration, 143
"Panther, The" (Nash), 115
Pantomime, 109
"Parsnip, The" (Nash), 100
Parts of speech
  and oral poetry, 94-95
  poems for, 158
"Passenger Pigeon, The" (Fleischman), 190
Pastoral poems, 112
"Paul Revere's Ride" (Longfellow), 82, 155
"Pebbles" (Worth), 62
Peer conferences, 124, 125, 134, 140
Pen names, 93
Pen pal exchanges with videocassette, 106
Penguins, 175
"Penguins" (Lewis), 177
Personification, 29, 67, 68, 123
Pet poems, 172-75
  and handling death, 174-75
"Pickety Fence, The" (McCord), 115
Picture books, 143, 184
"Pie" (Worth), 160
"Pied Piper of Hamelin, The" (Browning), 82
"Pig, The" (Nash), 100
Pipher, Tom, 44
Place My Words Are Looking For The (Katz), 113

"Places to Hide a Secret Message" (Merriam), 69
Poe, Edgar Alan, "Annabel Lee, 82
Poems
  acrostic, 83
  animal, 170-75
  audiotapes of, 9, 94, 108
  beach, 181
  bird, 175-77
  building self-esteem with, 45
  city, 53
  collaborative, 22
  concrete, 84
  discussing, 90, 92-93
  dinosaur, 180
  dramatic presentation of, 44
  family, 185-87
  finding, 35-37
  folders for, 26
  food, 159-61
  geography, 153
  history, 155
  holiday, 170
  illustrating, 143
  insect, 177-80
  list, 23
  math, 155-57
  memorizing, 97-99
  mountains and volcanoes, 180
  narrative, 31
  ocean, 180-82
  origins of, 12-15
  ownership, 40
  poets reading, 93
  question, 177
  rainbow, 165-66
  rhyming, 6, 64-66
  sandwich, 36
  science, 150-52
  singing and performing, 87
  social studies, 152-55
  space and time, 168-9
  spelling, 158
  tree, 182-84
  unrhymed, 67
  visual quality of, 60-62
  weather, 161-68
Poet tree, 184
Poetic
  devices, 64
  forms, 76-78, 85
  terms, 70-76
Poetry Day, 147
Poetry
  across the curriculum, 149
  by African Americans, 51
  anthologies of, 29, 144
  bilingual collections, 52, 53
  bridging cultures, 44-54
  by children, 8, 107
  circles, 25
  classical, 88
  devices and structures, 64-76
  to encourage reading, 30, 31
  enjoying, 29
  experimentation with, 49
  festivals, 147
  and global awareness, 53
  harmonizing in, 111
  by Hispanic Americans, 52
  multicultural, 49-54
  music in, 88
  by Native Americans, 49
  notebook for, 26
  oral, 87
  performing, 101-113
  and prose, 36, 51
  about Puerto Rico, 53
  readings, 107-108
  sources, 32, 33
  themes programs of, 111
  understanding, 91
Poets' lives, 93
Poison Tree, A (Mayer), 187
Pratt, Agnes T., "Fishing," 51
Pratt, E. J., "The Shark," 181
Prayers from the Ark (de Gasztold), 172
Prelutsky, Jack
  "Ah! A Monster's Life Is Merry," 94
  "Anna Banana," 153
  "The Beaver Bees," 178
  "Beneath a Blue Umbrella," 153
  "Electric Eels," 181
  "Fish," 181
  "Grasshopper Gumbo," 159
  "Happy Birthday, Mother Dearest," 159
  "The Hummingbird," 176
  "I Do Not Mind You, Winter Wind," 161
  "I Know All the Sounds That the Animals Make," 111
  "Life's Not Been the Same in My Family," 185
  "Louder Than a Clap of Thunder," 94
  "My Mother Says I'm Sickening," 94
  "Oysters," 181
  poems sung by, 112
  The Random House Book of Poetry for Children, 176, 190
  Read-Aloud Rhymes for the Very Young, 32, 66

Prelutsky, Jack (*continued*)
  Something BIG Has Been Here, 159, 171, 178, 185
  "The Spider," 178
  "Squirrels," 171
  story poems by, 42
  Tyrannosaurus Was a Beast, 180
  "When Dracula Went to the Blood Bank," 94
  "The Zoo Was in an Uproar," 111
Primary grades
  poetry workshops in, 34
Professional journals, 146
Prose, 23, 25, 70, 127
  and poetry, 51
  punctuation in, 16
  revision and, 123
Proximal development, 44
Publication celebration, 138, 146
  parties for, 146-47
  significance to children, 140
Publishing
  different ways for, 144-45
  and record keeping, 145-46
  revision and, 119-31
  students' poems, 12, 16, 119-21
Puerto Rico, poems about, 53
Punctuation, 9, 16, 37, 69, 139, 141, 174, 175
Puns, 115
Puppets, 110
Puppet shows, 109
Puppy poems, 172
"Purist, The," (Nash), 152

"Quest" (Merriam), 190
Question poems, 177

Rain and fog poems, 162-66
Rainbow poems, 165-66
Random House Book of Poetry for Children, The (Prelutsky), 176, 190
Rap songs, 104
"Raw Carrots" (Worth), 160
Read-Aloud Rhynes for the Very Young (Prelutsky), 32, 66
Reading
  poems out loud, 108
  and writing poems, 25-26
Record keeping, 27, 145-46
Recorder music, 112
"Red Wheelbarrow, The" (Williams), 94, 95

Reflection
  in poems, 41
  and writing, 141-42
Refrain, 66
Rehearsing for poetry reading, 20-21
Repetition, 29, 32, 38, 44, 45, 66, 67
  in big books, 31
  in chants, 104
  in choral speaking, 105
  of consonants, 75
Report cards, and self-evaluation, 136
Reptile poems, 172
Revising
  on computer, 120
  conferences, 124
  illustrataion and, 143
  lines, 59
  methods of, 60
  poetry, 10, 11, 22, 69, 122, 147
  and self-evaluation, 132-34
  student poems, 119, 122-26
Rhyme, 11, 29, 30, 32, 38, 43-45, 159
  in big books, 31
  chanting and, 104
  counting, 29
  in couplets, 79, 156
  in Dr. Seuss, 33
  finding, 6
  internal, 41
  jump-rope, 104
  nursery, 90, 128
  occasional, 7
  and poetic form, 64-66
  rules of, 85
  street, 53
  teaching, 70
Rhyming couplets, 31, 161, 181
Rhythm, 29, 32, 43-45, 88, 96, 99, 104, 159
  in big books, 31
  in Dr. Seuss, 33
  and song in poetry, 197
Robertson, Barbara, *The Wind Has Wings*, 181
Rocks and minerals, 180
Roethke, Theodore, 187
Rogers, Timothy, *Those First Affections*, 8, 9, 34, 35, 87
Rose, Where Did You Get That Red? (Koch), 24, 47
Rossetti, Christina, 190
  "Who Has Seen the Wind?," 161
Routman, Regie, 31
  Transitions, 30, 32
"Runaway, The" (Frost), 172

"Safety Pin" (Worth), 2, 58, 61
Samoan poems, 53
Sandburg, Carl, 9, 67, 68, 94, 104, 170
  alliteration in, 76
  "Arithmetic," 155
  "Bee Song," 178
  "Bluebird, What Do You Feed On?," 176
  "Bubbles," 69, 165
  "Bug Spots," 178
  city imagery in, 154
  "Cricket March," 178
  "Elm Buds," 184
  "Fog," 162
  "The Gong of Time," 170
  "Good Babies Make Good Poems," 152
  "Good Morning, America," 154
  "Hog Butcher for the World," 154
  "Joliet," 154
  "Just Before April Came," 67
  "Localities," 153
  "March of the Hungry Mountains," 180
  "Open Letter to the Poet Archibald MacLeish Who Has Forsaken His Massachusetts Farm to Make Propaganda for Freedom," 155
  "Prairie," 176
  "Slants at Buffalo, New York, 154
  "Webs," 178
"Sand Dollar" (Esbensen), 181
Sandwich poems, 36
School newsletters, 146
Science poems, 150-52
Sea-dwelling mammals, 181
Seagull poems, 182
Sea Is Calling Me, The (Hopkins), 181
Sea poems, 180-82
"Seashell" (Worth), 3
Seasons poems, 170
Seattle, Chief, *Brother Eagle, Sister Sky*, 51
Second-graders, poetry, 40-41
Second-language learners, 44. *See also* ESL learners
"Secret, The" (Livingston), 185
Self-esteem
  building with poems, 45-46
  and grades, 138
Self-evaluation
  criteria for, 136-37
  of student poems, 132-34, 147

Sendak, Maurice, *Chicken Soup with Rice: A Book of Months*, 31, 66, 170
Service, Robert, "The Cremation of Sam McGee," 155
Seuss, Dr. *See* Geisel, Theodor Seuss
Shakespeare, William, 24, 32, 99, 115, 130, 140, 170
Shape. *See also* Diamante
  of poems, 58, 59, 94, 168, 169, 184, 189
Shapiro, Arnold, "I Speak, I Say, I Talk," 74
Shark poems, 181
"Shark, The" (Pratt), 181
Shearer, Lynn, 35
Shell poems, 181
Shopper newspapers
  poems in, 145
Side by Side: Poems to Read Together (Hopkins), 29, 95
Silverstein, Shel
  "Band-Aids," 155
  "Dancing Pants," 110
  "For Sale," 185
  "Hippo's Hope," 110
  "Hungry Mungry," 159
  "I Must Remember," 159
  "A Light in the Attic," 110
  "Melinda Mae," 159
  "Sky Seasoning," 159
  "Sleeping Sardines," 159
  "Smart," 156
  "Spaghetti," 159
  Where the Sidewalk Ends, 32, 159
Simile, 9, 22, 39, 41, 70
  in cinquains, 81
  teaching about, 71-73
Sinatra, Frank, 88
Singer, Marilyn, *Turtle in July*, 170
Singing. *See also* Choral speaking
  poetry, 88, 94
"Sitting in the Sand" (Kuskin), 181
"Skeleton Train" (Johnston), 115
"Sky Seasoning" (Silverstein), 159
Sky Songs (Livingston), 81
"Slants at Buffalo, New York" (Sandburg), 154
"Sleeping Sardines" (Silverstein), 159
Sloth, 172
"Slug" (Worth), 3
"Smart" (Silverstein), 156
Smith, William Jay, "Laughing Time," 106
"Smog," 190

Sneve, Virginia Driving Hawk, *Dancing Tepees*, 51
"Snow" (Worth), 166
Snow and ice poems, 166-68
Social studies poems, 152-55
Some of the Days of Everett Anderson (Clifton), 51
Something BIG Has Been Here (Prelutsky), 159, 171, 185
Something New Begins (Moore), 154, 181
"Something there is that doesn't love a wall" (Frost), 98
Sonnet, 78
Soto, Gary, *Neighborhood Odes*, 52
Sounds
   and alliteration, 75
   awareness of, 99, 105
   for fun, 114, 115
   insects make, 178
   playing with, 115
   in poetry, 87-89, 94, 108, 113, 114, 116
   words, 7, 38
"Souvenir" (Merriam), 181
Space and time poems, 168-71
Space Songs (Livingston), 168
"Spaghetti" (Silverstein), 159
Spanish language poems, 52, 53
Spanish-speaking students, 47
Special education students learning poetry, 42-43
Spelling, 139, 140
   American and British, 140
   collaborative poems for, 158
   errors, 141
   invented, 36, 37, 126, 140
Spelling checker, 141
Spender, Stephen, 88, 187
"Spider" (Moore), 178
Spider poems, 178
Sports poems, 109
"Squirrel," 171
"Squirrels" (Prelutsky), 171
Standards, for student poems, 135
Stanzas, 39, 62, 63
   rhyme, 77
Starfish, 181
"Stars" (Worth), 168
"Status of the class" list, 146
Steig, Jeanne, *Consider the Lemming*, 172
Stein, Gertrude, 113
Stereotype, 90
Stick puppets, 110
"Stopping by Woods on a Snowy Evening" (Frost), 111
Story poems, 42
Street rhymes, 53

Street Rhymes Around the World (Yolen), 53
"Sun on Rain" (Moore), 165
Sunrises and Songs (McClure), 131, 143, 145
Swahili poems, 53
"Switch on the Night" (Bradbury), 82
Syllables, 80
   in haiku, 81
Syntax, 37, 128

Take a Number (O'Neill), 155
"Take a Word Like Cat" (Kuskin), 174
"Talking to His Drum" (Mitchell), 154
Tall-tales, 155
Tamarindo Puppy, and Other Poems, 52
Teachers' log, 146
Teasdale, Sara, "The Falling Star," 168
"Telling Time" (Moore), 74, 170
"Ten Billion Crows" (Kennedy), 176
Tennyson, Alfred
   "The Eagle," 176, 177
   "The Lady of Shalott," 82
"Tern, The" (Williams), 161
Themes
   in poetry collections, 145, 159
   in programs, 111
"There Was a Place and Other Poems" (Livingston), 180, 185
"Things" (Greenfield), 99, 100
"This Cat" (Kuskin), 173
"This little piggie went to market," 29
Thomas, Donna, 93, 94
Thomas-MacKinnon, Pat, 90
Those First Affections (Rogers), 8, 9, 34, 35, 87
"Three Little Kittens, The," 82
"Three Little Pigs, The," 31
Thunder and lightning poems, 162-63
Thurman, Judith, *Flashlight and Other Poems*, 154
"Tiger," 171
"Time" (Esbensen), 170
Time poems, 170
"Toad" (Worth), 3
Today We Are Brother and Sister (Adoff), 52
Tortillitas para Mama and Other Nursery Rhymes, 53
Transitions (Routman), 30, 32
Transportation poems, 152
"Tree at My Window" (Frost), 184
Tree poems, 182-84
Trinidad, poems about, 53
Tung - P'o, Su, 170

Turtle in July (Singer), 170
"Turtle Soup," 159
"Twinkle, Twinkle, Little Star," 29
Tyrannosaurus Was a Beast (Prelutsky), 180

United States, poems about, 152
Universe, poems about, 168, 169
Unrhymed poems, 67, 79
Updike, John, *A Child's Calendar*, 170
Usage, 140

Verbs, 94-96, 158
Videotaping, choral speaking, 106, 108
Viorst, Judith
   If I Were in Charge of the World and Other Worries, 173, 185
   "Mother Doesn't Want a Dog," 172
"Visit from St. Nicholas, A," 82
Visiting poets, 93-94
Visual drama, for poetry, 112
Visual interest, in poems, 17, 18, 143
Vocal production, of poetry, 101-108
Voice
   and sound of poetry, 87

"Walrus and the Carpenter, The" (Carroll), 82
"Watched Example Never Boils, A" (Nash), 165
Water creatures
   in poetry, 156
"Water Striders," 179
Water walker poem, 179
Watkins, Alyce, 43
"Way Down in the Music" (Greenfield), 89
Weather poems, 161-68
"Webs" (Sandburg), 178
"Wet" (Moore), 167
"Whale Ghost, The" (Moore), 190
Whale poems, 181
"What a Wonderful World" (Armstrong), 89
"When Dracula Went to the Blood Bank" (Prelutsky), 94
"Where the Sidewalk Ends" (Silverstein), 32, 159
"Where Would You Be?" (Kuskin), 161
"While You Were Chasing a Hat" (Moore), 162

Whispering Wind: Poetry by Young American Indians, The (Allen), 49, 154
White, E. B.
   "The Answer Is 'No'," 176
   Charlotte's Web, 97
   "Fashions in Dogs," 173
   "A Listener's Guide to the Birds," 176
White, Dr. Edward A., 140
White space, 58, 62, 69, 88
Whitman, Walt, 24, 53, 91
   "Leaves of Grass," 180
Whittier, John Greenleaf, "Barbara Frietchie," 155
"Who Has Seen the Wind?" (Rosetti), 161
Who Shrank My Grandmother's House?: Poems of Discovery (Esbensen), 174, 181
Whole language classrooms, 31, 37, 54
   ESL students in, 44
   and oral experience, 89
   themes for, 159
Williams, William Carlos, 9, 24, 67, 152
   "The Red Wheelbarrow," 94, 95
   "The Tern," 161
Wind (O'Neill), 161
Wind Has Wings, The (Downie and Robertson), 154, 181
"Windshield Wiper" (Merriam), 109
"Wind Song" (Moore), 162
Windy Day (Bauer), 161
Winslow, Nancy, 155
Winters, Yvor, 172
"Woman Work" (Angelou), 52
"Woodpecker" (Moore), 176
Word banks, 39
Wordplay, 32, 115, 150
Word processor, composing poems on, 37, 60
Words
   invented, 39
   sounds of, 7
"Worm" (Kuskin), 113
Worth, Valerie, 2, 6, 9, 33, 39, 67, 166, 176
   "Acorn," 184
   All the Small Poems, 3, 171, 179, 181
   "Amoeba," 151
   "Caterpillar," 179
   "Coins," 156
   "Crab," 181
   "Haunted House," 130
   "Magnifying Glass," 151
   "Mantis," 179
   "Mosquito," 179
   "Pebbles," 62
   "Pie," 160

Worth, Valerie (*continued*)
  "Raw Carrots," 160
  "Safety Pin," 58, 61
  "Snow," 166
  "Stars," 168
  "Tiger," 171
  "Wet," 167
Writing
  content of, 139
  evaluating, 132-35
  poems in primary grades, 34
  as process, 38, 85
  and reading poems, 9, 25
  and reflection, 141-42
  and revising poems, 10
  the sound of poems, 113
  with word processor, 37, 60
Writing: Teachers and Children at Work (Graves), 103, 145
Wuertenberg, Jacque, 89

Yiddish poems, 53
Yolen, Jane
  "Grandpa Bear's Lullaby," 111
  Street Rhymes Around the World, 53
You Come Too (Frost), 167
Young, Ed, 184
Young, Ree, 113
Yukon gold rush, 155

Zen
  and haiku, 81
Ziegler, Edie, 35, 41, 90, 91, 109, 141
Zimet, Ellie Kubie, 30, 38
Zoo Doings (Prelutsky), 111, 171
"Zoo Was in an Uproar, The" (Prelutsky), 111
Zuni poems, 53

ABOUT THE AUTHOR

Committed to teaching practices that enable all children to find their voices as writers, Maureen W. Armour has focused her professional energies on the reading and writing processes. She has taught elementary school, in-service workshops for teachers, and college-level courses in reading and language arts and has supervised teacher interns.

She graduated from Douglass College, received a master's degree from Fordham University, and continued her studies at New York University and Teachers College, Columbia University. A New Jersey Writing Project summer workshop in 1981 opened the door to the world of teaching writing as a process, which became a profound influence on her work.

Retired from public school teaching, she lives and writes in Florida.